IN THE SHADOWS
OF THE SUN

Other PACCA Books
from Westview Press

From Confrontation to Negotiation: U.S. Relations with Cuba, Philip
Brenner

The Dangerous Doctrine: National Security and U.S. Foreign Policy,
Saul Landau

*Crisis in Central America: Regional Dynamics and U.S. Policy in the
1980s,* edited by Nora Hamilton, Jeffry A. Frieden, Linda Fuller, and
Manuel Pastor, Jr.

IN THE SHADOWS
OF THE SUN

Caribbean Development Alternatives and U.S. Policy

Carmen Diana Deere (coordinator), Peggy Antrobus,
Lynn Bolles, Edwin Melendez, Peter Phillips,
Marcia Rivera, and Helen Safa

A PACCA BOOK

WESTVIEW PRESS
BOULDER, SAN FRANCISCO, & OXFORD

Copyright © 1990 by Policy Alternatives for the Caribbean and Central America

Published in 1990 in the United States of America by Westview Press, Inc., 5500 Central Avenue, Boulder, Colorado 80301, and in the United Kingdom by Westview Press, Inc., 36 Lonsdale Road, Summertown, Oxford OX2 7EW

Library of Congress Cataloging-in-Publication Data
In the shadows of the sun: Caribbean development alternatives and
  U.S. policy / Carmen Diana Deere, coordinator . . . [et al.].
     p. cm.
  "A PACCA book."
  Includes index.
  ISBN 0-8133-1029-6 (HC) — ISBN 0-8133-1028-8 (Pbk.)
    1. Caribbean area—Economic policy. 2. Caribbean area—Economic
  conditions—1945-   . 3. Caribbean area—Foreign economic relations—
  United States. 4. United States—Foreign economic relations—
  Caribbean area. 5. Poor women—Caribbean area. I. Deere, Carmen
  Diana.
HC151.I5 1990
330.9729′052—dc20   90-12429
                                                                  CIP

Printed and bound in the United States of America

The paper used in this publication meets the requirements
of the American National Standard for Permanence of Paper
for Printed Library Materials Z39.48-1984.

10   9   8   7   6   5   4   3   2   1

For Hilda

Contents

——— Tables and Illustrations

Features

Acknowledgments

THIS PROJECT HAS BEEN a truly collaborative effort between North Americans and Caribbeans. Although the seven of us, as co-authors, must take responsibility for the content of the book, we have had the privilege of drawing on the expertise and guidance of colleagues throughout the Caribbean and the United States.

Our Caribbean Project Board of Advisors included: Patricia Anderson, Robert L. Bach, Frank Bonilla, Juan Castañer, Miguel Ceara, Elsa Chaney, Rhonda Cobham-Sander, Margaret Crahan, Sonja Cuales, Isis Duarte, Joan French, Carmen Gautier, Norman Girvan, Eddie Green, Winston Griffith, Karen Judd, David Lewis, Lucille Mair, Beverly Manley, Joycelin Massiah, Kathy McAffe, Betsy Oakes, Emilio Pantojas-García, Marifeli Pérez-Stable, Magaly Pineda, Rhoda Reddock, Rony Smarth, Steve Stamos, Alex Stepick, Catherine Sunshine, Clive Thomas, Ilya Villar, Hilbourne Watson, and Sally Yudelman.

Most of the members of the board of advisors commented, if not on the whole draft of the manuscript at some stage, at least on one of the chapters. Many provided us with access to crucial data, including their own unpublished work. Over the past two years, we have had the privilege of meeting with many of them to discuss the ideas that went into the book; a number of the advisory board members served as commentators on panels organized around the manuscript at conferences or invited us to present the findings of the project at special seminars and workshops. In addition to our advisory board members, colleagues who commented on the alternative proposals include Andaiye, Geraldo Gonzales, Michelle Heisler, Rafael Hernández, George Huggins, Atherton Martin, Richard Newfarmer, and Bernardo Vega. We are also grateful to PACCA Executive Board members Xabier Gorastiaga, Manuel Pastor, and Kenneth Sharpe for their comments on various chapters. Our debt to all of them is large.

Special mention must be made of the various organizations and institutes that provided us with a forum for our work: the Caribbean Association of Economists, the Caribbean Studies Association, WAND (the Women and Development Unit, University of the West Indies), CIPAF (Centro de Investigación para la Acción Femenina), Instituto del Caribe of the University of Puerto Rico, and the Latin American Studies Association. We are also grateful to CEA (Centro de Estudios de las Américas), CEREP (Centro de Estudios de la Realidad Puertorriqueña), CIECA (Centro de Investigación Económica), and particularly PACCA's sister organization, CRIES (Coordinadora Regional de Investigaciones Económicas y Sociales) for their collaboration at various stages. The two policy alternatives presented in this book were the subject of a day-long conference at the University of Florida, Gainesville, in March 1989. Our special thanks to Terry McCoy, director of the Center for Latin American Studies, for inviting us to co-host the Center's 38th Annual Conference on Latin America.

A project of this dimension required the hard work of a number of research assistants. Our special thanks to Maribel Aponte who served as the principal research assistant during the first year of the project. Other graduate research assistants from the Economics Department at the University of Massachusetts included Jaime Benson, Nikoi Kote-Nikoi, Hector Saez, and José Tavara; we are grateful to the department for funding much of the research assistance that went into the project.

The PACCA Washington staff put extraordinary effort into this project. Robert Stark, PACCA executive director, was in charge of fundraising for the project and organized the various Core Team meetings. Colin Danby, publications coordinator at PACCA, was responsible for the production of the popular education tabloid which accompanies this book and for the final preparation of the manuscript. Both also provided crucial intellectual input to the project.

The manuscript was made more lively by the case studies prepared for us by Joan French, Paul Monaghan, Betsy Oakes, and Fafa Taveras. Both the manuscript and the case studies are much more readable due to the careful rewriting, editing, and comments by Karen Judd. It was also a pleasure to work with Barbara Ellington and Kathy Streckfus of Westview Press, which has published three previous PACCA books.

The project was funded by grants from the Ford Foundation, the John D. and Catherine T. MacArthur Foundation, the Samuel Ruben Foundation, and the Women's Division, General Board of Global Ministries, United Methodist Church.

The following publishers and authors have generously granted permission to reprint tables from copyrighted works. Table 2.2: from ECLAC (Economic Commission for Latin America and the Caribbean), "The

Impact of External Sector Developments on Caribbean Economic Performance 1983–1988," LC/CAR/G.278, October 1989, Table 3; reprinted by permission of ECLAC. Tables 3.1, 3.2, 3.4, and 3.6: from Omar Davies and Patricia Anderson, "The Impact of the Recession and Adjustment Policies on Poor Urban Women in Jamaica," paper prepared for UNICEF, 1987, later published in *The Invisible Adjustment: Poor Women and the Economic Crisis* (Santiago, Chile: UNICEF, The Americas and the Caribbean Regional Office, Regional Programme, Women in Development, 1989); reprinted by permission of UNICEF. Table 3.3: from Clara Baez, *La Subordinación de la Mujer Dominicana en Cifras* (Santo Domingo: Dirección General de Promoción de la Mujer and INSTRAW, 1984), Table 3.11; reprinted by permission of Clara Baez. Table 3.8: from Elsa Chaney, *Migration from the Caribbean Region: Determinants and Effects of Current Movements* (Washington, D.C.: Center for Immigration Policy, 1985), p. 21; reprinted by permission of Elsa Chaney.

Special thanks also to Nelcia Robinson for permission to reprint the first stanza of her poem "My C'bbean," which appears as the epigraph to Chapter 1.

The Authors

The Caribbean.

Source: W. Raymond Duncan and Carolyn McGiffert Ekedahl, *Moscow and the Third World Under Gorbachev* (Boulder, Colo.: Westview, 1990). Reprinted by permission of Westview Press.

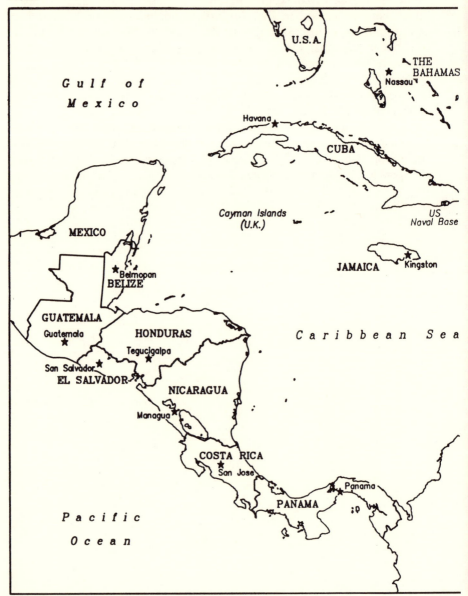

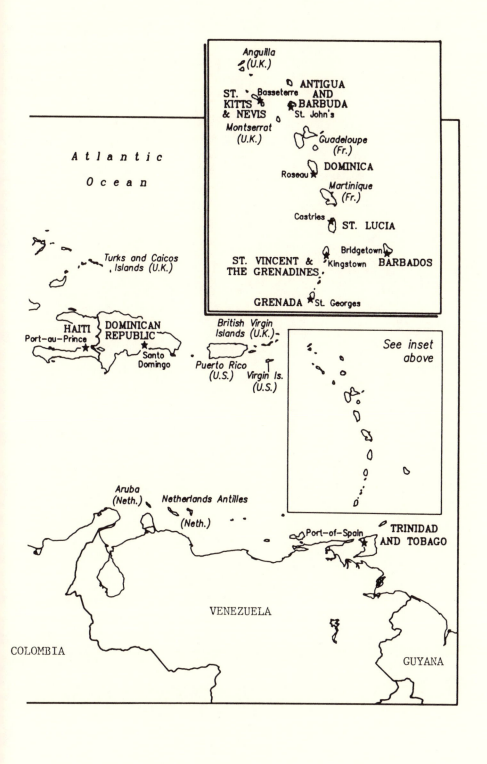

CHAPTER 1

The Setting

My Caribbean
What month
were you born
beautiful child
of the sun
cradling a friendly sea
crowded by land masses
whose motherhood
makes you jump and sing
Or whose shadows
Cause you to crawl
—Nelcia Robinson

CENTURIES OF COMMON HISTORY and close economic ties link the 35 million people of the Caribbean and the 250 million people of the United States. The countries of the Caribbean, like the United States, were colonized by European powers and had to fight for independence; some still have not achieved sovereignty. Also like the United States, the Caribbean nations are characterized by a rich mixture of ethnicities—African, Latin, Northern European, and Asian. The connections can be seen in music and sports, in the millions of U.S. citizens of Caribbean descent, and in migration patterns.

Puerto Ricans and Jamaicans staff the schools and hospitals of Brooklyn while immigrants from other Caribbean islands stitch garments in sweatshops in mid-town Manhattan. In Florida, Haitians cut sugarcane while Cubans have revitalized the businesses of Miami. It is no longer unusual to hear Spanish broadcast on U.S. radio or television, or Creole on the streets of Boston, Brooklyn, or Miami, while satellite dishes beam the CBS evening news into the living rooms of Port-au-Prince, Kingston, and Port of Spain.

Millions of North Americans flock to the beaches of the Caribbean each year as tourists. In a hotel in Montego Bay they may eat steak cooked from Iowa beef and sleep on sheets made in the Carolinas. Moreover, bathing suits bought in Seattle or St. Louis may have been stitched together in a free-trade zone of the Dominican Republic—in a factory furnished by used sewing machines from Maine.

As a result of migration, trade, and capital flows, wages and living standards in the Caribbean and the United States are inextricably linked. Low wages in the region spur Caribbeans to migrate and attract U.S. investors to the Caribbean. Runaway shops mean that U.S. workers lose jobs as garment and electronic factories leave for Caribbean free-trade zones—where workers are unorganized and the right to unionize is denied.

Capital flight has become an important mechanism in dampening real wage growth in the United States and breaking the power of organized U.S. labor. Between 1981 and 1986 the average real wage of U.S. production workers fell 14 percent while some five million workers were dislocated.[1] During the same period, Caribbean per capita income and real wages plummeted, and migrants from the Caribbean islands and Mexico, fleeing the lack of job opportunities at home, became the primary source of documented and undocumented immigrants to the United States. In the Caribbean islands, the average rate of unemployment exceeded 15 percent, in some places reaching as high as 40 percent.

The U.S. standard of living and very social fabric is linked to events in the Caribbean in other important ways. Geographical proximity has made the Caribbean attractive to drug smugglers and tax evaders as well as tourists. Deteriorating conditions on several of the islands have encouraged thousands to turn to the drug trade as a way of survival. International drug networks, such as the "Jamaica gangs," spur increased violence on the streets of New York and Miami as well as those of Kingston. Some Caribbean governments, eager to attract capital, have become booming financial centers where lax supervision has created new possibilities for laundering drug money in the region. These centers also provide new mechanisms and incentives for U.S. corporations to evade taxes in a time of growing U.S. budget deficits.

We all suffer the consequences of environmental degradation in the region. The dumping of U.S.-generated toxic wastes, periodic oil spills, and abuse of pesticides in efforts to grow more export crops all threaten the natural resources on which the people of the Caribbean depend, and to which U.S. tourists are attracted. Unchecked construction, together with the clearing and draining of swamps for the tourist industry, hurt both the region's natural beauty and its capacity to produce food and export crops. Deforestation, with its multiple ecological consequences, has long been a problem in Haiti and the Dominican Republic; tons of topsoil are washed to the sea every year.

While the problems that link the United States and the Caribbean region, such as the drug trade and environmental degradation, have intensified in scope in the 1980s, Caribbean governments have seen their ability to cope with these new challenges severely eroded. The region is poorer today than it was a decade ago, due to the combined effect of low export prices, external indebtedness, shrinking investment, and inflation. Austerity programs have led to rising unemployment and underemployment, falling real wages, and decreasing health and educational services. Growing poverty in the region has spurred increased migration to the United States and exacerbated social polarization at home, making the Caribbean potentially more unstable in the 1990s than it was at the beginning of the previous decade.

While a number of complex problems weave together the destinies of the United States and the Caribbean, and the two have many interests in common, there are also important points on which they differ. The majority of Caribbean people are poor. Caribbean economies, shaped by colonizing powers, remain highly dependent on international markets. Countries in the region that try to follow a more autonomous course find themselves in conflict with the United States. Washington's policy has been to bind the region more closely to the U.S. economy as a source of cheap labor and a market for U.S. goods. Whereas Caribbeans view poverty as the prime scourge in the region and call for alternative strategies to engender more egalitarian, participatory societies, U.S. policy-makers view the problems of the region through the prism of "national security."

The relationship between the United States and the Caribbean has always been one-sided: even before the Bolshevik revolution in the Soviet Union the United States had intervened in Cuba, Haiti, and the Dominican Republic a number of times. Cold War ideology only reinforced the view that governments not beholden to the United States, especially progressive ones, are threats. The practice of undermining governments that put a priority on the well-being of the poor majority has further limited the ability of Caribbean nations to chart their own course. On the other hand, it has been relatively easy for Washington, with its vastly greater wealth and military power, to pursue what it sees as U.S. interests in the Caribbean.

The Caribbean Produces
What It Does Not Consume

Throughout most of Caribbean history the region has functioned as an adjunct of external economic interests, producing agricultural products or relatively unprocessed minerals for export to metropolitan markets—whether Spain, France, England, or the United States. In the process, Caribbean countries developed extremely open and highly vulnerable economies. For most countries, one or two commodities— sugar, bananas, coffee, oil, or bauxite—still account for close to three-quarters of total exports in a context of extreme trade dependence; that is, trade constitutes a large proportion of national income, well over 50 percent in most cases.

It was not until the postwar years that determined efforts were made within the Caribbean to overcome the historical effects of colonialism upon the structure of economic life. Prior to that time, the circumstances of formal colonial rule, or of limited sovereignty as in the case of the Dominican Republic and Haiti, defined the traditional role of the Caribbean in the international division of labor. By virtue of their subordinate status, countries in the region were compelled to function as exporters of unprocessed or semiprocessed primary commodities and importers of manufactured goods. As the maxim runs, the Caribbean produces what it does not consume, and consumes what it does not produce.

Following the consolidation of a U.S.-centered world order after World War II, and also as a consequence of the nationalist upheavals which swept the region in the 1930s and 1940s, a new framework for economic development became generalized during the 1950s. The essential goal of the new strategies in the various territories was the creation of a modern industrial sector through a process of import substitution. Influenced considerably by the Puerto Rican "Operation Bootstrap" strategy to lure U.S. capital, "industrialization by invitation" became the main strategy for economic change. Foreign investors were invited to exploit the reservoir of cheap labor in the region by means of generous tax exemptions and other incentives.

By the end of the 1960s, however, these policies came under sharp criticism, as they consistently failed to meet their objectives of sustained industrial development and economic growth and to significantly relieve the unemployment problem of the islands. For the most part, these industries were relatively capital-intensive, depended on the import of raw materials and machinery, and developed few linkages with other sectors of the local economy. Thus, not only did the emerging industrial sector develop as a modern enclave with few linkages to the local economy, but the pattern of industrialization, by virtue of its primary reliance on foreign capital, served to reinforce foreign control over local economic activity.[2]

Despite the limited depth of import-substitution industrialization policies, the 1960s and early 1970s were a period of relative prosperity in the Caribbean, due first to the expansion of production and high price of raw materials such as bauxite and petroleum, and sugar for a brief period, second to the growth of tourism (particularly after the Cuban revolution and the U.S. embargo of that island), and third to accelerated migration, initially to England, but subsequently and more significantly to the United States.[3]

Even so, disappointment with the economic strategies pursued during the 1950s and 1960s formed the basis of a wave of social and political activism which swept the region toward the end of the latter decade. New social protest movements emerged, new ideologies—ethnic, nationalist, and socialist—developed, and political turmoil surfaced in many countries, as manifest in the 1965 revolt in the Dominican Republic, the 1970 protests by the Black Power Movement in Trinidad, and the 1974 election of Michael Manley as prime minister of Jamaica on a platform of democratic socialism. The 1970s were indeed a period of renaissance and experimentation, of constructing new utopias, and of rethinking development policy in different terms. After its peaceful revolution of March 1979, Grenada assumed a position of leadership in the search for social change in the Caribbean.

While the particular mix of policy initiatives pursued during the decade varied across countries, and the reorganization of policy was more comprehensive in some countries than in others, a common tendency was evident nonetheless. There was a steady expansion in the economic role of the state, a deepened commitment to and reevaluation of the role of Caribbean regionalism—leading to the formation of the Caribbean Community and Common Market (CARICOM) in the English-speaking Caribbean—and a general diversification of international relations.

The new policy directions of the 1970s met with varying degrees of success. Many of the new state enterprises and new industries oriented toward the regional market proved to be just as dependent on imported inputs and technology as those run by multinational corporations. Lack of diversified markets, a low level of domestic interindustry linkages, and deficiencies in managerial and entrepreneurial skills also limited the possibilities of these initiatives.[4]

The particular growth experiences of each country varied greatly, reflected in the exceptionally broad range of per capita income levels exhibited in the 1980s (see Table 1.1). At the top end of the scale are the financial centers and largely tourist economies of Bermuda, the Cayman Islands, the Bahamas, the British and the U.S. Virgin Islands, and more industrialized Puerto Rico. At the poorest end lie Haiti, Guyana, and St. Vincent-Grenadines among the independent countries, and the British territories of the Turks-Caicos Islands and Anguilla.

Table 1.1
Selected Indicators: Countries of the Caribbean

	Political Status	Population 1988 (in 000's)	GDP per Capita 1988 (US$)	Life Expectancy 1987	Infant Mortality 1987[1]
Independent Countries					
Antigua-Barbuda	1981 (UK)	82 [a]	3,399	73	19 [e]
Bahamas	1973 (UK)	234	11,317	70	29 [e]
Barbados	1966 (UK)	254	4,233	75	14 [e]
Belize	1981 (UK)	180 [a]	1,226 [2]	67	54 [e]
Cuba	1898 (Spain)	11,086 [a]	3,000 [3]	75	13
Dominica	1978 (UK)	82 [a]	1,550	74	14 [e]
Dominican Republic	1844 (Spain)	6,867	1,509	66	65
Grenada	1974 (UK)	106 [a]	1,346	69	34 [e]
Guyana	1966 (UK)	755	955	66	44 [e]
Haiti	1804 (France)	6,263	319	55	17
Jamaica	1962 (UK)	2,427	1,843	74	18
St. Kitts-Nevis	1983 (UK)	47 [a]	2,119	68	29 [e]
St. Lucia	1979 (UK)	145 [a]	1,400	70	23 [e]
St. Vincent-Grenadines	1979 (UK)	114 [a]	1,210	69	32 [e]
Suriname	1975 (The Netherlands)	359	3,420	67	42 [e]
Trinidad-Tobago	1962 (UK)	1,157	5,510	70	20
Territories, Possessions, and Colonies					
Anguilla	UK Dependency	7 [c]	630 [d4]	73 [f]	19 [f]
Aruba	Netherlands Dependency	60 [b4]	6,779 [d4]	76 [f]	8 [f]
Bermuda	UK Colony	56 [b4]	22,050 [f4]	76 [f]	11 [f]
British Virgin Islands	UK Dependency	12 [a]	9,492	73 [f]	15 [f]
Cayman Islands	UK Colony	22 [c]	18,200 [d4]	75 [f]	11 [f]
French Guiana	French Overseas Dept.	88 [b4]	n.a.	71 [f]	21 [f]
Guadeloupe	French Overseas Dept.	337 [b4]	3,300 [d5]	73	13 [f]

After the 1979 coup in Grenada, the triumph of the Sandinista revolution in Nicaragua, and the advances of progressive political forces in several Caribbean and Central American countries, U.S. efforts to control its "backyard," which had relaxed somewhat in the late 1970s, intensified. The Reagan administration intervened actively to prevent the consolidation of what were interpreted as models of development that operated against U.S. security interests, using destabilizing tactics in Jamaica and even military invasion in Grenada. In fact, experiments such as that of revolutionary Grenada or the first Manley administration in Jamaica were not threats to U.S. security—although they may have seemed threatening to those suspicious of any social experiment that is not "made in the U.S.A." Indeed, the U.S. government's hostile and militaristic posture toward progressive experiments has done little to

Table 1.1
Selected Indicators: Countries of the Caribbean (*Continued*)

	Political Status	Population 1988 (in 000's)	GDP per Capita 1988 (US$)	Life Expectancy 1987	Infant Mortality 1987[1]
Martinique	French Overseas Dept.	329 [b4]	4,280 [d5]	74	11 [f]
Montserrat	UK Colony	12 [a]	3,997	77 [f]	9 [f]
Netherlands Antilles	Netherlands Dependency	190 [b]	n.a.	66	9 [f]
Puerto Rico	U.S. Possession	3,294 [a]	5,574	75	16 [f]
Turks-Caicos Islands	UK Colony	8 [c]	500 [d5]	n.a.	n.a.
U.S. Virgin Islands	U.S. Territory	110 [b]	9,030 [d5]	73	18 [f]

Sources: Population and GDP per capita based on Inter-American Development Bank, *Economic and Social Progress in Latin America, 1989 Report* (Washington, D.C.: IDB, 1989), tables A-1 and B-1, except for data marked (a) Economic Commission for Latin America and the Caribbean (ECLAC), cited in Trevor Harker, "Caribbean Economic Performance," paper presented to the Second Conference of Caribbean Economists, Barbados, May 1989; (b) *World Development Report, 1989* (Washington, D.C.: World Bank, 1989), Box A.1 and Box A.2; or (c) 1986 statistics from United Nations, *1985/86 Statistical Yearbook* (New York: UN, 1988), table 18. Income figures from ECLAC unless noted (d) *Europa World Book Yearbook* (London: Europa Publications, 1989). Life expectancy and infant mortality statistics drawn from World Bank, *World Development Report 1989*, tables 1, 32, Box A.1 and Box A.2 and *The World Bank Atlas 1988* (Washington, D.C.: The World Bank, 1988); and for those marked (e) World Bank, *World Tables* 1988–89 edition, country pages; and (f) from Central Intelligence Agency, *CIA World Factbook 1989* (Washington, D.C.: CIA, 1989), p. 212.

1) Infant mortality indicates the number of infants per thousand live births who die before reaching one year of age
2) 1986 figure
3) Global Social Product per capita converted at official rates
4) 1987 figure   5) 1985 figure

redress the inequities which spur instability and revolution and thus has not made the Caribbean more secure.

Renewed recognition in Washington of the importance of the Caribbean also led to a new program to integrate the economies of the region more closely to the United States—the Caribbean Basin Initiative (CBI). CBI incentives, combined with the growth in external debt and the economic priorities imposed by the International Monetary Fund (IMF), the World Bank, and the U.S. Agency for International Development (AID) have reinforced traditional patterns of subordination in the relationship of Caribbean economies to metropolitan centers. Specifically, in the reliance on external markets, in the primacy of export production over production for local or regional markets, and in the preeminence given to the attraction of foreign capital, current development strategies advocated by Washington are repeating the errors of the past. The effect then and now has been to reinforce highly open and vulnerable economies at the expense of the welfare of Caribbean populations.

The historical subordination of Caribbean economies to external economic interests has also yielded a highly concentrated structure of ownership, often foreign-based, which in turn has resulted in an extremely unequal distribution of income within each country.[5] The unequal distribution of assets and income has very profound social consequences which resonate more clearly in the Caribbean than in other settings. For the fact is that, throughout most of the region, wealth and ownership has been historically associated with whiteness and maleness, and poverty and hard labor with women and black or other nonwhite racial groups such as East Indians and Chinese. This has yielded a very complex web of hierarchical relations that embrace class, race, and gender.

Class, Race, and Gender Hierarchies

The roots of the class, race, and gender hierarchies lie in the colonial domination of the Caribbean region for nearly five centuries from the time of arrival of Columbus in 1492 to, in the case of the English-speaking Caribbean, independence in the last half of this century. With colonial rule in the mid-seventeenth century came slavery to provide cheap labor for the region's sugar plantations, which flourished initially in Saint Domingue (Haiti), Jamaica, Barbados, and the Leeward Islands, and later moved to other areas, including Cuba, Trinidad, and Guyana. It is estimated that the Caribbean received 47 percent of the ten million African slaves brought to the Americas.[6] As a result, the white population became a numerical minority in almost all the islands, except for the Dominican Republic and Puerto Rico, where sugar plantations never assumed the same importance and slaves constituted less than 20 percent of the population. The racial hierarchy produced by slavery thus set up three basic social divisions—free whites, free nonwhites (or coloreds), and slaves—but the differences in their proportions varied considerably. Sugar plantations also initiated the pattern of large land-holdings, often absentee-owned, which continue to the present day and stifle the development of a viable small farming sector.

In addition to Spain and England, other colonial powers, such as France, Denmark, and the Netherlands, also obtained possessions in the Caribbean, several of which continue to be under metropolitan rule. While each of these countries followed a somewhat different colonial policy, we shall focus here on the Spanish-speaking and English-speaking Caribbean.

The abolition of slavery started with the slave revolt against the French in Saint Domingue from 1791 to 1804, and resulted in the first independent country outside of the United States in the Americas: Haiti. Slavery was abolished in the British Caribbean in 1834, the French Caribbean in 1848, the Dutch Caribbean in 1863, but not until 1870 in Puerto Rico and 1886 in Cuba. After abolition, in order to meet their continued need for cheap labor, the sugar plantations imported indentured labor from India and China, which further diversified the racial and ethnic composition of the population. East Indians today constitute almost half of the population of Trinidad-Tobago and Guyana; the majority of East Indians continue to live in rural areas and are often farmers. Where land was available, former black slaves also set up independent peasant villages, but these continued to be subordinated to the plantation economy.[7] The continued availability of cheap labor in the English Caribbean obviated the need for technological innovations to raise productivity introduced by U.S. capital on the sugar plantations of Cuba and Puerto Rico.

Until well into the twentieth century the Caribbean was essentially a labor-importing region. Intra-Caribbean labor flows followed the expansion of sugar plantations as Jamaican workers went to Cuba, Eastern Caribbean workers went to the Dominican Republic, Trinidad, and Guyana, and from all these islands, workers went to work on the Panama Canal. A relative labor surplus first became evident in the British Caribbean in the interwar years, when competition from other sources, including European and U.S. beet sugar, led to demographic changes and the collapse of the sugar plantation economy. Throughout the British Caribbean decreased levels of mortality resulting in population increases were due not to rising income levels but to public health measures, which reflected the growing economic role of the state.[8] These measures were part of the Colonial Development and Welfare Program initiated by the British government in response to the findings of the Moyne Commission, sent out to investigate spontaneous riots brought on by the dismal conditions in the 1930s. As a result of the Moyne Commission report, the British government also began a modified program of self-government, based on the extension of the franchise to all adults over the age of twenty-one.

Though the riots of the 1930s initiated the labor movement in the English-speaking Caribbean, this movement never assumed the strong class character it did in parts of the Spanish-speaking Caribbean, particularly Cuba, tending to ally with the state to gain reforms rather than confront capital directly. Part of the explanation for this may be traced to the tutelage of the British Labour Party, which encouraged "responsible reform" to avert the revolutionary character of some Cuban labor unions in the 1920s.[9] Also important was the rising political importance of the "colored" middle class, which sought labor's support against white colonialism, resulting in a close bond between political parties and trade unions that lasted until the late 1960s. Class differences in the English-speaking Caribbean thus appear muted in favor of nationalist solidarity against white colonialism.

Despite the nationalism of the elite in the English-speaking Caribbean, which was largely expressed in racial terms, class interests intersect with race and color divisions as in the rest of the region. Thus the elite of these societies have expressed their self-interest most often in racial terms, cutting across class lines. But the status of these brown-skinned ruling and middle classes is predicated on their difference from the black masses, not on their alliance with blackness. The elite have generally rejected the racial consciousness manifested in several pan-black movements which have swept through the region, including Marcus Garvey's Universal Negro Improvement Association, the Rastafarian religion, Black Power, as well as in a variety of other movements— Hindu, Mayan, Garifuna—depending on the ethnic make-up of the country.[10]

Compared to class and race oppression, gender subordination remained a secondary issue in the region and only began to assume importance after the initiation of the UN Decade for Women in 1975, when the participation of large numbers of women in the consciousness-raising and self-help development projects sponsored by outside agencies and local research institutes sparked a new awareness of women's subordinated position in Caribbean societies. Here again differences in the colonial heritage and in the importance of slavery have played a part in generating different forms of gender subordination in the English- and Spanish-speaking Caribbean.

In the British Caribbean, slavery established the importance of women as workers and providers, which was not seen as incompatible with their reproductive role as wives and mothers, as it was in the Hispanic Caribbean. In addition, poor women are often expected to take on the primary responsibility for providing for their families because of the high percentage of female-headed households which has resulted from high male Caribbean out-migration and the low level of legal marriages, the latter also a legacy of slavery. The relative economic autonomy of women in poor households has not resulted, however, in greater female visibility and participation in the public realm, in such arenas as politics or trade unions, which are dominated by males. This suggests that despite working women's relative economic autonomy, the English-speaking Caribbean is far from sexually egalitarian.[11] In the Spanish-speaking Caribbean in recent years women have been moving into the labor force in greater numbers and increasing their economic contributions to households. There is some evidence that their dependence on male breadwinners is also lessening, leading to more egalitarian household relationships.[12] However, in both regions the power and authority of women in the public sphere is very limited.

The current economic crisis in the Caribbean also has a class and gender bias. The deterioration in the standards of living has been much greater among the masses of the region than among the middle and upper sectors. This economic tension has yet to have generalized political expression, but recent events point in this direction. Riots and demonstrations in the Dominican Republic, Haiti, and Jamaica, protesting against the high cost of living and governments' acceptance of the terms of the IMF to meet debt payments, are everyday indicators of the desperate situation of the majority of Caribbean people. Women are increasingly playing an important role in mobilizing the population against IMF measures as they, usually the poorest of all poor, are facing the crisis in the most dramatic way.

Throughout the region, governments have been pushed to implement what are known as structural adjustment policies in order to obtain IMF credit, World Bank loans, and U.S. AID funding. In addition to a reordering of production toward exports for the world market and a lifting of import controls, these policies include reduced social spending, the end of consumption subsidies, and relaxed labor standards for employers. Higher prices for basic consumption goods have led to severe declines in real wages, at the same time that social welfare programs are cut back. Public housing, education and training programs, health services, and other social welfare programs have all been severely cut or reduced. It is women who are most deprived on account of these policies, as women bear the greatest responsibility for the care of children, the sick, and the elderly and head a large proportion of households in the Caribbean.

Increasingly large sectors of the Caribbean population are unable to meet their basic needs, or even to survive exclusively on income from wage work, given the reduction of formal employment opportunities and declining real wages. During the past decade the Caribbean has seen a dramatic increase in so-called informal sector activities, which for many families have become the only source of income. The critically unstable and competitive nature of these jobs requires a type of individual aggressive hustling that hinders the development of a sense of collective struggle. In some of the larger Caribbean countries such as Puerto Rico, Jamaica, and the Dominican Republic, the growth of the informal

sector has led to the fragmentation of the working class and a deterioration of its institutions, which further deepens the social crisis.

The Caribbean today is made up of sixteen independent countries
(including Belize, Guyana, and Suriname, besides the independent
island countries), comprising dozens of ethnic groups and five dominant
language groups: English, Spanish, French, Creole, and Dutch. Montserrat, Anguilla, Bermuda, the Cayman Islands, the Turks and Caicos
Islands, and the British Virgin Islands are still British colonies or
dependencies while the islands of the Dutch Caribbean are approaching
independence. Guadeloupe, Martinique, and French Guiana have been
incorporated as integral overseas departments of France; the political
status of Puerto Rico and the U.S. Virgin Islands remains unresolved.
Undoubtedly, this political fragmentation contributes to the linguistic,
ethnic, and racial diversity of the region and further undermines efforts
at regional integration. This political and cultural fragmentation in turn
adds to the vulnerability of these small states, with their limited
populations and natural resources, and facilitates external intervention.
In sum, the legacy of colonialism and slavery in the Caribbean is a
politically fragmented society, sharply divided along racial, ethnic, class,
and gender lines.

Beyond the Lost Development Decade

U.S. policy-makers seem to recognize that improving the standard
of living in the Caribbean is in both regional and U.S. interests.
However, the kinds of policies the various U.S. administrations have
adopted often have negative and contradictory effects for the people
of the Caribbean. The Caribbean Basin Initiative attempts to solve the
region's economic problems by integrating the region more closely to
U.S. markets. When the program was launched it was hoped that by
giving the region increased duty-free access to the U.S. market, Caribbean
exports, particularly of nontraditional products, would soar. Enhanced
export revenues in turn were expected to spur growth, investment, and
employment, while allowing these countries to continue servicing their
external debt.

While this policy has benefited U.S. capital by making U.S. corporations
more competitive and by generating a positive U.S. trade balance with
the region, it has done little to assuage the regional economic crisis.
Even before the CBI, the new insertion of the Caribbean in the
international division of labor implied a shift in production and exports
from traditional primary commodities to more diversified manufacturing
production. Over the past decade, free-trade or export-processing zones
have emerged throughout the Caribbean, and since 1984 have prolif-

erated in concert with the CBI. In contrast to the previous import-substitution industries, assembly industries in the export-processing zones employ a predominantly female labor force. As our subsequent analysis illustrates, female workers are preferred to male workers because they will work for lower wages and are less likely to organize against oppressive work conditions.

We also will argue that the majority of these assembly industries are inefficient generators of foreign exchange and employment as compared to the traditional export sector, due to their low value-added contribution to local economies. Moreover, the emphasis on export-processing zones as the panacea to the economic crisis has made Caribbean economies more vulnerable to the whims of multinational capital. The centralization and fragmentation of production under which multinational corporations operate, and the low level of capital investment which assembly operations require, mean that these industries can easily change location if conditions in other countries become more favorable. A significant sector of the garment industry of Puerto Rico, for example, has moved to Barbados, Haiti, and the Dominican Republic in pursuit of lower wages.

Export diversification toward nontraditional products may be *one* important component of a new model of development for the region. But it cannot be the central element in the quest for less vulnerable, internally self-sustainable economies. Moreover, restructuring U.S.-Caribbean economic relations around a new division of labor based on the Caribbean comparative advantage of cheap labor may make U.S. corporations more profitable but will not necessarily improve the standard of living of Caribbean peoples.

In addition, we will demonstrate that IMF, World Bank, and AID-supported structural adjustment policies have exacerbated poverty, with the costs falling unduly on the poor women of the region, who increasingly are the main economic support of their families. These anti-growth policies have also spurred the illegal migrant flow to the United States, made the drug trade an increasingly attractive survival strategy, and led to increased social and sexual violence as well as to the social polarization of Caribbean societies.

Structural adjustment policies must be questioned not only in terms of their effects, but also in terms of the underlying premises. An export-led cum stabilization strategy is premised on a rather optimistic set of assumptions about growth in the international economy and the willingness of the advanced countries to accept third world exports.[13] In addition, the effort to reduce the role of the public sector in development has been premised on a naive faith in the potential development role of the private sector. In countries where infrastructure is not well developed, the existing industrial base is small, and where managerial skills are scarce, it seems unlikely that the indigenous private sector can replace the state as a catalyst to engender growth with development.

Today, the development debate in the Caribbean is set forth in quite clear terms: on the one hand is the position that seeks to further the region's incorporation to the world economy, calling for a reduction in state intervention and less support for measures to reduce poverty or class, race, and gender inequities. On the other hand is a position that seeks to elaborate a regional economic alternative that responds to the social needs of the majority and not to the structural needs of capital. As the global economic crisis continues, as the number of migrants and refugees grows, and as the increasing spread of drugs, crime, and environmental degradation threatens the social and economic fabric of our societies, it is time for the United States to throw its weight behind those who are seeking alternative approaches to more sustainable and self-reliant models of development.

A new U.S. policy toward the Caribbean must start from the recognition that, given the complex and multifaceted links between the United States and the Caribbean, increasing the standard of living in the region is simply in the U.S. national interest, no matter what set of development strategies Caribbean countries choose toward that goal. Acting on this recognition requires a fundamental change in the aid, trade, finance, and military policies of previous U.S. administrations toward the Caribbean.

Above all, a new U.S. policy toward the region must be based on the acceptance of the view that when Caribbean governments place the interests of their people above those of U.S. capital they are operating within the framework of a political philosophy which believes in government by and for the people—a policy familiar to the people of the United States. An approach which accepts the right of governments to give priority to the needs and interests of their own people, and on this basis to identify and pursue common and mutual interests, is the only one which can lead to mutual respect for differences, a prerequisite for mutually beneficial relations between nations. The United States can start with this group of countries that share the Caribbean Sea.

For PACCA, this study breaks new ground in using the lens of gender in an analysis which seeks to link international policies to their consequences at the level of the poorest household, where their harsh impact is most severely experienced. This analysis reveals that it is women, especially poor women, who have borne the burden of policies based on a gender ideology which is fundamentally exploitative of women's time and labor—both paid and unpaid. It documents the ways in which women have used traditional networks of kinship and friend- ship, family and community, to cope with the devastating effect of policies which have had a severe impact on the very survival of these societies. And it is for this reason that we argue that it is these women— the poorest and most powerless of the poor and powerless—who must be consulted in the processes of defining alternative policies. It is their vision of a more equitable future which we try to project in this book.

Notes

1. "Testimony before the United States House of Representatives Subcom- mittee on the Caribbean Basin Initiative," by John H. Hovis, Jr., General President, United Electrical, Radio and Machine Workers of America (UE), mimeo, March 28, 1988.

2. The analysis of "Operation Bootstrap" and "industrialization by invitation" is further elaborated in Chapter 5. Also see Lloyd Best, "Size and Survival," *New World Quarterly* 2 (3) 1966, and José J. Villamil, "Los Límites del Crecimiento Dependiente," *Revista Ciencias Sociales* (San Juan), 1, 1976.

3. British Caribbean migration to Great Britain was cut off by the Com- monwealth Immigrants Act of 1962, and migration to the United States sub- sequently increased significantly, as discussed in Chapter 3. Also see Bonham C. Richardson, "Caribbean Migrations, 1838–1985," in Franklin W. Knight and Colin A. Palmer, eds., *The Modern Caribbean* (Chapel Hill: University of North Carolina Press, 1989), pp. 203–28.

4. *The Economist* Intelligence Unit, *The New Caribbean Deal*, Special Report No. 240, March 1986.

5. While consistent data on income distribution is not available for most Caribbean countries, a few examples illustrate the range of income inequality. In the late 1970s, less than 1 percent of the Haitian population accrued 44 percent of the nation's income; in Trinidad-Tobago, the wealthiest 10 percent of the population accrued 32 percent, while the poorest 20 percent earned only 4.2 percent. Josh DeWind and David H. Kinley III, *Aiding Migration: the Impact of International Development Assistance on Haiti* (Boulder: Westview Press, 1988), p. 104; World Bank, *World Development Report, 1989* (Washington, D.C.: World Bank, 1989), Table 30.

6. Franklin Knight and Colin Palmer, eds., "Introduction," *The Modern Caribbean* (Chapel Hill: University of North Carolina Press, 1989), p. 7.

7. Some Caribbean scholars argue that the peasantry was deliberately main- tained at low levels of productivity in order to assure their labor would be available to the plantations, a pattern which continued until well into the twentieth century. See Jay Mandle, "British Caribbean Economic History," in Knight and Palmer, eds., *The Modern Caribbean*, p. 233.

8. Ibid., p. 238.

9. Knight and Palmer, "Introduction," p. 13.

10. For an introduction to these issues see Rosina Wiltshire-Brodber, "Gender, Race and Class in the Caribbean," in Patricia Mohammed and Catherine Shep-

herd, eds., *Gender in Caribbean Development* (Trinidad: University of the West Indies, Women in Development Studies Project, 1988), pp. 145–48.

11. Helen Safa, "Economic Autonomy and Sexual Equality in Caribbean Societies," *Social and Economic Studies*, 35, no. 3 (1986).

12. Helen Safa, "Women and Industrialization in the Caribbean," in Sharon Stitcher and Jane Parpart, eds., *Women, Employment and the Family in the International Division of Labor* (New York: MacMillan, forthcoming 1990).

13. The assumptions behind the export-led growth stabilization strategy have been questioned in numerous reports. See U.S. General Accounting Office, *Foreign Assistance: U.S. Use of Conditions to Achieve Economic Reforms* (Washington, D.C.: GAO, 1986), pp. 42–43, and "Group of 24 Report," *IMF Survey*, August 10, 1987.

CHAPTER 2

The Economic Crisis

FOR MOST CARIBBEAN COUNTRIES and territories, the 1960s and 1970s were years of significant economic growth. During the 1980s, however, growth rates of Gross Domestic Product (GDP) per capita have declined, often to the point of being negative, while unemployment and inflation have increased and capital accumulation has slowed down. The generally adverse economic conditions prevailing in the Caribbean had their recent origin in the recession which gripped the advanced countries at the beginning of the decade. Given the degree of openness of Caribbean economies, periods of expansion and contraction in the international economy are quickly translated into fluctuations in the demand for Caribbean exports and changes in the prices of what the region sells and consumes. But current economic problems in the region are also a consequence of the structural crisis associated with the collapse of the previous structures of capital accumulation in both the advanced countries and in the Caribbean.

The economic crisis in the Caribbean has exacerbated the well-known characteristics of underdevelopment—the persistence of absolute poverty, generally high rates of unemployment and underemployment, and extremely skewed distributions of income, land, and wealth—in the context of the decline of the colonial economic model. The colonial economy was built around the primary export sector. Its collapse has been hastened by the profound changes in the world economy which have characterized the decades of the 1970s and 1980s.

The end of U.S. hegemony—signaled, for instance, by the United States going off the gold standard in 1974—coincided with a precipitous decline in growth rates of world production and trade, with world trade, which had grown at an average 8.7 percent a year from 1965 to 1973, declining to 4.6 percent between 1973 and 1980 and to 2.4 percent between 1980 and 1985.[1] The contraction of world trade generated increased competition as well as trade disputes and growing

Table 2.1
Growth Rate of Gross Domestic Product Per Capita, Selected Caribbean Countries, 1961–88

	1961–70[1]	1971–80[1]	1981–85[1]	1986	1987	1988[2]
Bahamas	2.6	–0.1	0.3	1.2	3.0	0.7
Barbados	5.9	1.2	–1.0	4.9	2.5	3.4
Dominican Republic	1.9	4.3	–0.8	0.8	5.7	–1.3
Guyana	1.0	0.9	–3.5	0.3	0.7	–2.9
Haiti	–1.2	2.8	–2.8	–0.9	–2.1	–2.1
Jamaica	4.0	–2.3	–1.3	0.4	3.7	0.4
Suriname	9.7	4.8	–0.3	0.6	–8.7	1.6
Trinidad-Tobago	2.5	5.1	–4.0	–4.3	–8.6	–5.1
All Latin America and Caribbean reported	2.8	3.4	–1.6	1.6	0.8	–1.5

Source: Derived from Inter-American Development Bank, Economic and Social Progress in Latin America, 1989 Report (Washington, D.C.: IDB, 1989), tables A-1 and II-3.

1) Average cumulative growth in 1988 dollars
2) Preliminary

protectionist sentiment among the advanced capitalist countries. It has also brought about significant changes in the international division of labor and in the structure of production as a result of technical change. Among the most important of the latter trends has been the radical decrease in the raw material intensity of industrial production with adverse effects for the Caribbean's major raw material exports (oil, sugar, and bauxite-alumina).[2]

The combination of internal and external, cyclical and structural factors has produced three types of interrelated macroeconomic imbalances, or financial crises, for the economies of the region: (1) a balance of payments crisis, (2) a fiscal crisis, and (3) a debt crisis. While the incidence and intensity of each has varied by country, the response of the governments of the region to these three types of financial crisis has been fairly uniform, with austerity or stabilization programs promoted by the International Monetary Fund (IMF) the norm. Structural adjustment policies—or austerity plus export diversification— have thus far produced only internal recessions with slower growth, less investment, growing unemployment, and falling real-wage levels, while export earnings continue to flounder.

The Making of a Crisis

In the first half of the 1980s the growth rate of per capita GDP throughout the region was negative, in marked contrast to previous decades (see Table 2.1). The decline in GDP per capita affected oil-producing economies (such as Trinidad-Tobago) and mineral-producing

Table 2.2
Percentage Change in GDP, 1980–88 (at constant prices)

	1980	1983	1984	1985	1986	1987	1988	Average[1]
Antigua/Barbuda	6.7	6.9	7.5	7.7	8.4	8.8	7.6	7.8
Bahamas	6.7	3.2	6.4	5.2	1.4	4.6	4.7	4.3
Barbados	4.3	0.4	3.6	1.2	5.1	2.5	3.5	2.7
Belize	2.4	0.8	0.8	2.3	1.5	5.0	7.6	3.0
Cuba[2]	−0.5	4.9	7.2	4.6	1.2	−3.5	2.3	2.8
Dominica	16.5	3.0	5.0	1.7	6.8	6.8	5.6	4.8
Dominican Republic	6.0	4.6	0.3	−2.6	2.0	8.1	0.9	2.2
Grenada	—	1.4	5.4	4.9	5.5	6.0	4.3	4.6
Guyana	1.9	−9.3	2.1	1.0	0.2	0.7	−3.0	−1.4
Haiti	6.7	0.6	0.4	0.5	0.5	0.1	−0.8	0.2
Jamaica	−5.4	2.3	−0.9	−4.7	1.9	5.2	1.5	0.9
St. Kitts-Nevis	3.9	−1.1	9.0	5.6	6.3	6.8	4.7	5.2
St. Lucia	−1.0	4.1	5.0	6.0	5.9	2.0	5.0	4.7
St. Vincent-Grenadines	3.3	5.8	5.3	4.6	7.2	5.7	8.4	6.2
Suriname	−6.6	−4.1	−1.9	−2.3	−2.0	−6.6	—	−3.4
Trinidad-Tobago	−6.5	5.2	−7.1	−4.5	−1.0	−6.1	−4.7	−3.0
British Virgin Islands	14.0	5.9	5.6	0.2	4.2	16.0	10.0	7.0
Montserrat	9.4	−5.3	2.8	5.4	5.1	10.8	12.1	5.2
Puerto Rico	1.6	1.7	6.6	2.2	7.0	7.6	5.2	5.0

Source: ECLAC, "The Impact of External Sector Developments on Caribbean Economic Performance 1983–1988," LC/CAR/G.278, October 1989, Table 3.

1) Average relates to period 1983–88, or 1983–87 in the case of Suriname
2) Global social product in 1981 prices

economies (Jamaica, Guyana), agricultural producers (the Dominican Republic and Haiti), and those diversifying production toward nontraditional exports (Barbados). In some countries, where growth in the 1970s already had been sluggish, such as Guyana, or negative as in Jamaica, the crisis of the 1980s wiped out the gains of the decade of the 1960s in terms of average per capita income; Haiti and Suriname lost the gains of the 1970s.[3]

The exception to this trend included a number of the Organization of Eastern Caribbean States (OECS) countries (Antigua, Montserrat, St. Kitts, and St. Vincent), the British Virgin Islands, and Puerto Rico, where growth in GDP after 1983 exceeded an average 5.0 percent (see Table 2.2). The economies of the countries of the Organization of Eastern Caribbean States (OECS) are primarily rooted in tourism, and they seem to be the least affected by the downturn. The most affected economies in the region were those that rely heavily on primary exports, with a relatively large industrial sector dependent on foreign inputs.[4]

Table 2.3
Rates of Unemployment, 1980–87 (percentages)

	1980	1981	1982	1983	1984	1985	1986	1987
Barbados	12.6	10.7	13.6	15.0	17.1	18.7^a	17.7^a	17.8
Belize	14.3	—	—	—	14.0	—	14.0	15.0
Dominica	23.0	23.0	15.0	—	17.5	—	—	—
Dominican Republic	—	20.7	—	—	25.0^b	27.2^b	28.7^b	28.0
Grenada	27.9	—	14.2	—	39.5	21.0	—	—
Guyana	—	—	—	—	—	—	30.0	—
Haiti	—	—	—	—	—	—	14.0	—
Jamaica	27.3	25.9	27.4	26.7	25.4	25.0^a	23.6^a	21.0
Montserrat	6.1	5.5^a	5.6^a	7.0^a	5.8^a	5.3^a	4.0	2.0
Netherlands Antilles	—	20.2^a	15.0^a	19.4^a	20.8^a	22.2^a	15.8	26.0
St. Kitts-Nevis	—	—	30.0	—	—	30.0	—	20.0
St. Lucia	—	—	27.0	—	18.9^b	18.7^b	18.6^b	18.3^b
St. Vincent-Grenadines	—	—	20.0	—	40.0^b	40.1^b	40.0^b	—
Trinidad-Tobago	10.0	10.4	10.4	11.1	12.7	15.5^a	22.0	22.3^a

Sources: 1980 to 1984 data from United Nations Economic Commission on Latin America, Economic Survey of Latin America and the Caribbean (Santiago: ECLA), various years; 1985 to 1987 data from Department of Commerce, Caribbean and Central American Databook (Washington, D.C.: Government Printing Office, 1988, 1989); data indicated (a) from International Labour Office, Yearbook of Labour Statistics (Geneva: ILO, 1988); and (b) from Department of Commerce, Foreign Economic Trends (Washington, D.C.: Government Printing Office, 1987, 1988).

Even acceptable growth rates of GDP did little to dampen high unemployment and underemployment rates in the region. Before the 1982 world recession, and despite increasing rates of international migration, measured unemployment rates in the Caribbean often exceeded 15 percent or even 20 percent of the labor force. After 1981–82 the rate of unemployment increased in Barbados, Trinidad-Tobago, the Dominican Republic, and Grenada (see Table 2.3). In 1984 St. Vincent-Grenadines and Grenada both exhibited unemployment rates of 40 percent, the highest in the region.

After relative price stability in the 1960s, inflation accelerated to two digits in most countries in the region in the latter half of the 1970s, carrying over until 1982, the year of the big slump in the U.S. economy and of plummeting Caribbean export earnings (see Table 2.4). Inflation was initially fueled by the rising price of imports, but in certain countries it was subsequently aggravated by structural adjustment policies, such as devaluation and the liberalization of imports, or rising budget deficits. Inflation remained intractable in Guyana, and beginning in 1984, in the Dominican Republic; in contrast, in Jamaica, which had exhibited the highest rate of inflation in the region in the 1970s, recessionary policies began to curb inflation in 1987.[5] High inflation had two main consequences: declining real wages and consumption

Table 2.4
Inflation Rates, 1961–88

	1961–70	1971–80	1981–85	1986	1987	1988[1]
Bahamas	6.2	7.5	5.9	5.5	6.0	5.1
Barbados	3.0	14.6	7.8	1.3	3.3	4.8
Dominican Republic	2.1	10.5	16.9	9.8	16.1	44.4
Guyana	2.3	10.3	19.7	7.9	28.7	40.1
Haiti	2.9	10.9	9.1	3.3	−11.5	−0.2
Jamaica	4.2	18.5	16.9	15.1	6.7	8.2
Suriname	4.2	9.9	7.0	18.7	53.3	7.3
Trinidad-Tobago	3.1	13.2	12.4	7.7	10.7	7.8

Source: Inter-American Development Bank, *Economic and Social Progress in Latin America, 1989 Report* (Washington, D.C.: IDB, 1989), table 11.7. Inflation rates are the annual averages of monthly consumer price indexes.

1) Preliminary estimate

Table 2.5
Rate of Growth of Gross Domestic Investment, 1961–88 (percentages)

	Cumulative			Annual		
	1961–70	1971–80	1981–88	1986	1987	1988[1]
Barbados	7.8	0.6	−4.8	7.4	2.5	2.1
Dominican Republic	12.2	10.0	4.2	11.7	39.5	6.7
Guyana	0.6	−0.7	−3.5	13.3	1.2	3.5
Haiti	4.5	11.8	0.3	−8.4	−1.8	−1.4
Jamaica	6.7	−9.4	3.7	−19.0	21.3	14.3
Suriname	2.1	3.5	−14.4	−20.4	−6.6	25.1
Trinidad-Tobago	1.2	16.6	−11.6	−0.9	−22.3	−4.0

Source: Inter-American Development Bank, *Economic and Social Progress in Latin America, 1989 Report* (Washington, D.C.: IDB, 1989), table III-1.

1) Preliminary estimate

standards among the majority of the population, and decreasing savings rates and capital flight among the wealthier minority.

Perhaps the best indicator of a stagnant capitalist economy is the rate of growth of investment, a measure of the rate of capital accumulation. Between 1961 and 1970 a number of Caribbean economies enjoyed relatively high rates of growth of gross domestic investment (see Table 2.5). Growth rates slowed down in the 1970s (with the exception of the Dominican Republic, Haiti, and Trinidad-Tobago) and came to a standstill in Barbados, with disinvestment occurring in Jamaica and Guyana. In the first half of the 1980s, new investment in the region slowed to a trickle—with disinvestment concentrated in Suriname and Trinidad-Tobago—a consequence of capital flight, decreased foreign investment, and the general contraction in state ex-

Table 2.6
Exports and Imports as a Percentage of Gross Domestic Product, 1985

	Exports as % of GDP	Imports as % of GDP
Barbados	67.5	59.8
Belize	55.3[1]	65.4[1]
Dominica	37.5[1]	71.9[1]
Dominican Republic	9.6	11.5
Grenada	44.9	76.9
Guyana	53.1	73.2
Haiti	23.2	34.1
Jamaica	58.0	67.8
Puerto Rico	87.6	124.2
St. Lucia	65.4[2]	83.2[2]
St. Vincent-Grenadines	75.9	82.9
Suriname	36.7	35.3
Trinidad-Tobago	32.9	28.8

Sources: International Monetary Fund, *International Financial Statistics*, vol. 41, no. 6 (Washington, D.C.: IMF, 1988), country tables; data for Puerto Rico from Junta de Planificación de Puerto Rico, *Informe Económico al Gobernador, 1987* (San Juan, P.R.: Junta de Planificación, 1987), table 2.

1) Figure for 1984
2) Figure for 1983

penditures throughout the region. In the late 1980s there were signs of a modest recovery in the Dominican Republic and in 1987 in Jamaica, induced by a rise in investment in tourism and free-trade zones.

The trends in growth rates of GDP, unemployment, inflation, and investment are important symptoms of the crisis in the Caribbean. In order to explain these outcomes, however, it is necessary to probe a bit deeper and examine the underlying structure of production in the region.

The Colonial Legacy

As noted earlier, the Caribbean economies are particularly open economies. Whereas exports constitute only around 10 percent of the U.S. GDP, it is not unusual for this ratio to be on the order of 50 percent in the Caribbean (see Table 2.6). In most cases, imports represent an even higher share of GDP, reaching 80 percent and more in the Windward Islands and more than 100 percent in Puerto Rico. The consequence of this degree of openness is that any change in international demand for the region's exports, a change in import prices, or the availability of external finance will have a disproportionate effect on the level of Caribbean income. In a recent study it was estimated that a decrease of one percent in the growth rate of the U.S. economy reduces the export earnings of Caribbean Basin countries by approximately $2.9 billion while reducing GDP by approximately $5.7 billion.[6] The ripple effect is of this magnitude because of the degree of openness and the importance of the United States as a trading partner.

What explains this degree of trade dependence and the minimal control these countries have over their economies? Trade dependence is unavoidable for countries with small populations and/or geographical size. The small size of the market limits the range of products which these countries can produce efficiently due to the presence of economies of scale in manufacturing production. This is certainly one factor. But the pattern of production of primary goods for export and reliance on imported raw materials and equipment as well as consumption goods is also a result of many centuries of colonial rule. European and North American colonialism imposed a productive structure designed to satisfy the demand of industrialized countries for primary goods such as sugar, bananas, coffee, bauxite, aluminum, and oil. More recently, tourism and labor-intensive manufacturing have been added to the list.

The most important characteristic of Caribbean economies is their production of only one or two main exports. In 1985, petroleum products accounted for 82 percent of Trinidad-Tobago's merchandise exports while bauxite and alumina accounted for 68 percent of Jamaica's, 76 percent of Suriname's and 43 percent of Guyana's export earnings. A number of countries are highly dependent on sugar exports, with sugar constituting 74 percent of total exports in Cuba, 46 percent in Belize, 35 percent in Guyana, and 21 percent in the Dominican Republic. Bananas accounted for 50 percent of export earnings in St. Lucia, 44 percent in Dominica, and 21 percent in St. Vincent-Grenadines, while coffee accounted for 22 percent of Haiti's exports. Only in Puerto Rico and Barbados (where electronic components accounted for 57 percent of merchandise export earnings in 1984) has there been a significant shift away from dependence on primary commodity exports.[7]

Export production has determined the structure of investment, imports, state expenditures and foreign aid. Foreign investors traditionally have owned a large proportion of the productive capacity in these countries, whether agricultural lands or mines. For example, about 70 percent of foreign investment in Jamaica between 1950 and 1968 was directed to bauxite and alumina production. In Trinidad-Tobago, where petroleum is by far the most important industry, United States direct investment in this industry at the end of 1981 amounted to $808 million or 87 percent of total U.S. investment in the country.[8]

The expansion of the export sector fueled by foreign investment shaped the demand for imports throughout the region. A large proportion of imports are machinery and raw materials for the export sector.

Moreover, the increased demand for labor and land in the export sector affected food production for local markets, increasing the need to import food. In the early 1970s imports of food ranged from 14 percent to 31 percent of total imports of the CARICOM countries.[9] More recently, the expansion of tourism has increased the demand for luxury manufactures and non-Caribbean food imports.

State expenditures and foreign aid also contributed to the expansion of the export sector, often at the expense of food self-sufficiency and industrialization. Agricultural and mining export industries required a relatively sophisticated infrastructure of ports, roads, and buildings; these were developed largely through bilateral or multilateral public borrowing or, in the case of the smaller islands, through international grants. Servicing the debt was not too problematic during the early period of postwar expansion, but became a burden when the tax base was eroded by falling export revenues and declining overall employment.

The colonial economic model in the Caribbean is also characterized by the coexistence of a modern export sector—on the larger islands, complemented by import substitution industries—with a highly fragmented domestic-oriented sector. Typically, such sectors as local food production, transportation, nonindustrial manufacturing, and construction are characterized by a large number of small independent producers who rely on the family labor force. Income in nonexport sectors is generally low and these workers and peasants are extremely poor. The neocolonial government is unable to nurture local, small-scale industries due to the infrastructure requirements of the export sector, the pressing demand for basic services, and an eroding revenue base. The weaknesses of the colonial economy model are evident during periods of crisis.

In contrast to periods of long-term expansion (such as during the early postwar years), in which stable flows of foreign investment and stable demand for exports allow macroeconomic stability, in crisis periods the decline in the demand for exports combines with falling investment levels and the drainage of economic surpluses to induce great macroeconomic instability on these islands. U.S. direct investment in the Caribbean has fallen sharply, led by disinvestment in offshore petroleum refining in the Netherlands Antilles in the late 1970s and in Trinidad-Tobago in the early 1980s; in this latter period U.S. investment in bauxite/alumina production in Jamaica also declined significantly (Table 2.7). In fact, during the 1980s, U.S. investment has been increasingly concentrated in the financial centers of Bermuda, the Bahamas, and the UK islands, while investment in the rest of the Caribbean has fallen drastically.

The effect of disinvestment is seen in the case of Trinidad-Tobago, where between 1956 and 1983 the inflow of foreign direct investment

Table 2.7
U.S. Direct Investment in the Caribbean, 1977–88 (in US$ millions)

	1977	1980	1983	1985	1986	1987	1988
Bahamas	997	2,712	3,762	3,795	2,991	2,706	2,244
Barbados	26	40	58	81	212	179	304
Belize	21	24	−46	2	n.d.	−15	−16
Bermuda	7,708	11,045	11,056	13,116	15,373	19,100	19,880
Dominican Republic	243	316	258	212	199	156	141
French Islands	12	21	13	9	12	26	22
Guyana	n.d.	n.d.	6	2	2	4	5
Haiti	14	34	17	26	29	34	27
Jamaica	378	407	310	122	106	102	156
Netherlands Antilles	−792	−4,336	−22,956	−20,499	−16,969	−14,257	−11,796
Trinidad-Tobago	971	951	862	484	424	388	429
UK Islands	336	979	1,960	3,490	3,794	3,953	3,577
(a) Total	9,914	12,193	−4,700	840	6,173	12,376	14,973
(b) Total Excluding Netherlands Antilles	10,706	16,529	18,256	21,339	23,142	26,633	26,769
(c) Total Excluding Netherlands Antilles and Financial Centers[1]	1,665	1,793	1,478	938	984	874	1,068

Sources: For 1977 and 1980, U.S. Department of Commerce, U.S. Direct Investment Abroad: Balance of Payments and Direct Investment Position Estimates 1977–81 (Washington, D.C.: Department of Commerce, 1986); for 1983–1988, "U.S. Direct Investment Position Abroad," Survey of Current Business (August), 1989, table 29.

1) The Financial Centers include the Bahamas, Bermuda, and the UK Islands

amounted to TT$5.3 billion, while the net investment outflow reached TT$6.1 billion. Similarly, between 1968 and 1980 total direct investment in Jamaica amounted to J$435 million while foreign investment income was J$996 million, producing a J$561 million deficit in little more than a decade.[10] These and other case studies suggest a significant long-term outflow of capital from the Caribbean economies.[11]

In short, underlying the severity of the 1980s recession on Caribbean economies is the hidden structure of the colonial economy. Long-term stagnation in the export sector, with its resulting decline in foreign investment, induces balance of payment deficits, a structural decline in state revenues, and increases in foreign debt.

The 1980s Recession

The recent recession well illustrates how "when the U.S. sneezes, the Caribbean catches a cold." The first jolt to the Caribbean economies came with the sharp increase in oil prices in 1972–73, which raised the import bill significantly for nonoil producers in the region. The second oil price increase, in 1979, was even more severe, for it was accompanied by a general rise in the price level of Caribbean imports, a product of the inflationary trends in the advanced economies in this period. This was then followed by the 1980–82 international recession, which severely reduced the demand for a number of regional exports, particularly bauxite, petroleum products, and sugar, as well as the number of tourists visiting the islands, and thus tourist earnings.

Caribbean economies felt the consequences of the recession in lower prices for their exports: sugar prices on the world market fell by an average annual 32 percent between 1980 and 1985, alumina by 10 percent, bauxite by 5 percent, and coffee by 4 percent.[12] The net effects of these changes were deteriorating terms of trade, lower export volumes, and declining foreign exchange earnings. The unfavorable external conditions affected most countries of the Caribbean, with the severity depending on the particular export product produced and the degree to which exports are concentrated in only one or two products.

Here it is useful to consider a few contrasting cases of how the composition and fate of the export sector has affected national economic performance. The Jamaican economy was doing reasonably well until 1973. In 1974 a large balance of payments deficit instigated by the oil price hike and a fall in exports marked the beginning of its current history of severe economic difficulties. The Michael Manley government was unable to restore external balance which, together with U.S. destabilization activities and Manley's new taxes on bauxite production, caused U.S. investors to lose confidence; production levels in the mineral export sector did not recover. The economy was thus in poor shape to withstand the onslaught of the early 1980s recession which brought an even more severe decline in the demand for traditional exports and deteriorating terms of trade.

Between 1980 and 1984 the value of Jamaican exports declined by an average 19.8 percent a year.[13] The decline in export earnings was only partially offset by increasing tourist revenues, once the government of Edward Seaga had replaced that of Michael Manley and the Reagan administration began to convince U.S. tourists of Jamaica's stability.[14] U.S. investors remained skeptical, however, and direct U.S. investment in the Jamaican economy continued to decline (see Table. 2.7). With aggregate demand severely reduced by the contraction in exports, investment, and government spending (due to austerity measures, subsequently discussed), the result has been low or negative growth rates of GDP (see Table 2.2).

The Trinidadian economy illustrates a somewhat different process, since it initially reaped the benefits of being an important producer of petroleum and petroleum products. It did not experience a drastic curtailment in external demand until 1981, which was then felt throughout the economy. Between 1980 and 1985 the value of petroleum exports declined by an average annual 14.4 percent, with the decline even more severe in 1986 and 1987.[15] Production of petroleum and petroleum derivatives declined from 87 percent of 1977 production levels in 1980, to 34 percent in 1983. As Table 2.2 shows, the only other economies which performed as poorly, on average, as Trinidad-Tobago in the 1980s were Guyana and Suriname.

Sectoral Changes

The relative performance of Caribbean economies depends on the composition and fate of their export sector as well as on government economic policies. Here we will examine in more detail the specific sectoral trends contributing to the economic crisis.

Agriculture. For the twenty countries which are members of the Caribbean Development and Cooperation Committee (CDCC) of the Economic Commission for Latin America and the Caribbean (ECLAC), the contribution of agriculture to GDP declined from around 18 percent in 1974 to 15 percent a decade later.[16] The decline, rather than a product of the expansion of other sectors—generally associated with the growth process—can be largely attributed to the displacement of food production and the stagnation of traditional export agriculture, particularly sugar.

Over the last decade the Caribbean has become a net importer of food. Four countries in particular have seen their imported food bill as a proportion of total imports rise between 1972 and 1982: Jamaica, Montserrat, St. Lucia, and Trinidad-Tobago.[17] The decline of sugar production and exports is partly related to severely reduced U.S. sugar quotas in the 1980s, falling world prices, and stagnation in terms of productivity levels. Caribbean earnings from sugar exports to the United States have fallen by 77 percent—from $408 million in 1980 to $93 million in 1987 as a result of reduced U.S. sugar quotas.[18] Moreover, U.S. protectionism has accelerated the trend toward expanded production of sugar substitutes, such as artificial and vegetable sweeteners, a trend which bodes ill for the long-term prospects of this industry.

A number of Caribbean countries have begun to rationalize the sugar industry, aiming to make production more efficient while liberating marginal sugarcane-producing land for agricultural diversification. In Jamaica, Trinidad-Tobago, and Barbados the plan is to produce sugarcane sufficient to meet only local consumption demand and quotas in preferential markets.

Whereas sugar exports have traditionally depended upon preferential access to the protected U.S. market (with the exception of Cuba since

1960, the main sugar producer in the region), 99 percent of CARICOM banana exports go to the protected UK market where they constitute 70 percent of British banana imports. After precipitous declines in the early 1980s (principally due to hurricane damage to the crop), banana exports climbed back up to their 1977–80 level in 1985. The recovery has been particularly strong in Dominica, St. Lucia, Belize, St. Vincent-Grenadines, and Suriname. However, yields in the Caribbean are less than in Central America, and CARICOM bananas are competitive only because of British trade preferences. These may erode after the unification of the European Common Market in 1992.

Manufacturing. In 1974 manufacturing contributed approximately 13 percent of GDP for the twenty CDCC countries; a decade later, this sector still accounted for only around 13.5 percent of GDP. The importance of the manufacturing sector differs widely across the region, with Cuba and Puerto Rico having achieved the most developed manufacturing sectors. The other larger economies of the region—the Dominican Republic, Haiti, Guyana, and Jamaica—all were above the 1974 regional average, at around 14 percent to 18 percent; the exception here is Trinidad-Tobago, where manufacturing accounted for only 5.3 percent of GDP in 1980, similar to the figure for the OECS countries.

Whereas the earlier import substitution industries geared either to the internal or regional market have generally stagnated over the last decade, growth in manufacturing has been concentrated in the free trade zones and in other assembly industries. These now account for 30 percent of total manufacturing production in Haiti, where assembly production is responsible for what growth occurred in manufacturing exports in the 1980s; a similar trend is apparent in the Dominican Republic and Jamaica. It is estimated that the output of the free-trade zones plus that of other assembled products accounted for 28 percent of total regional exports to the United States in 1984. However, the impact of this new manufacturing sector on domestic growth rates has been minimal, since value added to GDP is relatively small, given the few linkages to the rest of the economy, low wages, and the relatively small proportion of the economically active population employed in this sector.

Mining. The changing fortunes of the Caribbean mining sector, particularly its strong decline in the 1980s, can be attributed largely to changing structures of production in the advanced capitalist economies, rather than to those of the region. The fall in bauxite production—the most important mineral export in the region—was largely in response to the decline in international demand as a result of the world recession; in addition, a number of new aluminum producers came on stream in the early 1980s, leading to overcapacity in the industry and depressed prices. Moreover, a structural problem in this industry is the declining trend of the level of raw material per unit of manufacturing output in the advanced countries. Technical change has resulted in an increasing trend for plastics to replace aluminum.

The result of all of these factors was that between 1974 and 1984 the production of bauxite (from which alumina is derived) fell by 57 percent in Guyana, 42 percent in Jamaica, and 30 percent in Suriname, while it ceased entirely in Haiti and the Dominican Republic. Alumina production declined by 39 percent in Jamaica, ceased in Guyana, and has remained relatively constant in Suriname.

External factors have also contributed to the decline of the petroleum industry in the region. U.S. government efforts to discourage offshore refining in favor of the domestic refining industry (as well as periodic efforts to encourage energy conservation) have led to heavy disinvestment by U.S. multinationals that had built up the petroleum sector in Trinidad-Tobago as well as offshore refining in the Dutch Antilles, the Bahamas, and the U.S. Virgin Islands. In Trinidad-Tobago crude oil production declined by approximately 20 percent from 1974 to 1984; part of the decline was also due to the depletion of existing wells. The offshore refining component of the industry ceased operations in 1982. As a result, after the oil price increases which raised the contribution of this sector from 20 percent (1972) to 43 percent (1974) of Trinidadian GDP, petroleum's contribution had returned to 1972 levels in 1984. The decline in petroleum earnings accelerated after 1982 as prices started to fall, reaching new lows in 1986 and then again in 1988. The story of the offshore refining and transshipment depots in other Caribbean countries has been equally chaotic, going from the largest concentration of intermediate export refineries in the world to obsolescence in slightly over a decade.

Tourism. By 1985 this sector had become the single most important economic activity and major source of foreign exchange for many Caribbean countries, generating approximately $4.6 billion in revenues regionally in that year. Between 1983 and 1988 tourism earnings increased by an average annual 10 percent, with the fastest growth reported by the new entrants to the industry—Antigua, Dominica, the Dominican Republic, and the British Virgin Islands—and countries recovering from a previous slump, such as Cuba. Earnings were below average in Jamaica, Puerto Rico, and Haiti, and declined in Suriname and Trinidad-Tobago.[19]

It would not be an exaggeration to say that Caribbean economies are being sustained by tourist dollars. In 1984 tourism comprised 40 percent of the GDP of Antigua, 33 percent of that of the Bahamas, and 28 percent of that of Jamaica. Moreover, tourist expenditures in

1985 exceeded the total value of merchandise exports in Antigua, the Bahamas, Grenada, St. Lucia, and the British Virgin Islands. Even in those economies which are relatively diversified, tourist expenditures were equal to 84 percent of the value of merchandise exports for Barbados, 72 percent in Jamaica, 50 percent in the Dominican Republic, and 31 percent in Haiti.[20]

The tourism sector is an important source of employment in the islands, but it suffers from relatively weak domestic linkages (particularly to the agricultural sector). In 1982 the import content of tourist consumption was 61 percent in Antigua, 50 percent in Jamaica, 36 percent in the Virgin Islands and 34 percent in the Dominican Republic.[21] The foreign exchange generating potential of tourism is weakened by other structural factors such as advanced, fully paid bookings through tour agencies in the United States and the trend toward ship-board rather than island-housed visitors. In the Dominican Republic it is reported that only 15 percent of tourist revenues pass through the Central Bank; a 1982 study of twelve Caribbean islands, however, found that 42 percent of each tourist dollar was retained in direct, local value added.[22] The tourism industry is also sensitive to price and exchange rate considerations as well as to changing political conditions. Its health is also intimately tied to the state of the U.S. economy and U.S. disposable income levels, as well as to U.S. policies toward the various governments of the region.

Banking. A few countries of the region have benefited considerably from attractive inducements to U.S. finance capital. It is reported that in the Dutch Antilles the financial sector provides foreign exchange revenues three times greater than merchandise trade and, in the case of Curaçao, provides 53 percent of the total revenues of the government. The importance of this sector to the Bahamas is no less, although of smaller magnitude, and several other islands have recently changed their tax and disclosure policies to compete in this field. The advantages for international investors to locate their savings offshore in the region's financial havens have been eroded somewhat, however, by recent changes in U.S. policy; interest earnings on nonresident deposits in the United States are now exempt from U.S. taxation.

Government. In the 1974–84 period the share of government in the GDP of the twenty-country CDCC group increased from an average 16 percent to 19 percent. In that earlier year the government sector accounted for a greater share of GDP in the smaller countries of the region: Dominica (24 percent), St. Lucia (22 percent), Montserrat (23 percent), and, of course, in socialist Cuba where the state sector represents 80 percent. The growth of the government sector in GDP subsequently was concentrated in Suriname (which now claims the highest share in the region), Jamaica (until 1981), and Trinidad-Tobago, in all three cases associated with the formation of numerous state enterprises in the decade of the 1970s. As we will subsequently see, government expenditures consistently exceed revenues in most countries of the region.

In summary, the general trends indicate that agricultural diversification is proceeding more slowly than the decline in traditional exports; that import-substitution industries appear to be generally stagnant, with growth in manufacturing concentrated in export assembly industries that have a minimal impact on national growth rates; that traditional mineral exports are in decline, although petroleum will continue to be pro-cyclical (following periods of expansion and contraction in the world economy); and that tourism, which is also pro-cyclical, is the current growth industry, but it too is hampered by few domestic linkages. Despite recent sectoral changes, the structural factors underlying the economic crisis remain. Recent changes integrate the Caribbean as closely as ever to the U.S. economy, implying that the region will continue to be quite vulnerable to U.S. business cycles and changes in U.S. economic policies. Moreover, most Caribbean countries are expanding in the same sectors—competing in the production of winter crops, free-trade zone assembly industries, and tourism—while trying to attract the same type of foreign direct investment.

The Balance Sheet

The result of the prevailing adverse external conditions of the early 1980s, which aggravated underlying structural problems in many Caribbean economies, was typically a balance of payments crisis, a fiscal crisis, and/or a debt crisis.

The Balance of Payments Crisis

The decline in the demand for traditional exports, combined with deteriorating terms of trade, a net outflow of foreign capital, and rising freight and insurance payments, threw many Caribbean economies into a balance of payments crisis. In 1980 eighteen of the twenty CDCC countries exhibited negative trade balances (only Trinidad-Tobago and Suriname being exempt from this fate). In 1986, of the seventeen countries for which data is available, only Puerto Rico demonstrated a positive balance of trade. In most of the larger islands, the merchandise trade balance as well as the balance on current account were negative in the 1980–86 period (see Table 2.8).

Current account deficits are, of course, not new to the 1980s. For six of the largest economies in the region the current account deficit reached almost $3 billion over the 1973–79 period (Table 2.8). Changed international conditions simply aggravated underlying structural problems. Among the major domestic factors contributing to this chronic state of affairs is the high import content of industrial production and increasing food dependency throughout the region. Another factor aggravating the balance on current account is the large presence of multinationals in the Caribbean. For example, in 1982 (the last year for which precise data is available) 1,184 U.S. subsidiaries drained $1.7 billion from the region as direct investment income.[23] Considering the six countries shown in Table 2.8, net outflows of foreign capital reached $3 billion between 1973 and 1979 and $6 billion in the 1980 to 1986 period.

Only the contribution of tourism and migrant remittances (included in category "other" in Table 2.8), which doubled between the two periods, kept the balance on current account from exploding in the 1980s. Trinidad-Tobago was among the few countries in the region that could finance current account deficits through a run on reserves, the product of the oil boom years. At the other extreme were Jamaica and Guyana, which were literally bankrupt. The major alternative for most countries of the region was increased external indebtedness.

The Fiscal Crisis

As with balance of payments problems, fiscal deficits are not new to the region, partly a result of a generally weak tax base and the tremendous pressures upon these states to invest in infrastructure, social services, and sometimes, public enterprises. What turned these ever-present conditions into a fiscal crisis, however, was the loss of tax revenue on exports and the higher external debt-servicing requirements of the 1980s.

Many Caribbean countries rely heavily on taxes on foreign trade to generate government revenue. For example, both Haiti and the Dominican Republic generate over 50 percent of government revenues from this source.[24] The decline in export revenues thus directly and indirectly (through lower GDP and lower income tax revenue) produced a fiscal crisis. In the early 1980s, the only countries not running a significant deficit on current account were Barbados, the Dominican Republic, Trinidad-Tobago, and the British Virgin Islands. By 1986 Trinidad-Tobago had joined those countries running a central government deficit. Jamaica and St. Vincent have made the most significant gains, generating surpluses on the government current account by 1986,

Table 2.8
Balance on Current Account, Selected Caribbean Countries, 1973–79 and 1980–86 (in US$ millions)

	Bahamas	Barbados	Dominican Republic	Haiti	Jamaica	Trinidad-Tobago	Total
			1973–79				
Merchandise Trade							
Exports	935.4	613.8	5013.3	720.2	4982.2	6618.0	
Imports	2816.6	1671.1	5432.6	1095.5	5444.3	5645.1	
Net	−1881.2	−1057.3	−419.3	−375.3	−462.1	972.9	−3222.3
Freight & Insurance							
Credit	0.0	6.9	68.2	2.5	71.0	40.0	
Debit	156.0	146.9	846.3	188.3	783.2	546.6	
Net	−156.0	−140.0	−778.1	−185.8	−712.2	−506.6	−2478.7
Foreign Investment							
Income	1519.8	35.0	35.9	7.8	111.9	471.1	
Payment	2053.9	89.8	844.7	78.3	1050.1	1187.6	
Net	−534.1	−54.8	−808.8	−70.5	−938.2	−716.5	−3122.9
All Others[1]							
Credit	3866.0	1397.1	1347.8	887.1	2598.7	1923.4	
Debit	1077.7	344.6	917.2	462.8	1708.3	1427.5	
Net	2788.3	1052.5	430.6	424.3	890.4	495.9	6082.0
Balance for Period	217.0	−199.6	−1575.6	−207.3	−1222.1	245.7	−2741.9
			1980–86				
Merchandise Trade							
Exports	1643.2	1694.3	5988.6	1329.0	5219.3	15107.9	
Imports	5714.1	3835.3	9232.5	2252.8	7499.9	12547.8	
Net	−4070.9	−2141.0	−3243.9	−923.8	−2279.9	2560.1	−10099.4
Freight & Insurance							
Credit	0.0	35.2	78.8	20.3	93.0	6.5	
Debit	333.7	265.8	780.1	311.5	995.1	1533.3	
Net	−333.7	−230.6	−701.3	−291.2	−902.1	−1526.8	−3985.7
Foreign Investment							
Income	127.8	79.1	92.1	23.4	294.3	1436.4	
Payment	1074.9	201.0	1599.5	111.3	1691.5	3263.2	
Net	−947.1	−121.9	−1507.4	−87.9	−1397.2	−1826.8	−5888.3
All Others[1]							
Credit	7402.6	2701.1	3504.3	1572.8	5490.7	3260.7	
Debit	2120.1	742.7	1119.6	1012.4	2442.1	4769.1	
Net	5282.5	1958.4	2384.7	560.4	3048.6	−1508.4	11726.2
Balance for Period	−69.2	−535.1	−3067.9	−742.5	−1530.6	−2301.9	−8247.2

Source: Inter-American Development Bank, *Economic and Social Progress in Latin America*, 1980, 1981 and 1987 Reports (Washington, D.C.: IDB), various tables.

1) Includes tourism expenses, payments for transportation services other than freight, expenditures by diplomats and military personnel, royalties and other expenses not included in other accounts, and unrequited transfers

in both cases as a result of severe austerity programs, discussed below. The main alternatives for governments running large fiscal deficits were austerity policies which would threaten the growth process and/or increase external indebtedness. While most countries opted for borrowing to avoid an even more severe recession, increasing debt and austerity measures imposed by the IMF have generally prolonged macroeconomic instability.

The Debt Crisis

In the early 1970s the only relatively significant debtors in the Caribbean were Jamaica and the Dominican Republic. In one decade this picture changed considerably. Part of the reason for the increase in external indebtedness in the region lies with the problems analyzed above: the balance of payments and fiscal crises induced by the unfavorable external economic environment which aggravated underlying structural problems. The deterioration in the international economy in the late 1970s also explains why there was an increased supply of loanable funds available from international commercial banks for third world lending, and initially at negative real interest rates.

The genesis of the current debt crisis occurred in the mid-1970s, when many governments decided to use external financing to cushion the impact of the rising price of oil on domestic economies. Between 1975 and 1980 the external debt of Haiti increased fivefold, that of the Dominican Republic, Barbados, and St. Vincent tripled, while Jamaica's doubled in volume (see Table 2.9). Trinidad-Tobago's external debt also increased fivefold, but for different reasons: as an oil producer, it was considered particularly creditworthy by the commercial banks. External borrowing thus financed the steady expansion of state enterprises (natural gas, fertilizer, iron and steel) in this period. Jamaica also incurred debt in order to pursue state-led development projects. But in both Trinidad-Tobago and Jamaica debt was also fueled by capital flight, in the latter country accounting for 50 percent of the growth in the debt between 1977 and 1980.[25]

The public and publicly guaranteed long-term debt of the CARICOM countries almost doubled in the 1980s, with the outstanding debt increasing from $3.1 billion in 1980 to at least $6.5 billion in 1986. In this same period the debt more than doubled in both Haiti and the Dominican Republic. The largest debtor in the Caribbean, however, has continued to be Cuba, with its hard currency debt increasing from $3.9 billion to $6.4 billion just between 1986 and 1988. In 1988 its debt was followed in size by that of Jamaica ($3.5 billion) and the Dominican Republic ($3.2 billion).[26] These three countries, along with

Table 2.9
The External Debt of the Caribbean, 1970–88 (in US$ millions)[1]

	1970	1975	1980	1983	1984	1985	1986	1987	1988
Antigua	n.d.	46	56	51	65	134	n.d.	n.d.	n.d.
Bahamas	44	95	90	237	207	187	202	178	147
Barbados	13	27	98	293	305	361	465	497	566
Belize	4	5	47	76	76	95	108	139	122
Cuba[2]	n.d.	n.d.	3227	2790	2989	3621	3870	6094	6412
Dominica	n.d.	n.d.	18	41	44	49	57	n.d.	n.d.
Dominican Republic	212	411	1220	2198	2363	2689	2879	3151	3216
Grenada	8	8	13	43	42	47	52	65	65
Guyana	83	296	571	693	674	750	826	916	905
Haiti	40	57	341	429	475	520	573	672	683
Jamaica	160	695	1421	2361	2521	2936	3105	3569	3512
Montserrat	n.d.	n.d.	2	3	4	4	3	n.d.	n.d.
St. Kitts	n.d.	n.d.	10	12	17	19	19	n.d.	n.d.
St. Lucia	n.d.	n.d.	18	30	28	29	32	n.d.	n.d.
St. Vincent-Grenadines	1	3	10	22	21	23	27	37	42
Trinidad-Tobago	101	149	712	1026	1063	1299	1585	1639	1717

Sources: World Bank, World Debt Tables (Washington, D.C.: World Bank, 1988–89 and 1989–90), vol. 2, country tables, except for data for Antigua, Dominica, Montserrat, St. Kitts and St. Lucia, which is drawn from the Caribbean Development and Cooperation Committee, An Evaluation of Economic Performance of CDCC Countries (Trinidad: UNECLAC, 1988), table 2, and Cuba, which is drawn from Banco Nacional de Cuba, Cuba Quarterly Economic Report, various issues.

1) Public and publicly guaranteed long-term debt
2) Refers to convertible currency debt only in millions of pesos

Trinidad-Tobago and Guyana, account for around 90 percent of the region's external debt, now nearing $20 billion.[27]

Compared to the major Latin American debtors (Brazil, Mexico, Argentina), the outstanding external debt of the Caribbean may seem insignificant. Other indicators of indebtedness are useful to put it into perspective, however. In 1988 per capita debt stood at a high of $1,820 in Jamaica and $1,512 in Barbados—all in the range prevailing for the debt giants. It was actually even higher in the two countries of the region which are in significant arrears on debt repayment, $2,915 in Antigua-Barbuda and $2,249 in Guyana.[28] Caribbean countries also exhibit higher debt-to-GDP ratios than the Latin American average (which was 45.5 percent in 1986). In the Caribbean the highest debt to GDP ratio was in Guyana (187 percent), followed by Jamaica (145 percent) and then by Antigua (73 percent) and Dominica (63 percent).[29]

Most worrisome for a number of countries in the region was the debt-service ratio (the debt service as a percentage of earnings from

Feature

Two Special Cases of Debt: Cuba and Puerto Rico

Cuba and Puerto Rico differ in significant ways from the other Caribbean countries with respect to their external debt. The specificity of Cuba arises from its particular structure of trade, with over 80 percent corresponding to trade with the Soviet Union and other socialist countries. Moreover, trade agreements with socialist bloc countries peg the price of Cuba's main export, sugar, to an index of the prices of Cuban imports from these countries. Cuba was thus partly shielded from the adverse international economic conditions of the early 1980s. However, in the mid 1970s, as part of its import substitution program into capital goods, Cuba borrowed heavily from Western Europe and Japan. Expecting to repay these loans through increased exports to the West, it was caught, initially by the severe fall in sugar prices on the international market, and then by the fall in the price of oil—its second major export, through a re-export arrangement with the Soviet Union—and finally by the rising interest rates of the early 1980s.

Through successive reschedulings of debt obligations, Cuba's external debt with capitalist countries remained relatively stable at around $3 billion during the first half of the 1980s, and Cuba was able to avoid austerity measures, maintaining relatively high rates of growth (see Table 2.2). Between 1984 and 1987, however, Cuba's debt (over half which is owed to commercial banks) more than doubled, reflecting growing trade deficits. Cuba's hard currency exports fell 11 percent in 1986 and barely increased the next year, due to hurricane damage in late 1985 and subsequently, a severe drought. Moreover, export earnings continued to be affected by the extremely low prices for sugar and oil on the international market. Finally, the devaluation of the dollar against the yen and European currencies has also contributed to an increase in Cuba's debt, given that Cuban export earnings are mainly denominated in dollars while its debt obligations are in yen and European currencies.

In 1987 Cuba, for the first time in two decades, experienced a severe recession, as imports had to be cut rather drastically. These cuts have mainly affected investment, rather than consumption, since the Cuban government has attempted to protect the standard of living of its population. Overall, however, it is clear that Cuba's margins for policy discretion have narrowed, and it too is caught in the debt crisis.

(continues)

Puerto Rico's specificity is that due to its special relationship to the United States, it is considered a "domestic" borrower, with unique access to the U.S. bond market. Puerto Rico also has the highest public debt in the Caribbean: $10 billion in 1987. Moreover, the island experienced its debt crisis earlier than other Latin American or Caribbean countries, and in the 1980s the growth of public debt has been relatively moderate, to a large extent due to the U.S. government's subsidizing of its operating budget.

During the early 1970s both the Commonwealth and municipal governments borrowed heavily, with the rate of growth of public debt ranging from 26 percent in 1971 to 37 percent in 1975. During the same period, the interest rate for twenty-year Commonwealth bonds jumped from 5.3 percent to 9.0 percent. The sharp increase in interest rates reflected, in part, the substantial increase in total Puerto Rican debt in the bond market as well as expectations of higher risk due to increasing fiscal deficits. Pressure from the municipal bond market community forced a reorganization of the Commonwealth's finances to ensure repayment of the debt and to constrain public borrowing. The policies implemented included a reduction of government spending and public employees' wages, and an increase in revenues generated by reducing residential tax exemptions and increasing sales taxes.

Where the Puerto Rican case is very special, compared with its Caribbean counterparts, is that the Commonwealth government received more than $1 billion in U.S. government grants each year from 1979 to 1987, for a total of more than $10 billion during this period. In 1987, of the $1.2 billion received, 26 percent was allocated to education, 14 percent to social services, 8 percent to housing and urban development, and 10 percent to unemployment insurance. These figures do not include operating expenditures for federal agencies in Puerto Rico (which amounted to $640.5 million in 1987) or federal government transfers to individuals ($3.9 billion). Thus, the public debt crisis was avoided in Puerto Rico by the early intervention of the U.S. financial community, and by sizable United States' subsidies, subsidies not available to the rest of the Caribbean.

Sources: Richard Turits, "Trade, Debt and the Cuban Economy," in Andrew Zimbalist, ed., *Cuba's Socialist Economy: Toward the 1990s* (Boulder: Lynne Rienner, 1987); Economic Commission for Latin America (CEPAL), "Estudio Económico de América Latina y el Caribe, 1987: Cuba" (Geneva: United Nations, 1988); Banco Nacional de Cuba, *Cuba—Quarterly Economic Report*, June 1988; Comité Para el Estudio de las Finanzas de Puerto Rico, *Informe al Gobernador* (Rio Piedras: Ed. Universitaria, 1976); and Puerto Rico Planning Board, *Informe Económico al Gobernador, 1987* (San Juan: Planning Board, 1987).

exports of goods and services). This is the most critical index of the degree to which the debt is affecting national economies, since the larger the ratio, the higher the foregone imports (holding all else constant). According to World Bank data, Jamaica had the largest debt-service ratio in the region (30 percent in 1986), followed by Trinidad-Tobago (18 percent) and the Dominican Republic (16 percent).[30] According to other sources, Jamaica's debt service in that year should have been 59 percent of the value of exports, but due to reschedulings, it actually paid the still high figure of 42 percent.[31] Guyana was even in worse shape with a debt service ratio of 81 percent; it only managed to pay 13 percent of the value of exports in debt service in 1986.

The problem of debt servicing was compounded in the region, as in the rest of Latin America, by the sharp increase in interest rates in 1980 and 1981. For those countries having to reschedule previous loans, such as Jamaica, the terms of doing so, even under adverse international economic conditions, were much more severe. For example, in 1975 Jamaica paid an average interest rate of 6.1 percent on its commercial loans; in 1981 these loans averaged a 17.9 percent interest rate.[32] Moreover, in the 1980s many of the international banks were reducing their exposure in the region, making it extremely difficult for many countries to obtain the external resources to maintain debt servicing in the face of balance of payments and fiscal crises.

The extent of the damage caused by rising interest rates varied across the region, depending on the precise mix of the external debt with respect to public concessionary loans (bilateral and multilateral) as opposed to private commercial debt. The countries with the highest percentage of commercial debt in the region include the Bahamas (80 percent), Trinidad-Tobago (77 percent), and Cuba (56 percent) (see Table 2.10). This percentage is also quite high for the OECS countries (54 percent), but it is skewed by the high commercial debt of just one country, Antigua, which accounts for approximately one-quarter of the total outstanding OECS external debt. The countries most favored by concessional loans are Haiti, Belize, and Jamaica. Whereas the bulk of Haiti's debt is owed to multilateral institutions, the external debt of the latter two is principally bilateral. While official debt is contracted at lower interest rates and on more favorable repayment terms than commercial debt, it also means less flexibility when it comes to the need for rescheduling, a situation confronting Jamaica in the mid-1980s. This is particularly true of loans from multilateral agencies.

While there is general agreement that the Caribbean countries which are facing a severe debt crisis are only Jamaica and Guyana, and perhaps Antigua, the significance of the debt in the rest of the Caribbean should not be underestimated. Not only these three countries, but also the Dominican Republic and Cuba, have had to engage in repeated debt reschedulings as well as being forced to impose austerity policies.

Table 2.10
Composition of the External Debt of the Caribbean, 1987 (in US$ millions)[1]

	Multilateral	Bilateral	Subtotal Official	Commercial	Total
Bahamas	28	6	35	143	178
	(16%)	(4%)	(20%)	(80%)	(100%)
Barbados	161	120	281	216	497
	(32%)	(24%)	(56%)	(44%)	(100%)
Belize	54	72	126	13	139
	(39%)	(52%)	(91%)	(9%)	(100%)
Cuba[2]	23	2,657	2,680	3,414	6,094
	(0.4%)	(44%)	(44%)	(56%)	(100%)
Dominican Republic	752	1,549	2,301	850	3,151
	(24%)	(49%)	(73%)	(27%)	(100%)
Guyana	360	339	699	218	916
	(39%)	(37%)	(76%)	(24%)	(100%)
Haiti	417	187	604	68	672
	(62%)	(28%)	(90%)	(10%)	(100%)
Jamaica	1,161	1,816	2,976	592	3,569
	(32%)	(51%)	(83%)	(17%)	(100%)
OECS[3]	121	71	192	221	411
	(29%)	(17%)	(46%)	(54%)	(100%)
Trinidad-Tobago	72	312	384	1,254	1,639
	(4%)	(19%)	(23%)	(77%)	(100%)

Sources: World Bank, World Debt Tables (Washington, D.C.: World Bank, 1989–90), Vol. 2, country tables, except for data for the OECS, which is drawn from Association of Caribbean Economists (ACE), Working Group on External Debt, "Debt and Development Strategies in the Caribbean," paper presented to the Second Conference of Caribbean Economists, Barbados, May 1989, tables 8 and 9, and for Cuba, which is from Banco Nacional de Cuba, Cuba Quarterly Economic Report, December 1988, p. 28.

1) Public and publicly guaranteed long-term debt, debt outstanding and disbursed
2) Refers to convertible currency debt only in millions of pesos
3) Data for the OECS countries includes only Antigua-Barbuda, Dominica, Grenada, and St. Lucia

While debt-servicing ratios are generally lower in the Caribbean than in South America, Caribbean governments do not necessarily command all of the foreign exchange earnings presumed in this ratio to pay off the debt. Export earnings do not always pass through the Central Bank; moreover, profit remittances by multinationals as well as patent fees, royalties, and so on, may significantly reduce foreign exchange availability for debt repayment. It is thus important to keep in mind that the debt can become unserviceable at a low debt-service ratio if current revenues of a government are weak.[33]

The Role of the IMF

In 1970 only two Caribbean countries had entered into standby arrangements with the IMF, the Dominican Republic and Haiti; five years later, Jamaica and Grenada also had entered the fold. By 1980 at least seven countries in the region had signed IMF agreements, with the volume of IMF credit being both substantial and growing in the cases of Jamaica, the Dominican Republic, and Haiti.[34]

The mandate of the IMF is to promote world trade and the smooth transaction of international payments.[35] Its main objective in granting credit to third world countries is to provide short-term balance of payments relief in order to minimize disruptions to international trade. It also has a constitutional bias against unstable exchange rates and exchange controls since these represent restrictions on international transfers.

The IMF has a range of facilities for lending to members, which come with varying degrees of conditionality. The first so-called tranches (disbursements) are available almost automatically, but standby agreements and extended fund facilities are provided only if governments commit themselves to follow a program of adjustment acceptable to the fund. The basic components of IMF stand-by arrangements are as follows:

1. Abolition or liberalization of foreign exchange and import controls. This is always called for, since the basic objective of the fund is to remove barriers to free trade. The immediate effect of liberalization, however, is to worsen a country's shortage of foreign exchange, since demand for foreign exchange will usually exceed the supply. Moreover, the trade balance will worsen with the lifting of import controls. All the other components of the standby arrangement are needed to counteract the adverse effect of liberalization on the balance of payments.

2. Devaluation of the currency. This is a corollary to the liberalization of trade. With exchange controls dismantled, the demand for foreign currency increases sharply and a country must devalue its own currency to reach a "realistic" foreign exchange rate. Devaluation can provide a temporary boost to exports, since these will be relatively cheaper than those of competitors; if, however, another country in the region with a similar export structure is also implementing an IMF program and devaluing its currency, concurrent devaluations will prevent either country from realizing the positive impact of lower prices for their products. Moreover, devaluation will also have an inflationary impact on the domestic economy, since the price of imports will increase. Other measures are thus necessary to fight domestic inflation.

3. Domestic anti-inflationary programs. The IMF has no constitutional jurisdiction over internal policy, but an anti-inflationary program is the necessary corollary of liberalization and exchange stability. If the exchange rate is to be stable without controls, domestic demand for foreign currency has to be reduced, which usually requires a strong

dose of austerity. The usual measures prescribed include (a) control of bank credit, usually through higher reserve requirements and subsequently, higher interest rates; (b) control of the government deficit by curbing spending by the end of consumption subsidies, reducing social services, and increasing taxes; (c) control of wage increases; and (d) the dismantling of price controls.

The effect of an anti-inflationary program is to induce an internal recession and thus slow growth. The justification is that this short-run adjustment is necessary in order to reduce the demand for imports and thus restore balance to the current account of the balance of payments, and to promote exchange rate stability. In return for pursuing these policies a country gets to draw on its quota with the IMF to cover temporary balance of payments deficits. It also gets an IMF "stamp of approval" which can encourage greater foreign aid, foreign investment, and commercial bank credit. Either one of these, should it generate a surplus in the capital account to balance the deficit on current account, will assist a country in putting its balance of payments in order. Public and commercial loans, however, increase the external debt, thereby increasing future debt-servicing commitments.

It is rather remarkable that the IMF has maintained its basic recipe for solving balance of payments difficulties over three decades, in spite of significantly changed international economic conditions—principally the debt crisis—and a rather poor record in meeting its stated goals. The only significant changes in IMF operations have been a special expanded credit facility created in the late 1970s to ease the impact of short-term recessionary programs, and coincident with the Reagan era, an even stronger emphasis within the basic recipe on privatization of government assets and deregulation. But in response to the criticism that its policies offer no basis for long-term growth (with perhaps the exception of the encouragement to increased foreign investment), the IMF has added on an additional component in the 1980s: a focus on encouraging the development of nontraditional exports.

Critics of the IMF argue that the institution is blatantly hostile to the third world, being both anti-growth and anti-development, and that its sole purpose is simply to integrate the third world more tightly to the international economy. In the current crisis the imposition of austerity measures is seen to serve only one purpose—to squeeze out an internal surplus to repay the external debt, thus maintaining the profitability of international banks and the stability of the international system.

One of the most rigorous analyses of the IMF stabilization programs in Latin America and the Caribbean over the 1965–81 period demonstrated that IMF programs have had mixed results in terms of enabling a country to achieve the IMF's stated goals of balance of payments stability, reduced inflation, and increased growth.[36] The majority of countries did show some improvement in their balance of payments subsequent to signing standby arrangements, but this was usually due to increased capital inflows and not to improvements in the trade balance or the balance on current account. In general, the programs were associated with accelerated inflation rather than its reduction. In terms of the impact on growth rates, the results were mixed. The most significant result of this study was that the IMF stabilization programs were consistently associated with a decline in the wage share; that is, they resulted in a redistribution of income from labor to capital.

IMF stabilization policies in the Caribbean in the 1980s have generally compounded the economic crisis, a conclusion that is particularly well illustrated in the cases of Jamaica and the Dominican Republic. The Manley government signed an IMF agreement in April 1977, after the international banks, responding to U.S. pressures, stopped granting credit to Jamaica. The conditions for this two-year IMF agreement required Jamaica to devalue its currency, impose higher taxes, and reduce public expenditures. The IMF canceled the agreement in December of that year, accusing the Manley government of noncompliance. It then required even more drastic conditions in subsequent renegotiations, terms which Jamaica was forced to accept in June 1978, and when implemented, contributed to the fall of the Manley government.[37]

The political favoritism practiced by the IMF was blatantly apparent in the more favorable agreement which it negotiated in 1981 with the Seaga government. Two more standby agreements were signed in June 1984 and July 1985, making Jamaica a significant recipient of IMF credit. Concomitantly, the Reagan administration pressured the international banking community to reopen lines of credit to Jamaica in order to support its "model of democracy" in the region.

The IMF stabilization policies in Jamaica contributed to rising unemployment and inflation in that country. Unemployment increased from 21 percent in 1975 to 27 percent in 1980, stabilizing at around 25 percent in 1984.[38] The rate of growth of the consumer price index shot up from 6.6 percent in 1982 to 28.9 percent in 1984. After a slight recovery in 1983, GDP growth rates were subsequently negative, and gross domestic investment grew at a meager 3.7 percent per year between 1981 and 1988. Not until 1987 did domestic investment increase significantly, contributing to a brief spurt in the growth rate of GDP (see Tables 2.1, 2.3, 2.5).

The Dominican Republic first entered into a standby arrangement with the IMF in 1983, accepting the usual conditions of devaluation plus reductions in the fiscal deficit.[39] Given the high import content of domestic production in the Dominican Republic, inflation soared following devaluation, increasing from 4.8 percent in 1983 to 37.5 percent in 1985.[40] Moreover, devaluation initially resulted in only a small increase in export earnings in 1983 and then a fall in these earnings in 1984. Due to the extent of popular protest, the government was unable to reduce the fiscal deficit significantly. In 1985, facing contractions in production, a growing trade deficit, and a sharp rise in debt-servicing as old loans reached maturity, the Dominican Republic was forced into an even more severe austerity program in order to renegotiate its external debt obligations.

Among the new IMF conditions were unification of the exchange rate for all types of importers, a foreign exchange surcharge on some exports and imports (geared to favor nontraditional exports), elimination of Central Bank credit to the public sector, an increase in the marginal reserve requirement to 100 percent, the expansion of indirect taxes and an increase in the price of fuel and electricity, the elimination of subsidies on a number of other basic goods as well as to state enterprises, and limits on the public sector deficit and international reserves held at the Central Bank. But rather than the stability promised by IMF technicians, the Dominican Republic has seen increased inflation and unemployment and negative GDP growth rates. Measured unemployment increased from 21 percent in 1981 to 27 percent in 1985 (Table 2.3). Even though foreign investment in the export-processing zones boomed in the 1980s, gross domestic investment was negative between 1980 and 1985, recovering only in 1986.[41] The main accomplishment of this austerity program was that the Dominican Republic was able to meet its debt-servicing commitments—$571 million, amounting to 76 percent of export earnings, was repaid in 1985—and the country's external debt was rescheduled thanks to the "good offices" of the IMF.[42]

In analyzing the on-going crisis of the Caribbean economies, it is important to note that in 1983 the advanced capitalist countries were entering a phase of economic recovery, with declining inflation, lower interest rates, and moderately rising growth rates. Yet these more favorable external conditions, while generating a slight improvement in regional export performance, failed to have a significantly positive effect on GDP growth rates for the majority of Caribbean countries (Table 2.2). This must be at least partially attributed to the role of the IMF in the region and the austerity policies pursued by even those countries not subject to IMF conditionality.

Moreover, it is becoming increasingly clear that even the IMF "stamp of approval" granted for undertaking stabilization policies is insufficient to generate the external capital flows to the region which are necessary to promote growth. It is generally well-known now that since 1982 the commercial banks have been increasingly unwilling to maintain, let

Table 2.11
Resource Flows to the Caribbean,[1] 1981–86 (in US$ millions)

	1981	1982	1983	1984	1985	1986
Official Donors/Creditors	1318	1389	1063	928	779	394
Bilateral	764	807	462	628	441	334
Net Loans	536	578	324	386	116	36
Grants	228	229	138	242	325	298
Multilateral	554	582	601	300	338	60
Net Loans	487	528	555	249	284	3
Grants	67	54	46	51	54	57
Private Creditors	172	171	155	16	220	162
Suppliers	36	6	3	13	67	−23
Banks and Other	136	165	152	3	153	185
Total All Sources	1490	1560	1218	944	999	556
Outflows (interest paid)	392	439	519	525	587	653
Net Resource Flow	1098	1121	699	419	412	−97

Source: Clive Thomas, "Economic Crisis and the Commonwealth Caribbean: Impact and Response," paper presented to the ISER-UNRISD conference on Economic Crisis and Third World Countries," Kingston, April 1989, table 6; based on World Bank data.

1) Includes Antigua and Barbuda, the Bahamas, Barbados, Belize, Dominica, Dominican Republic, Grenada, Guyana, Haiti, Jamaica, St. Kitts-Nevis, St. Lucia, St. Vincent-Grenadines, Suriname, and Trinidad-Tobago

alone increase, their level of debt exposure to third world countries. Much less attention has been paid to the decreasing level of official credit, particularly with regard to the Caribbean. Bilateral and multi-lateral loans and grants to fifteen Caribbean countries fell from a high of $1.4 billion in 1982 to $394 million in 1986 (Table 2.11). Combined with the decrease in commercial bank credit over this period, the result was that in 1986 the capital outflow from the Caribbean ($653 million) exceeded the external inflow ($556 million); that is, the region paid creditors in the advanced countries almost $100 million more in interest payments than it received in new resources.

Deepening the Crisis:
Structural Adjustment Policies

Meeting in the Bahamas in July 1984, the heads of government of the CARICOM countries declared their commitment to pursue policies of structural adjustment in what is known as the "Nassau Understanding." The term "structural adjustment," as noted previously, refers to the package of IMF stabilization policies (for short-run balance of payments adjustment) plus a commitment to export diversification (as the long-run source of growth). According to the Nassau Understanding, structural adjustment "is an integral part of the development process" and represents a "conscious shift to a new development path to accelerate development."[43]

Whether structural adjustment is a viable development path for the Caribbean is the subject of much current debate. In its most positive light, it represents an understanding that Caribbean balance of payments problems are not just temporary disequilibria which can be corrected through the short-run contraction of internal demand, but rather, that these problems are structural; that is, rooted in the existing structure of production geared to the production of primary goods for export. The solution posited is the diversification of exports toward nontraditional agricultural and manufacturing products.

The underlying rationale for export diversification is that it lessens the vulnerability of economies which rely on only one or two export products for the generation of foreign exchange; moreover, it represents a response to the poor prospects for traditional exports in world markets. The prospects for sugar, oil, bauxite, and alumina are indeed quite bleak, given the trend toward the production of substitutes in the advanced economies. Certain tropical agricultural exports, such as bananas, have been suffering from a different problem, namely, increased international competition among suppliers. Most Caribbean products are also affected by the widespread protectionist tendency among governments of the advanced economies.

The issue for the Caribbean is not whether export diversification is a good thing—it is—but rather, whether it can be the pivotal element in a new development strategy, one which could benefit the majority of Caribbean people. The underlying assumption behind structural adjustment, as promoted by the U.S. government, the IMF, and the World Bank, is that an increased orientation toward exports of any kind, and the corresponding enhanced integration into the world economy, is a necessary component of any long-term Caribbean growth strategy. A second assumption, even more ideologically rooted, is that increased reliance on market mechanisms for price determination and resource allocation, both domestically and internationally, will increase efficiency and promote growth. A third is that the private sector will always be more efficient than the state, leading to the blanket prescription for "privatization" of state enterprises. The fourth assumption, which is perhaps the most troubling, is that somehow the growth of new export sectors based on the Caribbean's comparative advantage of cheap labor will generate benefits that will trickle down to benefit the majority of the population.

What is interesting about the Nassau Understanding is that it does recognize that structural adjustment policies will reduce the standard of living of the majority of the population in the short run. There is thus at least a nominal commitment to cushion the adverse effects on the most vulnerable groups, notwithstanding the fact that social programs must uniformly be curtailed to reduce fiscal deficits.[44] Moreover, all sectors of society are asked to make a contribution to income restraint—companies, by limiting the distribution of dividends and freezing executive salaries (although many of these decisions are made in New York or London); unions, by moderating wage demands; and the state, by restricting government wages and salaries—in the hopes of developing more competitive cost structures to boost investment, employment, exports, and growth. However, the Nassau Understanding is strangely silent with respect to the issue of *how* development can take place if it is based on low wages and a structure of production which is divorced from that of consumption. Moreover, while calling for the compliance of all social groups in meeting the objectives of structural adjustment, most governments in the region have done little to enhance the participation of all sectors of Caribbean society in designing and implementing the policies that will so drastically affect their futures.[45]

The Caribbean region indeed faces a structural problem—linked to the structure of production as well as the distribution of assets and income—but the focus of current debates around structural adjustment is quite misplaced. Export diversification might reduce the degree of Caribbean vulnerability to fluctuations in the international economy, but it can do little to foster a structure of production that can withstand the volatility of world markets, for decisions as to what is best to produce and at what price still remain external. Moreover, efforts to diversify exports have generally focused on attracting new assembly operations to be located in free-trade or export-processing zones. These industries—garment, electronics, and so on—tend to have few linkages to local economies, and while they generate employment, the low wages of the largely female labor force they employ mean that the domestic value added component is extremely small.

In addition, to lure foreign capital into these zones, Caribbean governments have had to offer very generous incentives, such as duty-free import of raw materials and capital goods, the exemption from taxation or any restrictions on profit repatriation, and the waiver of labor legislation. Caribbean countries are induced to compete against each other by offering the most advantageous conditions to foreign capital and through devaluations to reduce low wages still further, in a strategy based on the "competitive" advantage of misery rather than comparative advantage, the latter which must be rooted in enhancing the skills and productivity of the workforce.[46]

Finally, a development strategy which focuses exclusively on increased trade will do little to solve the region's recurring balance of payments problem if, at the very least, it is not tied to aggressive import substitution at the regional level, heavily focused on the agricultural sector. An inward-looking strategy, geared to the needs of the majority of the population and built on enhanced regional economic integration, complemented by export diversification, would seem to provide much more stable foundations for more equitable future growth in the Caribbean.

Notes

1. World Bank, *World Development Report 1989* (Washington, D.C.: IBRD, 1989), table A.8.

2. Clive Thomas, "The Economic Crisis and the Commonwealth Caribbean: Impact and Response," paper presented to the ISER-UNRISD conference on "Economic Crisis and Third World Countries," Kingston, April 3–6, 1989, pp. 8–9. Thomas also argues that the region has lost its wage cost-location advantage in relation to the U.S.-Canadian market due to technical changes in the areas of robotics, information, and transportation as well as agriculture.

3. Inter-American Development Bank, *Economic and Social Progress in Latin America, 1989 Report* (Washington, D.C.: IDB, 1989), table B-1.

4. Association of Caribbean Economists (ACE) Working Group on Debt, "Debt and Development Strategies in the Caribbean," paper presented to the Second Conference of Caribbean Economists, Barbados, May 1989, p. 7.

5. The experience of the smaller OECS states with inflation is quite different from that of the larger Caribbean economies. While inflation rates were substantially higher in the Eastern Caribbean in the 1970s, by 1982–83 inflation was running below 10 percent in almost all OECS countries. See United Nations Economic Commission for Latin America and the Caribbean (ECLAC), *Economic Survey of Latin America and the Caribbean* (Santiago: ECLAC, various years), and ECLAC, *Statistical Yearbook* (Trinidad: ECLAC, 1985).

6. Richard Newfarmer, "Economic Policy Toward the Caribbean Basin: the Balance Sheet," *Journal of InterAmerican Studies and World Affairs* 27, no. 1 (1986), pp. 76, 89.

7. Trevor Harker, "The Caribbean in the Context of the Global Economic Crisis," in George Beckford and Norman Girvan, eds., *Development in Suspense: Selected Papers and Proceedings of the First Conference of Caribbean Economists* (Kingston: Association of Caribbean Economists, 1989), p. 25.

8. See Ramesh F. Ramsaran, *U.S. Investment in Latin America and the Caribbean* (New York: St. Martin's Press, 1985).

9. Trinidad-Tobago was an exception to this trend, with food imports constituting only 9.1 percent of total imports in 1972. Data is drawn from Clive Thomas, *The Poor and the Powerless: Economic Policy and Change in*

the Caribbean (New York: Monthly Review Press, 1988), p. 138, based on ECLAC agricultural statistics.

10. Ramsaran, *U.S. Investment*, pp. 145, 159.

11. Just considering foreign profits and investment, the net capital outflow in Puerto Rico in 1983 amounted to $3.26 billion. In Puerto Rico Planning Board, *Income and Product: 1983* (San Juan: Government of Puerto Rico, 1983), Tables 1 and 19.

12. Organization of American States (OAS), *Statistical Bulletin of the OAS*, (Washington, D.C.: OAS, 1987), 9 nos. 3,4, table A–12.

13. Ibid., table A–8.

14. The number of visitors increased from 543,000 in 1980 to 844,000 in 1984 (with the United States accounting for 78 percent). Tourist expenditures increased from an estimated $136 million to $407 million over this same period. ECLAC, *Economic Survey of Latin America and the Caribbean*, 1982 and 1984 reports, Table 12.

15. OAS, *Statistical Bulletin of the OAS*, 1987.

16. Eighteen of the twenty members of the CDCC are listed in Table 2.2; missing from the list are the Netherlands Antilles and the U.S. Virgin Islands. Puerto Rico is not an official member. The sectoral data presented in this and subsequent sections are drawn from CDCC data for 1974–84, presented in the draft paper by Trevor Harker, "The Caribbean in the Context of the Global Economic Crisis," presented to the First Conference of Caribbean Economists, Kingston, Jamaica, July 1987, pp. 13–24; much of this data was deleted in the final version of the Harker paper in Beckford and Girvan, *Development in Suspense*.

17. Thomas, *The Poor and the Powerless*, p. 138.

18. Trevor Harker, "Caribbean Economic Performance: an Overview with Special Emphasis on the External Sector, from 1983–1988," paper presented to the Second Conference of Caribbean Economists, Bridgetown, Barbados, May 1989, p. 14.

19. Harker, "Caribbean Economic Performance," 1989, p. 21.

20. Ibid., calculated on the basis of Tables 8 and 11.

21. World Bank, *The Dominican Republic: An Agenda for Reform* (Washington, D.C., World Bank, 1987), Table 8.8, based on data provided by the Inter-American Development Bank.

22. Harker, "Caribbean Economic Performance," p. 23.

23. U.S. Department of Commerce, *U.S. Direct Investment Abroad: 1982 Benchmark Survey Data* (Washington D.C.: Government Printing Office, 1985), table 5.

24. OAS, *Statistical Bulletin of the OAS*, 1978, tables B–15-b and B–23-b.

25. ACE, Working Group on Debt, "Debt and Development Strategies," p. 8. In a recent study, capital flight between 1980 and 1986 was estimated as approximately $2.2 billion in Trinidad-Tobago, $810 million in Barbados and $469 million in Jamaica; this represented 215 percent, 182 percent, and 22 percent, respectively, of the increase in external debt over this same period. See Lester Henry, "Capital Flight from Beautiful Places: a Case Study of Four

Caribbean Countries," paper presented to the History and Development Workshop, University of Massachusetts, Amherst, 15 November 1989, p. 32.

26. These figures do not include the private, nonguaranteed debt. The only two Caribbean countries where this nonguaranteed debt is important are Jamaica and the Dominican Republic, although in the 1980s the volume of such credit dropped significantly. See the World Bank, *World Debt Tables,* 1988/89, (Washington, DC: World Bank, 1989), Vol. 2, Country Tables.

27. ACE, Working Group on Debt, "Debt and Development Strategies," p. 3.

28. Derived from Trevor Harker, "Caribbean Economic Performance," 1989, tables 2 and 15.

29. Data for Jamaica and Trinidad and Tobago is from the World Bank, *World Debt Tables,* 1988–89, Vol. 2, and refer to public and publicly guaranteed long-term debt, outstanding and disbursed as a percentage of GNP. The data for Antigua and Dominica are from Caribbean Development and Cooperation Committee, "An Evaluation of Economic Performance of CDCC Countries: with Special Reference to the Genesis and Evolution of the External Debt between 1977–1986," November 1988, p. 3. According to this latter source, if one includes arrears Guyana's debt to GDP ratio would be 293 percent.

30. World Bank, *World Debt Tables,* 1988/89, Vol. 2, Country Tables.

31. ACE, Working Group on External Debt, "Debt and Development Strategies, table 7. Data on debt servicing ratios often differ among sources depending on the components of debt included, and the valuation of exports.

32. World Bank, *World Debt Tables,* 1988/1989, vol. 2, Country Tables.

33. Owen Jefferson, "A Note on the External Debt of the English Speaking Caribbean," in Beckford and Girvan, eds., *Development in Suspense,* p. 52.

34. In 1980 Jamaica borrowed $309 million from the IMF, increasing to $678 million in 1986. In the latter year, the Dominican Republic borrowed $304 million and Haiti, $67 million. See World Bank, *World Development Report, 1988,* table 16.

35. This section draws largely on Cheryl Payer, *The Debt Trap: The International Monetary Fund and the Third World* (New York: Monthly Review Press, 1974).

36. Manuel Pastor, "The Effects of IMF Programs in the Third World: Evidence from Latin America," *World Development* 15, 1987.

37. Norman Girvan, Richard Bernal, and W. Hughes, "The IMF and the Third World: the Case of Jamaica, 1975–1980," *Development Dialogue,* 1980, p. 2.

38. ECLAC, *Economic Survey of Latin America and the Caribbean, 1984,* p. 251.

39. This section is based largely on Apolinar Veloz, "The Effects of Adjustment Programmes Applied in the Dominican Economy," paper presented at the First Conference of Caribbean Economists, Kingston, Jamaica, July 1987.

40. Inter-American Development Bank, *Economic and Social Progress in Latin America,* 1986 Report, table 11–7, and 1988 Report, table II–9.

41. Inter-American Development Bank, *Economic and Social Progress in Latin America,* 1989 Report, table III–1.

42. Miguel Ceara Hatton, "Hacia una Nueva Dinámica de la Economía Dominicana (1987)," paper presented to the Dominican College of Economists, Santo Domingo, May 1987, p. 5.

43. "The Nassau Understanding—July 7, 1985," in Caribbean Congress of Labour, *A Trade Union Programme*, appendix 4, paragraph 5.

44. Ibid., paragraph 9.

45. Caribbean Congress of Labour, *A Trade Union Programme*, ch. 4.

46. This important point was stressed by Norman Girvan at the conference on "Puerto Rico and the Caribbean," sponsored by the Institute of Caribbean Studies, University of Puerto Rico, May 1989.

CHAPTER 3

Impact of the Crisis on Poor Women and Their Households

POOR WOMEN, ESPECIALLY THOSE WITH FAMILIES, have had to bear the major brunt of the regional economic crisis and the structural adjustment policies instituted in the Caribbean. The economic crunch has hit women harder than men because women's disadvantaged occupational distribution, and more limited access to resources, makes them more vulnerable; moreover their roles as producers and consumers are different. In addition, women have always assumed a primary role in household survival strategies, securing and allocating usually meager cash and other resources to enable their families to make ends meet.

The economic crisis has made it extremely difficult for families to survive on a single wage, forcing additional women into the labor force to meet the rising cost of living and the decreased wage-earning capacity of men due to unemployment or wage cuts, or due to their absence as a result of migration. At the same time structural adjustment policies are forcing families to absorb a greater share of the cost of survival as a result of the cutbacks in social services, such as health and education, and the elimination or reduction of subsidies on food, transportation, and utilities. By shifting more responsibility for survival from the state to the household, structural adjustment policies are increasing the burden on the poor, especially women.[1]

In this chapter we shall examine the impact of the economic crisis and structural adjustment policies on poor women and their households in the Caribbean, focusing on Jamaica and the Dominican Republic, two of the countries most severely affected by the crisis. As we saw in Chapter 2, in order to deal with severe balance of payments difficulties, both governments signed standby agreements with the International Monetary Fund (IMF): Jamaica in 1977–78, 1981, and 1984–85, and the Dominican Republic in 1983 and 1985. Similar structural adjustment policies were instituted in both countries, including cutbacks in social services, continuing devaluation of the national currency, liberalization of regulations regarding imports, removal of food subsidies and price controls on basic consumer goods, and the promotion of nontraditional exports.[2]

As a result of the crisis in the external sector, austerity measures, and high debt-servicing payments, GDP per capita declined in both countries, but more precipitously in Jamaica than in the Dominican Republic, since the economic crisis generally has been more severe and of longer duration in Jamaica. In 1988, per capita Gross Domestic Product (GDP) in the Dominican Republic was $1,509, below that of Jamaica, which was $1,843. Jamaica's GDP per capital in 1988, however, was lower in real terms than it had been in either 1980 or 1970.[3] The resulting economic crunch has dramatically highlighted the structures of female subordination and exploitation which have long characterized both countries.

How the Crunch Is Felt

The impact of the crisis and structural adjustment policies has been devastating for poor women due primarily to three factors: (1) a sharp fall in wages and rising female unemployment; (2) the unequal burden which the rising cost of living imposes on women; and (3) the reductions in public spending for services on which women rely.

Declining Wages and Rising Unemployment

Despite the fact that they have slightly higher educational levels and outnumber men in white-collar occupations such as professional, clerical, and sales workers, Jamaican women are at a distinct disadvantage in the labor market, earning less and being more vulnerable to job loss than men.[4] In 1985, average weekly earnings for men stood at J$86.9, compared to J$68.3 for women (see Table 3.1). Female unemployment in 1985 reached 36.6 percent, over twice the rate for men. Among the young, aged fourteen to nineteen years, unemployment rates in 1985 approached 80 percent for women, and many of these young women have never been employed.[5]

High unemployment rates for women are especially critical in Jamaica because of the high percentage of female-headed households. In 1985, 39 percent of all Jamaican households were headed by women, reaching

Table 3.1
Comparison of Average Weekly Earnings, Jamaica, 1983–85 (in Jamaican $)

	1983	1984	1985
Male			
Current dollars	72.3	86.9	86.9
Constant dollars (1983 = 100)	100.0	94.1	74.9
Female			
Current dollars	49.2	65.4	68.3
Constant dollars (1983 = 100)	100.0	103.9	86.6

Source: Omar Davies and Patricia Anderson, "The Impact of the Recession and Adjustment Policies on Poor Urban Women in Jamaica," paper prepared for UNICEF, 1987, table 14.

Table 3.2
Distribution of Monthly Income Among Household Heads in the Kingston (Jamaica) Metropolitan Area, March 1984

Jamaican Dollars	Male Household Heads %	Female Household Heads %
less than $200	14.6	40.8
$200–$399	24.7	31.8
$400–$599	23.2	11.3
$600–799	14.6	7.0
$800 or more	23.0	9.2
Total	100.0	100.0
	N = 562	N = 444

Source: Omar Davies and Patricia Anderson, "The Impact of the Recession and Adjustment Policies on Poor Urban Women in Jamaica," paper prepared for UNICEF, 1987, table 9, based on ISER Mobility Survey.

45 percent in the Kingston metropolitan area. In many cases, these women may be the sole source of income in the family. The labor-force participation rate for female household heads in Kingston is very high, standing at 82 percent, not far below the level of 92 percent for male household heads, who in most Caribbean societies are traditionally viewed as the primary breadwinners.[6] Nevertheless, poverty is particularly severe among female heads of households, three-quarters of whom had a 1984 monthly income under J$400, or the equivalent of US$18 a week, compared to only 39 percent of male household heads at that income level (Table 3.2). This finding is confirmed by another study which showed that the average monthly income of female-headed households in urban Jamaica was 22 percent less than that of households headed by a co-resident couple.[7] Lower incomes among female heads reflect not only lower wages but a reduced number of wage earners per household.[8]

Table 3.3
Average Monthly Income of Male and Female Household Heads, Dominican Republic, 1980
(in Dominican pesos)

| Zone | Household Head | | Male/Female Income Ratio |
	Male	Female	
Urban	266	138	1.9
Rural	73	67	1.1

Source: Clara Baez, La Subordinación de la Mujer Dominicana en Cifras (Santo Domingo: Dirección General de Promoción de la Mujer and INSTRAW, 1984), table 3.11.

Unemployment rates in the Dominican Republic are among the highest in all Latin America, and reached 29 percent in 1986. As in Jamaica, unemployment is higher for women than men, especially in rural areas, where in the 1981 census, the rate was 21 percent for men and 29 percent for women.[9] Underemployment is estimated at about 40 percent, and is thought to be higher for women than for men, because of the high percentage of women in the informal sector. Average wages in the informal sector are estimated to be 56 percent lower than in the formal sector, though both have declined since 1980.[10]

Despite several increases in the minimum wage, the real wage in the Dominican Republic in July 1987 was estimated to be only 70 percent of that earned in January 1980.[11] This may be leading men to withdraw from the labor force; their participation rate has declined 10 percent since 1960, to 81.2 percent in 1980.[12] At the same time, female labor-force participation rates have increased dramatically, growing from 11 percent in 1960 to 37.5 percent in 1980.[13]

As in Jamaica, major salary differentials continue to exist between women and men in the Dominican Republic, especially in urban areas where the average monthly wage for women in 1980 was DR$150 compared to DR$234 for men.[14] At that time nearly 60 percent of urban women and 88 percent of rural women earned less than the monthly minimum wage of DR$125. This has a particularly negative effect on female heads of households, who in 1980 represented about one-fifth of all Dominican households.[15] While this percentage is still lower than in Jamaica, it is increasing, especially in urban areas. The average monthly income of urban female heads of households in 1980 was DR$138, nearly half that of urban male heads of households (Table 3.3).

Growing unemployment and falling real wages have exacerbated income inequality in the Dominican Republic. In 1984, the poorest 20 percent of households absorbed 9.6 percent of total income, while the richest 20 percent absorbed 42.4 percent.[16] The percentage of families

Table 3.4
Changes in Minimum Food Costs for a Family of Five and in the Minimum Wage, Jamaica, 1979–85

Period	Cost of Basic Set of Meals (J$)	Weekly Minimum Wage (J$)	Cost as Percentage of Minimum Wage
June 1979	24.27	26.4	91.9
September 1983	65.31	30.0	217.7
December 1983	77.00	30.0	256.7
August 1984	101.46	40.0	276.2
July 1985	128.43	52.0	247.0

Source: Omar Davies and Patricia Anderson, "The Impact of the Recession and Adjustment Policies on Poor Urban Women in Jamaica," paper prepared for UNICEF, 1987, table 10.

under the poverty line increased from 23.3 percent in 1976–77 to 27.4 percent in 1984.[17]

In short, the economic crisis has had a particularly devastating effect on the poor, particularly women, because in both countries they represent a more vulnerable segment of the labor force, earning lower wages and being subject to higher unemployment.

The Rising Cost of Living

Though legal minimum wages have been increased several times in both Jamaica and the Dominican Republic, they have been unable to keep up with continuous increases in the cost of living. Consumer prices from 1982 to 1985 rose 74 percent in the Dominican Republic and close to 100 percent in Jamaica.[18] In Jamaica, the weekly cost of a basic set of meals for a family of five virtually doubled in less than two years (between September 1983 and July 1985), reaching J$128.43, while the weekly minimum wage was J$52 (Table 3.4). In the Dominican Republic, the weekly cost of a family food basket more than doubled in a six-year period, from DR$166.94 in January 1980 to DR$397.64 in June 1987 (Table 3.5). This was higher than the monthly minimum wage, which stood at DR$350 in 1987. However, not even fully employed persons always receive the minimum salary, due to lax government regulation.[19] Moreover, more women are employed in jobs not even covered by minimum wage legislation.

Cost of living increases have resulted primarily from devaluation, which has an especially severe impact on economies that are import-dependent. The minimum wage in the Dominican Republic, for example, declined from a value of US$98.43 in January 1980 to US$67.20 in July 1987.[20] The decline of the Jamaican dollar has been even more precipitous, falling 207 percent between January 1983 and February 1986.[21]

Table 3.5
Indicators of the Rising Cost of Living, Dominican Republic, 1980–86 (in Dominican pesos)

	Cost of Family Food Basket	Price Index	Purchasing Power of Dominican Pesos
1980	162.00	1.3652	1.00
1981	156.94	1.4681	0.93
1982	167.44	1.5802	0.86
1983	173.48	1.6897	0.80
1984	212.81	2.1027	0.65
1985	291.75	2.8918	0.47
1986	334.24	3.1735	0.43

Source: Miguel Ceara, "Situación Socioeconómica Actual y su Repercusión en la Situación de la Madre y el Niño," paper prepared for UNICEF (Santo Domingo: INTEC, 1987), table 18.

As a result, the increase in the cost of living in the Kingston metropolitan area between January 1983 and December 1985 was 68 percent, roughly twice the average for the previous three-year period. Price increases affected not only food, fuel and, clothing, but public utilities, which have been financed by external loans. Because of high debt-servicing payments, there was an 116 percent increase in electricity charges within the space of five months in 1983, while water rates in Kingston and St. Andrew increased 218 percent between September 1984 and October 1985.[22]

Increases in food prices are due both to increased dependence on imports, and thus to the effect of devaluation on imported food, and to the removal of subsidies and controls on food prices. In 1981 there was a 40 percent increase in food imports, due to the government's decision to remove existing import restrictions on a range of foodstuffs that could be produced in Jamaica. This resulted in a 12 percent decline in domestic agriculture the following year, due to competition from cheaper imports.[23] In 1986, locally produced foods represented only 14 percent of total foods consumed annually.

Food production for the internal market has always been accorded lower priority than export-oriented agricultural production. Women are particularly affected by this distinction, not only as consumers but as producers. In Jamaica, they produce 60 to 75 percent of the food for the local market, and are responsible for over 80 percent of its distribution.

Domestic food production has also declined in the Dominican Republic, particularly since the beginning of the industrialization process of the 1970s; here as well it has been aggravated by the emphasis on export production in structural adjustment policies. Production of root crops such as batata, yucca, and potatoes, staples of the Dominican diet, has fallen. Cheaper imports of soybean and vegetable oil have replaced locally produced peanut oil for cooking. At the same time, nontraditional exports such as melon, tomatoes and pineapples have grown from 15 percent of total commodity export earnings in 1978–80 to 19 percent in 1982.[24] These new exports are grown on the basis of production contracts with small farmers or in large-scale, wage-based agroindustries which often employ a high percentage of women.[25]

The decline in domestic food production also contributed to an increasing reliance on food imports, which rose from RD$63 million in 1973 to RD$151 million by 1980.[26] Growing import dependence has been accompanied by a sharp increase in food prices which, at the height of the economic crisis between 1984 and 1985, rose 43 percent. In the six months between April and September of 1988, the cost of staples such as beans doubled, from RD$1.65 per pound to RD$3.40, while rice rose from 75 Dominican centavos to RD$1.45.[27] Price rises are due not only to the effects of devaluation, but to the reduction of state price controls on items such as rice and sugar. According to a 1976–77 survey of household income and expenditure, the poorest half of Dominican households spend 60 percent or more of their budget on food.[28] Undoubtedly the percentage of income spent on food has increased with the economic crisis.

In both countries there were declines in per capita consumption due to the rising cost of living, though these drops occurred in different time periods; the decline was most severe in Jamaica in 1979 and 1980, whereas in the Dominican Republic, the initial 1979 decline was exceeded in 1982. It is also noteworthy that per capita consumption is consistently higher in Jamaica than in the Dominican Republic. For example, in 1980, at the height of the economic crisis in Jamaica, per capita consumption (in 1982 U.S. dollars) was $1,580 compared to $1,026 in the Dominican Republic.[29] This comparison, like the GDP figures given earlier, appears to reflect a higher standard of living in Jamaica than in the Dominican Republic, although these per capita figures conceal sharp income inequalities.

Reductions in Public Expenditure

The poor in Jamaica and the Dominican Republic have suffered not only from increases in the cost of living, lower wages, and higher unemployment, but also from reductions in public expenditures, which provide essential social services that the poor cannot afford to buy. According to UNICEF, real expenditure in Jamaica on services such as education, health, and social security fell from J$662 million in 1981–82 to J$372 million in 1985–86, a reduction of 44 percent over the last five years.[30] Health clinics and hospital wards were closed without warning and even the most basic supplies were unavailable in schools and hospitals. Health services and drugs at public hospitals and health centers which were previously free now had to be paid for, making them inaccessible to those who could not afford them. We have already mentioned the cut in government subsidies on basic food items, though some of these were restored in early 1986 after growing public protests.

Services related to economic infrastructure were also cut, including transport and communications, roads, and agricultural and industrial services. In real terms the 1985–86 expenditure for this category was 57 percent lower than the 1981–82 level. As part of this reduction, the Jamaican government divested itself of certain operations formerly run by the state, such as street cleaning, maintenance of markets, and urban public transportation, which have led to further unemployment and other hardships. For example, the decision to close the Jamaica Omnibus Service and allocate routes to individual minibus owners has resulted in wholesale congestion at certain transit points, overloading, and delays.[31]

Comparable figures for the Dominican Republic show a reduction in per capita public expenditure for education from RD$17.67 in 1982 to RD$13.30 in 1986, while in health the figures were reduced from RD$16.41 to RD$12.99 over the same period.[32] There has been a serious deterioration in the health care system during this period. Hospitals cannot supply medicines, sheets, or even surgical supplies, and patients are being forced to buy their own. Over half of the vital equipment in hospitals and clinics is out of order, including such critical items as incubators, x-ray machines, sterilizers and lab equipment. Hospitals are estimated to be operating at 50 percent capacity, with a severe shortage of nurses; moreover, all medical personnel are underpaid.

Not only has the quality of public health care in the Dominican Republic declined, but it has never reached the population it was designed to serve. The Ministry of Public Health is responsible for 80 percent of the population, but its coverage in 1986 was estimated at 40 percent. The Social Security system (IDSS) is designed to cover wage earners through a combined contribution from employees, employers, and the state, but in 1981 it covered only 22 percent of salaried wage earners.[33]

The reduction in public expenditures has also resulted in lower salaries and the laying off of government employees. In the Dominican Republic the average real monthly salary paid by the state sector has declined 51.3 percent from 1970 to 1984.[34] In Jamaica, employees of local government departments were the hardest hit, as this part of the state sector was the prime target for budget cuts. Many of those laid

Table 3.6
Distribution of Female Employment by Industry in 1981 and 1985, Jamaica

Industry	October 1981 %	October 1985 %	Change in Numbers of Employed Females
Agriculture	21.1	22.2	+8,100
Mining, Quarrying, and Refining	0.2	0.2	—
Manufacture	7.0	8.7	+6,800
Construction	0.1	0.2	+100
Transport, Communications and Public Utilities	2.7	1.7	−2,200
Commerce	23.4	25.1	+10,700
Public Administration	19.3	13.4	−14,100
Other Services	25.8	28.2	+13,100
Not Stated	0.4	0.3	−200
Total	100.0	100.0	+22,300
	N = 285,400	N = 307,700	

Source: Omar Davies and Patricia Anderson, "The Impact of the Recession and Adjustment Policies on Poor Urban Women in Jamaica," paper prepared for UNICEF, 1987, table 12, based on 1985 STATIN Labor Force Survey.

off were women receiving the lowest wages, such as cleaners at hospitals and schools. Between 1981 and 1985 there has been a decline of 14,100 in the number of women employed by the public sector in Jamaica, higher than in any other sector. Whereas public administration accounted for nearly 20 percent of female employment in 1981, in 1985 this figure was reduced to 13 percent (Table 3.6). A major reason for the cutbacks in public expenditure for social services and in the number of state employees is the increasing expenditure allocated to debt servicing. By the most conservative estimate, in 1986 debt servicing commitments consumed 16 percent of the Dominican Republic's export earnings and 30 percent of those of Jamaica (see Chapter 2).[35]

Despite severe cuts in social services in both countries, Jamaica appears to have a higher commitment to public health than does the Dominican Republic. Even before the crisis, per capita government health expenditure (excluding social security) has always been much higher in Jamaica than in the Dominican Republic, and in 1984 such expenditure stood (in 1982 U.S. dollars) at $52.70 and $12.87 respectively.[36] Cuts in health expenditure in the 1980s have also been more severe in the Dominican Republic, where they amounted to more than 40 percent compared to about 20 percent in Jamaica. This is particularly difficult to understand when it appears, as we noted earlier, that the crisis has been more severe and of longer duration in Jamaica.

Growing Hunger and Poorer Health

The combined effect of the rising cost of living, particularly rising food prices, and decreased health care is that malnutrition as well as mortality from curable diseases is on the rise. UNICEF, in its studies on the impact of the economic crisis in Latin America and the Caribbean, has well documented the often dramatic changes in consumption and dietary patterns induced by the crisis, with severe implications for health and nutrition. There is a growing concentration on cheap sources of calories such as rice or yucca in the diet, and declining intakes of protein, such as milk or meat. Women and young girls are the family members most likely to be affected by declining food consumption, since preference is given to male wage earners.[37]

In Jamaica, a decline in the nutritional status of children under the age of four years, with the percentage of malnourished rising from 38 percent in 1978 to 41 percent in 1985, sums up the effects of these policies.[38] This trend was confirmed by hospital admissions; the proportion of children under five admitted to the Bustamante Children's Hospital for malnutrition and malnutrition/gastroenteritis, for example, rose from 2.7 percent of all admissions in 1980 to 8.4 percent in 1985. In addition, the percentage of pregnant women screened at prenatal clinics who were deemed anemic rose from 23 percent in 1981 to 43 percent in 1985.[39] Moreover, the infant mortality rate has increased from 16 per thousand in 1980 to 18 per thousand in 1987.[40]

In the Dominican Republic, despite dramatic improvements in mortality and life expectancy rates starting in the 1950s, infant mortality in 1987 still stood at 65 per thousand, a figure which is surpassed only by Haiti (see Table 1.1). Moreover, the rate of infant mortality tends to be generally underreported and is considerably higher in rural areas and among the lowest income groups.[41] Maternal mortality, which also differs significantly in urban and rural areas and by income group, stood at 56 per 100,000 in 1980 in the Dominican Republic.[42] In one major maternity hospital in the capital of Santo Domingo, maternal mortality, while much lower than in rural areas, increased from 15 to 22 per 100,000 from 1981 to 1985.[43]

According to a study conducted by the Central Bank in 1976–77, 90 percent of the Dominican population consume less than the recommended minimum of 2,300 calories and 60 grams of protein per day, with the poorest Dominicans significantly below this minimum standard. Among children aged one to four, the level of malnutrition in 1984 reached 40.8 percent.[44] A 1981 U.S. Agency for International Development (AID) study found the highest prevalence of malnutrition among infants aged five to eight months. The authors attribute this to a variety of causes: the abrupt cessation of breastfeeding as mothers are forced by economic circumstances to return to work, dilution of baby formulas to make them stretch, and lack of potable water used in infant feeding.[45] Also, it is estimated that one-fourth of all babies born in the Dominican Republic are children of malnourished mothers.[46] Finally, in 1983, one-fourth of all children admitted to a major children's hospital in Santo Domingo died, not of incurable diseases but of the combined effects of poverty, ill health, and poor health care.[47]

How Households Survive

Caribbean women are not simply victims of economic hardship; they and their families are devising innovative strategies for dealing with it. Four main strategies can be detected: (1) women are entering the labor force in increasing numbers, particularly as workers in export-processing industries; (2) along with men, they are engaging in a wide variety of activities in the informal sector; (3) households are diversifying their survival strategies, changing living and consumption patterns; and (4) women are joining, and even predominating in, the international migration stream, especially to the United States. All of these constitute important economic and social changes of the last decade.

Increasing Labor-Force Participation

At first glance the growing number of women in the labor force may appear contradictory in view of increased unemployment and under-employment in the Caribbean generally. However, women are forced into the labor force precisely because of increased unemployment among men and because real wages of employed household members are decreasing, contributing to an overall reduction in household income. Women are able to find jobs even when men are not, because they work for lower wages, because the labor market in the Caribbean (as elsewhere) is highly segregated by gender, and because a high percentage of women work in the informal sector.

Several factors in the development process in the Dominican Republic have favored the dramatic increase in the number of women entering the labor force (from 11 percent in 1960 to 37.5 percent in 1980), including urbanization, the growth of the service sector, and the growth of export-processing industries. At the same time, changes have taken place in the female population in the last two decades which have made them more employable, including a rise in educational levels, and a marked decline in fertility.[48] It would seem that many of these same factors help explain the high percentage of Jamaican women in

the labor force. In the English-speaking Caribbean, however, women's labor-force participation rates traditionally have been high, and in Jamaica in 1985 stood at 62 percent for women over fourteen years of age.[49]

Export manufacturers have shown a preference for women workers because they are cheaper to employ, less likely to unionize, and have greater patience for the tedious, monotonous work involved in assembly operations. Although Jamaica was initially targeted as the showpiece of the Caribbean Basin Initiative (CBI), export manufacturing never took off on the scale anticipated. The bulk of employment created in export manufacturing in Jamaica in recent years has occurred, not through the CBI (which excluded textiles and garments from its duty-free provisions) but rather, through the preferences created by U.S. Tariff Code 807 for apparel assembled overseas from U.S. components.[50] Between 1981 and 1985, an additional 6,800 women found employment in the manufacturing sector, so that the proportion of women employed in manufacturing rose from 7 percent to 8.7 percent of the female labor force (see Table 3.6), the majority presumably employed in apparel production.

While data are unavailable on whether the increased number of women employed in export manufacturing are located in formal vs. informal (domestic homeworkers) sector jobs, there is some evidence that garment manufacturers appear to be turning to the use of domestic homeworkers as a way of cutting their labor costs. By contracting out to homeworkers, they avoid the payment of fringe benefits and the costs of factory installations as well as any possible threat of unionization. Moreover, homeworkers offer manufacturers considerable flexibility in managing the size of their workforce, which can be scaled up or down with market fluctuations, clearly offering these women workers little stability of employment. The bulk of these manufacturers appear to be Jamaican nationals who are linked to U.S. companies through subcontracting arrangements. Free-trade zones in Jamaica have had less appeal to U.S. firms than have their counterparts in Haiti or the Dominican Republic. In 1987 total employment in foreign-owned firms in the Kingston Export Free Zone was only 8,500, far lower than in the Dominican Republic.[51]

A study done for AID of the apparel industry in Jamaica revealed that U.S. firms see unions as a major obstacle to investment, although only one of the twenty-two factories in the Kingston Export Free Zone is unionized.[52] Nonetheless, fear of labor unrest may explain the preference of U.S. firms for subcontracting because there have been frequent public protests against such work abuses as low pay, excessive and forced overtime, occupational health hazards, arbitrary suspension and dismissal for protesting, and absence of trade union representation. Such complaints are common among workers employed in export manufacturing, and have also been voiced in the Dominican Republic.

The Dominican Republic has seen a dramatic growth in export manufacturing in recent years. The greatest increase has taken place precisely during the years of structural adjustment, when the number of firms in the free-trade zones increased from 103 in 1983 to 224 in 1988, and the number of employees more than quadrupled, reaching an estimated 85,000 in 1988.[53] The overwhelming majority (84 percent) of these workers in export manufacturing are women.

One of the reasons for the explosion of export manufacturing in the Dominican Republic is the general wage reduction resulting from devaluation. Between 1981 and 1984 there was a 17 percent reduction in the average real wage in manufacturing, despite increases in the minimum wage. At the rate of exchange prevailing in August 1986, the average wage in free-trade zones was approximately US$90 monthly.[54] In addition, succumbing to pressure from industrialists in the free-trade zones, the Dominican government granted them access to the parallel currency exchange market, which enabled them to buy local currency at an even more favorable rate. This new exchange rate policy lowered operating costs by approximately 30 percent, and is another major factor behind the rapid growth in activity in the zones in the last few years. Because of devaluation, average hourly wages in the Dominican Republic are now at approximately the same level as in Haiti, the poorest country of the hemisphere (see Table 5.3).[55]

In addition to low wages and various government incentives, the weakness of the labor movement in the Dominican Republic attracts U.S. investors to the free-trade zones. There are no unions in the Dominican free-trade zones and workers are fired and blacklisted with other plants if any union activity is detected. Women who have tried to take complaints of mistreatment or unjust dismissal to the government Labor Office have generally been rejected in favor of management. Workers complain of the lack of public transportation, proper eating facilities, adequate medical services, and child care. Labor turnover is high, since many workers cannot withstand the pressure of high production quotas, strict discipline, sexual harassment, and a forty-four hour work week, with overtime sometimes imposed in addition.

In a study of Dominican free-trade zones conducted in 1981, it was found that most of the workers are under thirty years old, but in a departure from the global pattern of young, single women, over one-half are married and one-fourth are female heads of household.[56] Their need to work is demonstrated by the fact that nearly three-fourths of the female heads of households and nearly half of the married women

64

Feature

María

María arrived in the free-trade zone of La Romana in the Dominican Republic as a young woman with two daughters, aged two and one. She had married at age fourteen, but her husband drank and mistreated her, so she left him and went to live with her sister in La Romana. She started working almost immediately, tried a number of factories, but has been at the same blouse factory for about ten years.

María is very critical about the conditions in this factory. She says the manager, a Cuban exile, is very strict, and does not give them food or pay their transportation home when they have to work overtime. He uses various ways to degrade his workers, such as denouncing them publicly over the loudspeaker and calling them by number. María was fired once several years ago along with sixty other women for trying to organize a union. The women received no support from the Ministry of Labor and María was blacklisted from working in any other factories in La Romana. As the manager told them when they were fired: "La que se meta en sindicato sabe que va a perder su empleo aquí y no va a trabajar más en Zona Franca, porque ustedes saben que el peje grande se come al peje chiquito." (Whoever gets involved in unions here knows she will lose her job and will no longer work in the free-trade zone, because as you know the big fish eats the little fish.)

María is a skilled operator, and managed to find work in the free-trade zone in San Pedro de Macorís, about one hour's drive from La Romana, where the manager was not concerned about her union activities. The pay there was also better. Still, when the manager from La Romana came to ask her to return, she accepted. María says she prefers this factory, despite its bad reputation, because she has worked there so long and is able to do some business on the side, such as lending money at interest, or participating in *san*, the rotating credit association. Although these activities are not permitted, she can get away with them in this factory because she knows the personnel. At this point she earns as much or more from these activities as from her meager salary of RD$57 pesos (then about $20) a week. As María says: "Si yo viviera atenida a lo que me pagan en mi fábrica yo no pudiera sostener mi casa." (If I tried to live from what they pay me in the factory, I couldn't support my household.)

María now has four children, the younger two with a man with whom she lived for fourteen years. Although he did not want her to work initially, she convinced him of the need. María said she felt much more secure working, especially since two of the children were not his. "Me
(*continues*)

sentía bien segura porque sabía si el se va por lo menos mis hijos no van a pasar hambre." (I felt very secure because I know that if he goes my children at least would not go hungry.) Like María, women rarely feel secure in their relationships with men, and have come to depend on themselves for supporting their family. Four years ago, María and this man separated and she basically supports her four children.

María thinks it is very important for women to work. She says there are women working in the zone who support men through their employment. She feels that many of these young women have a distorted vision of liberation, that permits them to do the same as men. According to María, these women maintain: "Tu te vas, yo me voy, tu bebes yo bebo, tu llegas tarde, ah! yo trabajo y yo gano, yo también, yo soy liberada y yo puedo hacer lo mismo con mi dinero." (You go, I go, you drink, I drink, you come late, ah! I work and I earn, I am also liberated and I can do the same with my money.) According to María, these are the women that fill the discotheques on Friday evening. Many of them have left children with their relatives in the country.

After he left her for another woman, María's second partner threatened to take his children away from her, and at one point tried to force his way into her home. María told him: "No, mijito, no, eso no es verdad, no. Tu te fuistes, tu te quedas. Y no es verdad que después que yo he vivido contigo catorce años yo voy a ponerme de amoríos. Ah, no cuando tu te casaste con otra, yo voy a entonces a vivir contigo como una amante, eso no es verdad." (No, my son, no that is not true. You left, you stay. It is not the case that after having lived with you for fourteen years I am going to make love. Oh, no, when you married another, I should live with you like a lover, that is not the case.) It is clear that María is very independent and she says she has no interest in another man. Even so, she sends her twelve-year-old son to his father's TV repair shop during the day so he will not be alone and get into trouble.

María plans to continue working indefinitely in the free-trade zone. She says there are many problems that could be dealt with through a union, such as the lack of transportation and food, but the women are afraid. "Uno no se quiere exponer a perder el pan de sus hijos." (One does not want to risk losing the bread of your children.) She also notes the need for wage increases, and says that many women are paid as little as RD$35 pesos a week because they are in training which can last three months. She claims there is high turnover among these women, since by keeping them in training the manager can save a lot of money.

While María has a strong collective sense of solidarity with her fellow workers, she is now primarily engaged in a struggle for her family's survival; everything is more expensive and she now pays for her children to go to a private school. She has begun selling things like beer and other consumer items from her house, and is constructing an addition to set up a small store. She thinks her daughter can attend to the

(*continues*)

business during the week and she can work weekends and evenings. The oldest daughter already works in the free-trade zone, which bothers María, but they need the money.

María is glad that her older daughters, now seventeen and sixteen, have not yet married and had children, although she hopes they will marry some day. She knows she can count on little support from their fathers, even though her second partner has his own business. María is more resourceful than most, and never loses an opportunity to earn extra money. While she also sees the value of collective action, the repression she and other women have faced has made her depend on more individualistic strategies. Paid employment is her primary life line, because, as she says, "Las que no producen tienen que adaptarse a los que el marido le da." (Those [women] who don't produce have to adapt themselves to what the husband gives them.)

Source: Helen Safa, based on interviews conducted in July 1986.

claim they are the principal breadwinners for their families. In fact, employers in the Dominican Republic indicate a preference for women with children because they feel their need to work ensures greater job commitment.[57]

While growth in demand for female labor has been greatest in manufacturing, women in the Dominican Republic have also been employed as wage laborers in the new agroindustries that have flourished recently due to the CBI. A 1985 study of rural women revealed that wages in these agroindustries are even lower than in manufacturing, averaging three to six pesos daily in 1985, and the work is very unstable, concentrated in the harvest season. Many women also work as unremunerated family labor on small farms, some of which produce for agribusiness on a contract basis.[58]

In short, the growth of employment for women in domestic homework, in the free-trade zones, and in agribusiness, represent strategies by industries to reduce production costs at a time of intense international competition. The growth in export manufacturing employment also represents the adaptation by poor women to the need to augment their earnings to meet the increasingly high cost of living and the high unemployment and reduced real wages of male partners and kin. But while export promotion has increased the demand for female labor, it has also taken advantage of women's inferior position in the labor market and reinforced their subordination through poorly paid, dead-end jobs.

Women workers in the free-trade zones of both the Dominican Republic and Jamaica have received little or no support from their governments in their efforts to achieve better wages and working conditions. Indeed, both governments have attempted to control labor unrest in order to attract foreign investment. Under these circumstances it is understandable why workers have not organized nor protested more vehemently, although in March 1988 there were widespread strikes among Jamaican garment workers in favor of higher wages and better working conditions. Thus the failure to improve working conditions lies more with the lack of support women workers receive from government, political parties, and unions than with the women themselves. At present these women workers have no adequate vehicles to express their grievances or to transform their sense of exploitation (which is very real) into greater worker solidarity. These difficulties are compounded for women workers employed in the urban and rural informal sectors.

Surviving in the Informal Sector

Despite its disadvantages, most women still regard jobs in export processing, particularly the free-trade zones, as preferable to work in the informal sector. The informal sector in the Caribbean still includes a high percentage of domestic servants and petty vendors, as well as other self-employed workers whose activities range from food preparation for sale on the streets to home repairs and other services, as well as artisan production. Working in this sector generally provides no labor protection, minimum wages, social security, or other benefits, but for growing numbers of men and women, there is little alternative.

In Jamaica, the percentage of women (38 percent) working in the informal sector is much higher than that of men (12 percent).[59] Undoubtedly this reflects the high percentage of Jamaican women who work as "higglers" or petty vendors, trading in homegrown foodstuffs and local manufactured goods. Women's involvement in the marketing of foodstuffs for the domestic market dates back to the days of slavery, and has traditionally provided them with the flexibility needed to manage their dual roles and a certain degree of independence. Studies on higglers in the English-speaking Caribbean suggest that women comprise over 80 percent of the population engaged in trading and commercial activities.[60]

In recent years the role of higglers itself has been transformed, as some women now travel internationally, buying clothing and other consumer goods in Miami to sell in Jamaica or selling Jamaican goods in Haiti and other areas.[61] The complex web of interrelationships in which these women engage at different levels and their creativity in managing their businesses is quite impressive—finding loans, identifying

68

Feature

Martha

Martha is a twenty-six-year-old school teacher, who now lives with her parents and small son in a rural parish in Jamaica. Her father cultivates five acres of land with help from Martha and her brother, whenever the brother is unable to get some other job. Her mother describes herself as a housewife, but she manages the reaping and sale of produce with help from Martha. In addition to the five acres, Martha has started farming on her own, on a plot of family land, in order to supplement her low wages as a teacher. This family is fortunate in having land on which to grow food for themselves.

Martha has three brothers altogether. Two left to work as migrant farmworkers on a contract basis in Canada and the United States. Both attempted to stay on illegally, but only one succeeded. The other one was discovered and deported, and now uses the family home as his main base when he is not away working on temporary jobs—as a mechanic, welder, or painter. The brother who stayed abroad sends money home to the family from time to time.

Martha graduated from teacher training college, but was unable to get a job in town, which would have allowed her to continue her university courses. She worked for a year in a rural community, on the outskirts of the capital. In 1983 she became pregnant, and as a single mother was subjected to extreme harassment by the principal of the school. At that time, conservative elements in Jamaica were pressing to reverse the provisions of the Maternity Leave law, passed in the 1970s, which provides for six weeks maternity leave. Tired of the harassment, Martha left the job. She remained unemployed until 1985.

During part of the period when she was out of work Martha and her child were supported entirely by an elderly relative in town. Eventually, however, she was obliged to send her son to her mother in the country, and finally she herself returned to the country, where she could get free shelter and food from the land.

In 1986 Martha had three temporary jobs, each lasting three months—two as a teacher and one as a clerk in the Ministry of Social Security. To get this last job she had to "stoop to smiling up with the man in charge" as she put it, when he made sexual overtures. Finally, towards the end of that year she gained employment in a primary school some six miles away. She often walks the distance "over hill and gully" because transportation is not reliable, and she cannot afford to reach school late. In the evening, when she can afford it, she takes a taxi from the nearest transportation point, but this cannot be done often as it costs J$30.

(continues)

Her father is an epileptic, and it is Martha who has to take him to a private doctor in the nearby town, as the clinic has been closed. However, the fee is J$50, and the pills cost J$100 for each prescription. He should go to the doctor every three months, but can afford to go only at six-monthly intervals. Often Martha cannot afford to fill the prescription.

Martha is now pregnant again, and receives some financial support from the "baby father," though she is not sure how long this support will last. Like many poor women in Jamaica, Martha decided to find a boyfriend and have a baby, knowing that the man would give her some money for the baby—for a while at least. When he gets tired of supporting the child, Martha will have to try to find another man, and begin the cycle again. Meanwhile, she has more children to support. But what else can she do? As she says, "I don't really want this baby. It's mainly an economic thing."

Source: Joan French, based on interviews conducted in 1986.

"sure sells," bargaining wholesale purchases, devising book-keeping and accounting systems, learning the intricacies of air and boat travel, and learning new languages.[62]

In the Dominican Republic, the economically active population in the informal sector has grown from 39 percent in 1980 to 45 percent in 1983, with men outnumbering women. Unemployment in the 1980s would surely have been much higher were it not for the growth of this sector. Nevertheless, jobs in the informal sector pay 60 percent less on average than those in the formal sector. Seventy percent of women in the urban informal sector earn less than the estimated poverty level of income.[63] The majority of women working in the informal sector are employed in domestic service, which pays the lowest wages and has practically no labor protection.[64]

The growth of the informal sector in the Dominican Republic may also reflect state policy, since international development assistance has increasingly been encouraging the growth of microenterprises in Latin America and the Caribbean. Because of their capacity for absorbing labor and their very low costs, microenterprises have been identified as enjoying a comparative advantage in a highly competitive international market. Microenterprise development has thus been getting increasing support from both the public and private sector in terms of credit, access to raw materials and foreign exchange, and other privileges formerly reserved exclusively for the formal sector.[65]

The Intensification
of Household Survival Strategies

The increasing "informalization" of Caribbean economies has brought the household to the limelight, as it is here that strategies for generating incomes are conceived and coordinated by men and women, and across generations. In the context of the economic crisis, the household has acquired new importance as a center for small-scale entrepreneurial activity, as women and men prepare foods for the market, organize and package agricultural produce, sew and embroider, do macramé and craft jewelry, grow and sell ornamental plants, collect aluminum cans, and as we have noted, engage in industrial homework for garment, electronic, and computer industries. Women in poor Caribbean households have always sought to stretch family income by producing goods at home rather than purchasing them in stores and by making use of extended family and neighborhood networks. The economic crisis has obliged women to intensify these activities in order to cope with declining household income, increasing prices, and cuts in government services.

An understanding of Caribbean concepts of "family" and "community" is important here in understanding women's responses to the crisis. The structures of the family and of the community in the Caribbean have emerged out of the history and culture of the region. They represent reconstructions of human communities out of the dehumanizing experience of slavery, the destruction and reconstruction and resistance of the African family, and the specific realities and requirements of the local economy.[66] For the majority of the black, working-class population of the Caribbean, the concept of family often extends beyond the household unit or nuclear family, beyond the neighborhood or village, and even beyond the country, to encompass a network of mutually supporting members. Similarly, the concept of "community" may transcend spatial dimensions to include people who are linked together in communities of interest—savings groups, the sports club, or closely knit religious groups.

The persistence of these networks and associations has been important in building links among different social classes and in enabling women to respond creatively to the current crisis. For a central feature of women's survival strategies is the extent to which they draw on networks of family and community in times of hardship. These networks provide both a mode of survival and a source of affirmation—crucial for emotional support as well as for the empowerment of women.

However, by providing a retreat from an exploitative system, Caribbean forms of the family and community also facilitate the continuation of exploitation and the inequitable distribution of resources. It appears that governments have in fact taken advantage of women's ability to draw on traditional networks of support to introduce policies which have been particularly devastating to women and those for whose care they have been traditionally responsible—children and the elderly.

In Jamaica, for example, women have extended household exchange networks, which increases the amount of goods, services, and occasionally cash that flows among relatives, friends, and neighbors. Many women have taken advantage of commissaries at their place of work to purchase scarce items such as dairy goods or baby-care products whether or not they need them themselves in order to exchange them for food, child care, or other needed services. Rural and urban kin have linked up, with higglers providing their urban kin with fresh vegetables in return for manufactured goods such as flashlight batteries. A conscious attempt is made to avoid market transactions because of the increasing scarcity of cash.

Survival strategies vary with household composition, and one emerging response to the crisis is to increase household size. Expanding the number of people living in a household potentially increases the number of income earners as well as those available to undertake household chores and child care. Dominican sociologist Isis Duarte believes that the incorporation of additional members into the household as a survival strategy may be one explanation for the continued large size of households in the Dominican Republic, which has remained at about 5.3 persons since 1920, despite the sharp decline in fertility levels since the 1960s.[67] Large households generally consist of extended families, among whom 69 percent have five or more members. Extended families continue to account for approximately 30 percent of all households, and the percentage is higher in urban than in rural areas, which runs counter to most demographic expectations. The increasingly high cost of housing may be one factor that forces families to double up and results in severe overcrowding among the urban poor.

In a 1981 study in Kingston it was found that there was a greater tendency among female-headed households than among those headed by a stable co-residential couple to incorporate additional kin into the household.[68] Additional kin are added for two reasons: they free women from some domestic chores and child care so that they can be full-time workers, and they often contribute to household income through informal sector activities. Whenever possible, new household members are expected to help with the payment of rent and utilities; this is particularly expected of men joining households, whether they are stable partners or boyfriends in visiting unions, or fathers of one or more of the woman's children. However, because of the high rate of unemployment among men, particularly in the urban areas, many men are unable to fulfill these traditional financial obligations. In this study, less than a quarter of the women living in visiting unions, and none of the single women then living alone with their children, received regular support from their boyfriends or the fathers of their children.

Hence, while a series of sexual partners may have been a traditional means by which Jamaican women sought financial support, it would seem that the devastating decline in male earning capacity in recent years has made women even more reliant on their own wages and other sources of income. In the study just cited, over 80 percent of the women who headed households were directly responsible for all major household expenditures, and 63 percent of the women in the stable unions also assumed this responsibility. Throughout the English-speaking Caribbean, women express the need to be economically "independent" as one central to their lives.[69]

In the Dominican Republic, although women have been joining the workforce in increasing numbers, the role of the male breadwinner has remained more intact. The 1981 study of Dominican free-trade zones referred to earlier found that husbands are still considered the principal economic provider in many if not most households, and are responsible for providing such basic items as food and housing. However, the great majority of working women also maintain that their families could not survive without their wages, suggesting that their wages are not just supplementary, but rather, crucial to the household's well-being.[70]

Nonetheless, women's contribution to the household economy is greatest among female heads of household, and as mentioned previously, the proportion of such households has been increasing since the 1970s. While the 1981 Census puts the figure at 20.6 percent, other estimates reach as high as 33.5 percent.[71] It may be that the increased difficulties men are facing in fulfilling their roles as economic providers are partly responsible for this increase. Although female heads of household have higher rates of labor-force participation than married women, they are a particularly vulnerable group, with lower incomes, higher rates of unemployment, and twice as likely to find employment as only occasional laborers as are male heads (see Table 3.3).[72]

International Migration

International migration is the bottom-line survival strategy for the poorer households throughout most of the Caribbean and has been for many years; the region as a whole sends out a greater percentage of its population than does any other world region.[73] Several changes have taken place in the nature of this migration since 1960, however, which

Feature

Jasmine

In 1979, Jasmine, her boyfriend Bob, and their two children lived in one room in an old house just off Torrington Bridge in Kingston, Jamaica. The room was complete with bed, crib, table, vanity, two chests of drawers, refrigerator, radio, cassette recorder, plenty of clothes, and enough to eat. Jasmine worked in a chicken processing plant, which was then operating sporadically, so that she could not rely on her pay check to be the same each week. Bob worked as a waiter in the almost-empty luxury hotel in New Kingston. His biggest tips came from Miami-based Cubans who overnighted in Kingston on their way to visit relatives in Cuba. Earlier that year the United States had normalized visiting rights for Cubans to go home and then return to the States.

Because of the nature of their relationship and their unreliable wages, Bob and Jasmine shared household expenses. Jasmine also has two other children living in the countryside. One lived with Bob's relatives even though Bob was not the child's father. Jasmine sent her children in the country "what she can."

Bob had taped pictures of Bob Marley and other Rasta musicians on the walls of their room. Influenced by Rastafarianism, Bob also supported the Peoples' National Party (PNP), led by Michael Manley. But a Miami-based businessman wanted to help him migrate—undocumented—to work for him in his Florida factory. Bob had his passport, no air fare, and just the man's business card. Bob said if he could work in Miami six months, he could really buy all those things he, Jasmine, and the kids need. Jasmine went along with the idea, saying the money was worth the hardship and waiting during Bob's planned absence. He was good to her and the children, was not "stingy with his money," and did not see other women. In the hotel, Bob said, all the white women were always after the male help (meaning seeking sexual favors), a common boast. As for other Jamaican women, he said he was not interested.

By 1985, Jasmine had experienced four years on her own. In 1980, the workers at the chicken processing plant voted out the established trade union for one associated with the Workers' party of Jamaica—a Communist party. Management then closed the shop down and filed for bankruptcy. A "new" set of managers bought the factory and rehired only workers who had never spoken a word against the company. Jasmine had been vocal about the poor working conditions and sporadic pay. She was not hired back.

(continues)

Jasmine tried to find other factory work, but no one was hiring: 36 percent of the female labor force was unemployed. She and the children lived on Bob's small, unreliable wages. Bob became increasingly harassed by the extra burden imposed upon him by Jasmine's unemployment. Soon, Bob caught the eye of a woman who was not looking for rent or food money. One day in 1981, Jasmine returned home to an empty room. All that she and Bob bought together, he had taken with him.

Four years later, Jasmine has found a place to live after "moving from pillar to post," carrying her things up and down the road. Bob had not sent any money to her "for the kids" in two months. For a while, Bob kept the boy with him, but returned him to Jasmine without explanation, and without his clothes. Jasmine earns money by doing favors for people—such as shopping, child care, hairdressing—literally surviving on tips from other poor people. She is bitter about her relationship with Bob and has become fierce in her attacks on his character. As for politics, she lives in "PNP country," a neighborhood partisan to Manley. The neighborhood is an impoverished one, where there is political warfare, and often violence, but Edward Seaga, then prime minister, and Michael Manley, his rival, were minor "man worries" in Jasmine's life.

Source: Lynn Bolles, based on interviews conducted during 1979 and 1985.

have particular significance for women. In the first place, the volume has greatly increased since the early 1980s; moreover, the rate of female migration has increased rapidly during this period, now surpassing that of men. In addition, more middle-class family members are leaving for the United States than before 1960, when migration was primarily an escape for the poor and unskilled.

Table 3.7 shows that legal migration to the United States from the Caribbean began to increase significantly after 1976, when the region began to experience its economic downturn, and shows little sign of abating. Over a million legal migrants entered the United States during the ten years from 1976 to 1986, which represents slightly over half the total since 1960. As a result, an important share of Caribbean people now reside in the United States. The total number of persons who migrated legally from Jamaica and from the Dominican Republic is about the same, but since the total population of Jamaica is smaller, this represents a much higher percentage of Jamaicans (12 percent) than Dominicans (5 percent).[74] If estimates of illegal migration— 400,000 Haitians, 225,000 Dominicans, 250,000 Jamaicans over this same ten-year period—are added to this figure, it becomes clear how strongly labor flows have integrated the United States and the Caribbean.

Table 3.7
Legal Immigration by Country of Birth from the Caribbean, 1960–87

	1960–65	1966–70	1971–75	1976–80	1981–83	1984–86	1987	1960–87
All Countries	1,715,710	1,871,365	1,936,281	2,557,033	1,750,494	1,715,620	601,516	12,148,019
Caribbean	159,354	381,386	341,631	608,127	244,673	290,718	115,637	2,141,526
Caribbean Share of Total Migrants	(9.3%)	(20.3%)	(17.6%)	(23.9%)	(14.0%)	(16.9%)	(19.9%)	(17.6%)
Bahamas	n.a.	n.a.	n.a.	n.a.	1,628	1,602	556	3,786
Barbados	2,377	7,312	7,878	13,070	6,204	4,797	1,665	43,303
Cuba	84,979	180,073	110,691	290,886 [1]	28,045	64,047	28,916	787,637
Dominican Republic	36,128	58,744	67,051	80,965	57,729	73,109	24,858	398,584
Guyana	1,434	5,760	14,320	33,211	25,782	27,310	11,384	119,201
Haiti	10,820	27,648	27,130	41,786 [2]	23,886	32,670	14,819	178,759
Jamaica	9,675	62,676	61,445	80,550	61,815	58,340	23,148	357,649
Trinidad-Tobago	2,598	22,367	33,278	28,498	11,287	8,622	3,543	110,193
OECS:								
Antigua	n.a.	n.a.	1,969	4,131	6,171	2,722	874	15,867
Dominica	n.a.	n.a.	1,182	3,399	1,836	1,546	740	8,703
Grenada	n.a.	n.a.	2,388	5,377	3,340	2,959	1,098	15,162
Montserrat	n.a.	n.a.	932	1,007	503	n.a. [3]	n.a.	2,442
St. Kitts-Nevis	n.a.	n.a.	1,960 [4]	4,474	4,679	2,990	589	14,692
St. Lucia	n.a.	n.a.	1,305	3,642	1,981	1,485	496	8,909
St. Vincent-Grenadines	n.a.	n.a.	1,613	3,122	2,285	2,023	746	9,789
Other[5]	11,343	16,806	8,489	14,009	7,502	6,496	2,205	66,850

Source: Robert Pastor, "Introduction: The Policy Challenge," in R. Pastor, ed., *Migration and Development in the Caribbean: The Unexplored Connection* (Boulder: Westview, 1985), table 1.3; 1984–1987 update and revisions on earlier years drawn from U.S. Department of Justice, *1988 Statistical Yearbook of Immigration and Naturalization Service* (Washington, D.C.: Government Printing Office), table 3.

1) Includes 124,789 entrants from Cuba in the Mariel exodus of 1980
2) Includes 10,211 Haitian entrants legalized simultaneously with the Mariel Cubans in 1980
3) Beginning in 1984, Montserrat is listed in "other"
4) Prior to FY 1977, historical data for Anguilla were included in St. Kitts-Nevis
5) From 1960 to 1970, "other" probably includes the OECS nations, which were not yet independent. There is no specific reference to that effect. From 1971 to 1981, "other" includes Anguilla, Bahamas, Belize, Bermuda, British Virgin Islands, Cayman Islands, Guadeloupe, Martinique, Netherlands Antilles, Puerto Rico, Turks-Caicos Islands, and the U.S. Virgin Islands. For 1982 on, it includes all of the latter countries except the Bahamas.

Table 3.8
Distribution of Migrants by Sex: Comparison of Three Decades

Sending Country	1950s	1960s	1970s	Total
Jamaica				
Male	59.6	41.3	45.6	48.3
Female	40.4	58.7	54.4	51.7
Dominican Republic				
Male	59.2	51.5		54.7
Female	40.8	48.5		45.3
Grenada				
Male	55.9	48.2	49.0	50.6
Female	44.1	51.8	51.0	49.4
St. Lucia				
Male	59.8	54.4		56.7
Female	40.2	45.6		43.3
Trinidad-Tobago				
Male		53.8	44.4	49.6
Female		46.2	55.6	50.4
Barbados				
Male	65.5	47.0	50.2	53.2
Female	35.5	53.0	49.8	46.8

Source: Elsa Chaney, *Migration from the Caribbean Region: Determinants and Effects of Current Movements* (Washington, D.C.: Center for Immigration Policy, 1985), p. 21.

International migration has a long history in the English-speaking Caribbean, dating back to the nineteenth century when Jamaicans migrated to Panama to build the canal or to Cuba to cut sugarcane. In the immediate postwar period, most of Jamaican migration was to the United Kingdom, but this was sharply curtailed by British immigration controls in 1962. After 1962, most migration was to the United States and Canada and it has constituted close to half the natural increase in Jamaica's population since 1962 to the present.[75]

Before 1950 migration was dominated by men, and is one of the factors accounting for the high percentage of female-headed households in Jamaica and other areas of the English-speaking Caribbean. Since 1960, however, the percentage of women emigrating from Jamaica has been much higher than that of men (see Table 3.8). This change is partly due to the U.S. Immigration Act of 1965, which gave higher preference to better educated, more skilled immigrants that, in the case of Jamaica, included large numbers of female teachers and nurses. Domestic workers were given special labor certification in Canada as well. The U.S. law also gave preference to family reunification, so that wives, mothers, and other female relatives joined earlier male migrants. Family reunification is the primary reason for female migration from the Dominican Republic, which is also now predominantly female;

according to the 1980 U.S. Census, women constitute 55 percent of the Dominican population resident in the United States.[76]

The U.S. and Canadian preference given to the more skilled labor force suggests that it is not only the unemployed and very poor who migrate. In fact, legal migration from Jamaica since the 1970's has been notable both for its volume and for its high proportion of skilled and educated workers. These Jamaicans have been propelled by the discovery that domestic mobility has been blocked with the cutbacks in jobs and wages in both the public and private sectors as well as by the social upheaval and political violence of the last years of Michael Manley's first administration. Between 1976 and 1985, professionals and managers accounted for 9.7 percent of all Jamaican migrants to the United States and Canada, while craftspeople and operatives represented 12 percent; these two categories alone represent a serious loss of educated and skilled labor power. In the health sector, for example, over the 1975–85 period, the number of doctors and nurses who migrated represented 78 and 95 percent, respectively, of those trained in these professions during this period.[77] Clearly this loss of labor power seriously reduces the adequacy of health care in Jamaica, and reflects Jamaica's inability to retain and effectively utilize its skilled labor at adequate levels of compensation.

Recent studies of migration from the Dominican Republic indicate the growing importance of middle-class migration from that country as well. Middle-class migration has been attributed to the nature of dependent development in the Caribbean, which both created and then restricted the expansion of the educated middle class.[78] With the general economic downturn in the 1970s, cutbacks in the public sector meant many lost their jobs, and the falling standard of living made it harder to maintain middle-class status on government salaries.

A 1981 survey of Dominican migrants in New York City, aged twenty to forty-five, revealed that women constituted 55.8 percent of the Dominican migrants to New York City, most apparently not drawn from the poorest segments of the population.[79] Women originated mainly from urban areas, and had an average of nine years of schooling, which is much higher than the national average. The labor-force participation of these women before they left the Dominican Republic was 31 percent; it increased to 49 percent in New York City, where they were employed primarily in the garment industry. Thus while family reunification may be the primary reason for migrating, paid employment is also an important motivation for those who go to New York and remain there. Thirty-seven percent of these migrant households are headed by women, among whom household income is lower than for co-resident households.[80]

Those who migrate are usually in their most productive ages (twenty to thirty-nine), and often leave behind the very young and old. This results in much higher dependency ratios in the Caribbean than in the United States. The high number of dependents left behind also explains the high level of remittances. Some of the smaller Eastern Caribbean islands such as St. Kitts-Nevis are known as remittance societies, since so many people have left and the remaining population is almost entirely dependent on remittances.

The level of remittances is much higher in the Dominican Republic, reaching US$205 million in 1985, than in Jamaica, where it is US$26 million.[81] In addition to serving as an important source of household income, remittances have a significant impact on these countries' balance of payments. In 1985 remittances amounted to 5 percent of the value of merchandise trade of Jamaica and 28 percent of the Dominican Republic. Data from the Bank of Jamaica suggests that the value of remittances in foreign exchange has shown a marked decline since 1975, which was only partially offset by the increased value of farm-workers' remittances.[82] These are seasonal farmworkers temporarily admitted into the United States under the H2 contract workers program.

In contrast, a study by the Central Bank in the Dominican Republic shows that the level of remittances has been increasing steadily since 1970, when it stood at only US $8.5 million.[83] The 1981 study of Dominican migrants in New York City found that 59 percent of male heads of households sent remittances compared to 44 percent of female heads of households, and that the average annual amount is nearly double for the former (US$1,124) than for the latter (US$687). Undoubtedly, this reflects the lower income level of female heads, over half of whom were receiving some form of public assistance.[84] A more recent 1985 study found that the average monthly remittance had increased to US$183, which would be nearly double the amount reported in 1981.[85]

Remittances appear to be most often spent on household expenses and consumer goods, and when current needs are met, on improved housing. Therefore they do not appear to contribute to productive investment in the Caribbean.[86] There is also little effort to pool remittances, creating funds for community projects as is common in some Mexican rural communities. Remittances may in some cases reduce the need to seek local sources of employment, increasing dependency on this external source of income. A 1980 study of migrants from Santiago, the second largest city in the Dominican Republic, found a much higher percentage of unemployment among heads of households with members who had migrated compared to households without migrants.[87] The mean amount remitted per household was nearly equal to the 1979 median monthly wage in the city.

The increasing level of remittances to the Dominican Republic has largely sustained the local housing industry in the 1980s. People who had left the country received 60 percent of the housing loans issued in 1984 (a year in which construction permits issued had dropped by more than 50 percent compared to 1981). Since the houses built by migrants may be rented in their absence, this housing constitutes an important source of moderate-income housing. Migrants also constitute 22 percent of the tourists to the Dominican Republic in recent years, and the money they spent constituted nearly 29 percent of total tourist income.[88]

With the increasing integration of Caribbean economies into the U.S. economy, there has been a rise in circular migration, with frequent short-term movements to and from. The economic crisis is making it more difficult for migrants to return to live in the region, however. In 1980 return migrants to the Dominican Republic already reported a high rate of unemployment, especially among female heads of household, nearly four-fifths of whom were unemployed.[89] This induces many to think of leaving again, and confirms the inability of the economy to absorb even these experienced workers, about a third of whom are in professional and managerial categories.

As the possibilities of permanent return are dimmed, migration represents a contradictory picture for Caribbean countries. If the better educated and more skilled continue to migrate, they constitute another subsidy that poorer countries are supplying to the richer, advanced countries like the United States. In addition, while remittances help reduce deficits in the balance of payments, they also increase demand for imported goods, ultimately having a negative effect on the balance of trade.[90] Thus migration and the remittances it generates may simultaneously alleviate the crisis and generate new problems.

In sum, the impact of the regional economic crisis and of consequent structural adjustment policies has been devastating for poor women and their families. Women suffer higher rates of unemployment and earn lower wages than men, and have been the most affected by cuts in government services and increases in the cost of living. In response, they are working even harder, spending and eating less, and migrating more. The toll this is taking in terms of increased malnutrition and other indices of poor health and the loss of skilled labor power will be paid by these households and by their countries for decades to come.

As this analysis of the impact of structural adjustment measures has demonstrated, it often seems that governments and international agencies are taking advantage of women's traditional responsibility for household reproduction as well as their survival skills, and their relative lack of organization, to introduce policies that have been particularly devastating for women and children. Moreover, proposed solutions to the crisis—such as the encouragement being given to nontraditional exports which are labor intensive—seem to be built on women's "comparative disadvantage," their need and thus willingness to work for wages that are lower than what men might work for.

Women's traditional survival strategies and support networks are also providing, however, the basis for new forms of confronting the crisis. Women are creating new support mechanisms every day, sharing child care, creating "common pots" for feeding children and elders, dividing community tasks, becoming active beyond the realm of the household into that of the community. In so doing, as we will see in the next chapter, women are increasingly leading many community efforts, and taking to the streets to protest IMF policies and their devastating consequences.

Notes

1. Omar Davies and Patricia Anderson, "The Impact of the Recession and Adjustment Policies on Poor Urban Women in Jamaica," paper prepared for UNICEF (Kingston: University of the West Indies, 1987), p. 1.

2. Ibid., p.5; see also Miguel Ceara, *Situación Socioeconómica Actual y Su Repercusión en la Situación de la Madre y el Niño* (Santo Domingo: INTEC and UNICEF, 1987).

3. Inter-American Development Bank, *Economic and Social Progress in Latin America, 1989 Report* (Washington, D.C.: IDB, 1989), table B–1. This comparison is based in 1988 dollars.

4. Davies and Anderson, "The Impact of the Recession," p. 26.

5. The Jamaican Census definition of the unemployed, which includes those not actively looking for work as well as those never employed, substantially raises labor-force participation rates, especially for women. According to Patricia Anderson (personal communication), in the Jamaica labor-force surveys, the category of unemployed includes persons who did not actively look for work during the reference week of the survey, but who wanted work and were able to accept it. This group, usually referred to as "non-seekers" is larger for women than for men. However, even when non-seekers are excluded from the unemployed and from the labor force, the differential between levels of male and female unemployment remains. In October 1985, using this narrower definition of the labor force, the "job-seeking rate" stood at 13.3 percent, with the male rate at 8.5 percent and the female rate at 17.9 percent.

6. Davies and Anderson, "The Impact of the Recession," p. 26.

7. B. Miller and Carl Stone, "The Low-Income Household Expenditure Survey: Description and Analysis." Staff Paper No. 25, Jamaica Tax Structure Examination Project, Metropolitan Studies Program, Syracuse University, 1985.

8. Lynn Bolles, "Kitchens Hit By Priorities: Employed Working-Class Jamaican Women Confront the IMF," in June Nash and Maria Patricia Fernandez-Kelly, eds., *Women, Men, and the International Division of Labor* (Albany: State University of New York Press, 1983).

9. According to a 1980 survey, rural unemployment among women actually reaches 53 percent. As in Jamaica, this estimate of unemployment includes all those who indicated a willingness to work if they had some chance of being employed, even if they were not currently looking for work. (See Isidoro Santana, *Tendencias Recientes y Perspectivas de la Situación Ocupacional en R.D.*, Santo Domingo: Instituto de Estudios de Población y Desarrollo, Boletín 9, 1985.)

10. Santana, *Tendencias Recientes*, p. 10.

11. Ceara, *Situación Socioeconómica*, p. 27.

12. Baez, *La Subordinación de la Mujer Dominicana en Cifras* (Santo Domingo: Dirección General de Promoción de la Mujer and INSTRAW, 1984), p. 45.

13. Baez, *La Subordinación de la Mujer*, table 3.3.

14. Ibid., p. 55.

15. Ibid., p. 31.

16. Ceara, *Situación Socioeconómica*, p. 217.

17. Nelson Ramírez, Isis Duarte, and Carmen Gómez, *Población y Salud en República Dominicana* (Santo Domingo: Instituto de Estudios de Población y Desarrollo, Boletín 16, 1986), p. 11.

18. Bernardo Vega, *El Ajuste de la Economía Dominicana (1982–1986) dentro de la Crisis Financiera Latinamericana* (Santo Domingo: Fundación Cultural Dominicana, 1988), p. 38.

19. Santana, *Tendencias Recientes*, p. 21.

20. Ceara, *Situación Socioeconómica*, p. 26.

21. Derrick Boyd, "The Impact of Adjustment Policies on Vulnerable Groups: The Case of Jamaica, 1973–1985," in Giovanni Cornia, R. Jolly, and F. Stewart, eds., *Adjustment with a Human Face*, Vol. II (N.Y.: Clarendon Press/UNICEF, 1988), p. 133.

22. Davies and Anderson, "The Impact of the Recession," p. 35.

23. Ibid., p. 12.

24. World Bank, *Dominican Republic: Economic Prospects and Policies to Renew Growth* (Washington, D.C.: World Bank, 1985).

25. Belkis Mones and Lydia Grant, "Agricultural Development, the Economic Crisis, and Rural Women in the Dominican Republic," in Carmen Diana Deere and Magdalena León, eds., *Rural Women and State Policy: Feminist Perspectives on Latin American Agricultural Development* (Boulder: Westview Press, 1987), pp. 35–50.

26. Ramirez et al., *Población y Salud.*

27. Linda Whiteford, "Sugar and Survival: The Economic Crisis and Health in the Dominican Republic," draft, University of South Florida, 1988, pp. 21–22.

28. Philip Musgrove, "Household Food Consumption in the Dominican Republic: Effects of Income, Price and Family Size," *Economic Development and Cultural Change* 34, no. 1 (1985), p. 92.

29. Philip Musgrove, "The Economic Crisis and Its Impact on Health and Health Care in Latin America and the Caribbean," *International Journal of Health Services* 17, no. 3 (1987), p. 418.

30. Boyd, "The Impact of Adjustment Policies," p. 145.

31. Patricia Anderson, "Minibus Ride: A Journey through the Informal Sector of Kingston's Mass Transport System," Institute of Social and Economic Research, University of the West Indies, Kingston, Jamaica, paper no. 2, 1987.

32. Ceara, *Situación Socioeconómica*, p. 27.

33. Ramírez et al., *Población y Salud*, pp. 68, 80.

34. Whiteford, "Sugar and Survival," p. 18.

35. The World Bank, *World Debt Tables 1988/89*, Vol. II, country tables.

36. Musgrove, "The Economic Crisis," pp. 426–27. Higher per capita expenditures on health and education in Jamaica as compared to the Dominican Republic may be at least partially explained by differences in historical background. British colonial policy in Jamaica and other areas of the English-speaking Caribbean instituted social welfare policies following the workers' riots of the 1930s, on the advice of the Moyne Commission and the British Labour Party. In contrast, in the Dominican Republic, the social security and labor legislation was designed by the Trujillo regime primarily to legitimize his dictatorship and to contain labor struggles. See Isis Duarte, *Trabajadores Urbanos* (Santo Domingo: Ed. Universitaria, 1986), ch. 1.

37. To combat growing malnutrition, the government of Edward Seaga instituted a Food Aid Program for primary school children, nursing mothers, and the indigent. Although half the total population of Jamaica qualifies for this program (about one million people), in the first six months of the program it was reaching only 20 percent of the targeted population. See Boyd, "The Impact of Adjustment Policies," p. 141.

38. Giovanni Cornia and Francis Stewart, "Country Experiences with Adjustment," in Cornia, Jolly, and Stewart, eds., *Adjustment with a Human Face*, Vol. 1, p. 115.

39. Joan French, "The CBI and Jamaica: Objectives and Impact," Report prepared for the Development Group for Alternative Policies (Washington), 1987, pp. 50–51.

40. World Bank, *The World Development Report*, 1982 and 1989 eds. (Washington, D.C.: World Bank, 1982 and 1989), table 32.

41. Ceara, *Situación Socioeconómica*, p. 55, p. 28.

42. The World Bank, *World Development Report 1989*, table 32.

43. Ceara, *Situación Socioeconómica*, p. 29.

44. Ramírez et al., *Población y Salud*, p. 12.

45. Quoted in Whiteford, "Sugar and Survival," p. 15.

46. Whiteford, "Sugar and Survival," pp. 22–23.

47. Ibid., p. 16.

48. Duarte, "Crisis, Familia y Participación," p. 12.

49. Davies and Anderson, "The Impact of the Recession," p. 37.

50. Section 807 of the U.S. Tariff Code is discussed in more detail in Chapter 5. The Reagan administration gave garment producers located in the Caribbean increased access to the U.S. market in 1986, giving CBI-designated countries expanded quotas in the U.S. market for garments assembled from U.S.-formed, made, and cut cloth; see discussion in Chapter 6.

51. French, "The CBI and Jamaica," pp. 31–32.

52. Ibid., pp. 33–34.

53. Alfonso Abreu, Manuel Cocco, Carlos Despradel, Eduardo García Michel, and Arturo Peguero, *Las Zonas Francas Industriales en la República Dominicana: El Exito de una Política Económica* (Santo Domingo: Centro Internacional para el Desarrollo Económico, 1989), pp. 63–67, 141.

54. Susan Joekes, *Employment in Industrial Free Zones in the Dominican Republic: A Report with Recommendations for Improved Worker Services* (Washington, D.C.: International Center for Research on Women, for USAID/Dominican Republic, 1987), p. 55.

55. Other sources show Dominican wages being slightly higher than in Haiti for that same year; see Abreu et al., *Las Zonas Francas,* p. 130.

56. The 1981 study of women in the free-trade zones of the Dominican Republic was conducted by CIPAF (Centro de Investigación para la Acción Femenina), a feminist research center directed by Magaly Pineda. Two members of the CIPAF research team, Quintina Reyes and Milagros Ricourt, along with Lorraine Catanzaro, wrote MA theses at the University of Florida using this data. See Quintina Reyes, "Comparative Study of Dominican Women Workers in Domestic and Free Trade Zone Industries," MA thesis, Center for Latin American Studies, University of Florida, 1987; Milagros Ricourt, "Free Trade Zones, Development, and Female Labor in the Dominican Republic," MA thesis, Center for Latin American Studies, University of Florida, 1986; and Lorraine Catanzaro, "Women, Work, and Consciousness: Export Processing in the Dominican Republic," MA thesis, Center for Latin American Studies, University of Florida, 1986.

57. Joekes, *Employment in Industrial Free Zones,* p. 59.

58. Mones and Grant, "Agricultural Development," pp. 43–45. Also see Francis Pou, et al., *La Mujer Rural Dominicana* (Santo Domingo: CIPAF, 1987). This study, based on the first national sample survey of rural women, found that the percentage of rural women listed as economically active in the 1981 Census was grossly underestimated because of the failure to include all of the ways in which women contribute economically to the household.

59. Patricia Anderson and Derek Gordon, "Economic Change and Labour Market Mobility in Jamaica, 1979–1984," paper presented to the First Conference of Caribbean Economists, Kingston, Jamaica, 1987.

60. See Economic Commission for Latin America and the Caribbean (ECLAC), *Women in the Inter-Island Trade in Agricultural Produce in the Eastern*

Caribbean (Trinidad: ECLAC, 1988), and the papers presented at the ECLAC Advisory Group Meeting on Women Traders in the Caribbean, Grenada, 9–11 May 1988, particularly: Alicia Taylor, "Women Traders in Jamaica: The Informal Commercial Importers;" Monique Lagro, "Women Traders in St. Vincent and the Grenadines;" and Daphne Phillips, "Women Traders in Trinidad and Tobago."

61. ECLAC, *Women in the Inter-Island Trade* .

62. The dimensions of the Caribbean higgling trade are not to be underrated. A recent study found that approximately 1,200 to 1,500 Haitians (the majority of whom are women) regularly travel to Puerto Rico, purchasing approximately $13 million worth of goods annually, which are then resold in Haiti. See Paul Latortue and Luis Luna Rosado, "Los Comerciantes Ambulantes Haitianos en Puerto Rico," Centro de Investigaciones Comerciales, University of Puerto Rico, mimeo (1985).

63. PREALC, "Empleo y Política Económica de Corto Plazo," memorandum prepared for ONAPLAN, Santo Domingo, 1983, pp. 8, 15.

64. Baez, *La Subordinación de la Mujer*, p. 50.

65. Helen Safa, "Urbanization, the Informal Economy and State Policy in Latin America," in Michael P. Smith and Joseph Feagin, eds. *The Capitalist City* (New York: Basil Blackwell, 1987).

66. Among East Indians, their physical and social isolation from the wider society of Trinidad and Guyana allowed them to retain much of their traditional cultures and religion. However, family structures such as visiting unions and common-law marriage are now becoming a part of the East Indian marital pattern as among Afro-Caribbeans.

67. Duarte, "Crisis, Familia, y Participación," p. 17.

68. See Bolles, "Kitchens Hit By Priorities," p. 156.

69. Christine Barrow, "Finding the Support: Strategies for Survival," *Social and Economic Studies*, 35, no. 2 (June 1986).

70. See Catanzaro, "Women, Work, and Consciousness."

71. Baez argues that the percentage of female-headed households is underestimated because it relies on the opinion of the informant surveyed (*La Subordinación de la Mujer*, p. 31). The higher figure is obtained, utilizing a method suggested by the United Nations, which measures the percentage of households where there are women with younger children and no adult men. If we assume that headship connotes family authority and responsibility, it could be argued that many women and men are sharing this responsibility. However, census data does not capture these changing patterns of family authority and responsibility, and we have followed the conventional usage of "male head of household," which was used in most studies we consulted. See Helen Safa, "Women and Industrialization in the Caribbean," in Jane Parpart and Sharon Stichter, eds., *Women, Employment and the Family in the International Division of Labor* (New York: Macmillan, forthcoming).

72. Carmen Julia Gómez and María Gator, "La Mujer Jefe de Hogar y la Vivienda," *Población y Desarrollo*, no. 19, (1987), p. 13.

73. Elsa Chaney, *Migration from the Caribbean Region: Determinants and Effects of Current Movements* (Washington, D.C.: Center for Immigration Policy and Refugee Assistance, 1985), p. 15.

74. Compiled from Inter-American Development Bank, *Economic and Social Progress in Latin America, 1987 Report.*

75. From 1943 to 1960, there was a net migration loss of 195,000 or nearly a third of the natural increase of the population of Jamaica; the net outflow reached 280,000 during the 1960s comprising 53 percent of the natural increase and has remained at this high level since then. See Patricia Anderson, "Manpower Losses and Employment Adequacy Among Skilled Workers in Jamaica, 1976–1985," in Patricia Pessar, ed., *When Borders Don't Divide: Labor Migration and Refugee Movements in the Americas* (New York: Center for Migration Studies, 1988), pp. 101–4.

76. José Del Castillo and Christopher Mitchell, eds., *La Immigración Dominicana en los Estados Unidos* (Santo Domingo: Universidad APEC, 1987), p. 54.

77. Anderson, "Manpower Losses," pp. 106, 113–14.

78. David Bray, "Economic Development, the Middle Class, and International Migration in the Dominican Republic," *International Migration Review* 18, no. 2 (1984), p. 221.

79. Douglas Gurak and Mary Kritz, "The Caribbean Communities in the United States, "*Migration Today* 13, no. 2 (1985), p. 8.

80. Douglas Gurak and Mary Kritz, "Dominican and Colombian Women in New York City," *Migration Today* 10, no. 3/4 (1982), pp. 17–19.

81. World Bank, *World Development Report, 1987* (Washington, D.C.: World Bank, 1988), pp. 220, 230. Remittances are also very important to Haiti where they represented 22 percent of the value of merchandise trade in 1985.

82. Patricia Anderson, "Migration and Development in Jamaica," Institute of Social and Economic Research, Working Paper No. 2. (University of West Indies, 1985), pp. 24–5; Del Castillo and Mitchell, *La Immigración*, p. 68.

83. Del Castillo and Mitchell, *La Immigración*, pp. 69–71.

84. Gurak and Kritz, "Dominican and Colombian Women," p. 18.

85. Del Castillo and Mitchell, *La Immigración*, p. 69.

86. Chaney, *Migration from the Caribbean Region*, p. 69.

87. Sherri Grasmuck, "The Consequences of Dominican Urban Outmigration for National Development: the Case of Santiago," in Steven E. Sanderson, ed., *The Americas in the New Division of Labor* (New York: Holmes and Meier, 1985), p. 155.

88. Del Castillo and Mitchell, *La Immigración*, pp. 69–71.

89. Grasmuck, "The Consequences of Dominican Urban Outmigration," p. 166.

90. Ibid., p. 156.

CHAPTER 4

Structural Adjustment and the Quest for Participation

IN THE EARLY HOURS OF APRIL 23, 1984, in the neighborhood of Capotillo, one of the poorest in Santo Domingo, more than 100 community organizations began a strike intended to last twelve hours, from 6:00 A.M. to 6:00 P.M. Their demands, directed to then President Salvador Jorge Blanco of the Dominican Revolutionary Party (PRD), were as follows:

1. To rescind the recent increases in the price of rice, beans, cooking oil, milk, tomato sauce, flour, soap, and other basic necessities.
2. To increase the minimum wage to DR$200 and to create new jobs.
3. To repair the streets of Capotillo, and to extend electricity and potable water to the neighborhood.
4. To abrogate the agreement signed with the International Monetary Fund (IMF).[1]

Notice of the strike and its demands were broadcast by radio, and within hours, acts of solidarity were taking place in many of the neighborhoods of the Dominican capital. Businesses closed, transportation was paralyzed, the schools were empty, and growing numbers of people gathered at the entrances to the poorer neighborhoods to put up barricades.

The police responded immediately and attempted to break up the protests, first with tear gas and then with bullets. By midday ten people were dead and twenty-five injured by gunshot wounds. The population

responded by assaulting the posts of INESPRE (Instituto de Estabili-
zación de Precios or Institute for Price Stabilization), from where
subsidized food was distributed in low income neighborhoods, by
blocking more roads, and by burning some government vehicles and
local offices. That evening the smell of burning tires from bonfires in
the poorer neighborhoods permeated the capital.

The next day the city was completely paralyzed. The accumulated
indignation of the people coalesced in a collective popular protest
without precedent, which by then included not only the organized
groups in poor neighborhoods, some of which were Christian base
communities, but also women's groups, the labor syndicates, teachers,
nurses, and professionals from all sectors, as well as a number of
political parties. Moreover, the strike had spread to many of the interior
cities of the Dominican Republic; peasant groups throughout the country
had also rallied in its support.

The government's response was to close all radio and television
stations; it then sent out the army to take back the streets. By the end
of the second day of the protest, 74 people were dead, 300 injured,
and thousands had been arrested. The next day the government sent
in tanks, the air force, and the marines, with orders to shoot on sight.
By noon of April 25 the protest had been suppressed. The final body
count was 114 dead—including 27 women and 5 children; 500 people
had been wounded by bullets, while over 5,000 had been taken prisoner.

The government, political parties of all persuasions, and the labor
unions had been caught completely by surprise, underlining their lack
of awareness of the depth of public anger. The inability of organized
labor or opposition political parties to channel this anger, and to give
the protest a clear political direction in the face of government repression
undoubtedly facilitated its containment. Following the April 1984 riot,
the Dominican government did moderate some price increases, but
new price increases were announced three months later, after further
arrests of community activists, leftist politicians, and labor leaders.
However, the government's handling of the riots split the ruling party
into factions, contributing to the PRD's defeat in the 1986 election.

Today, Caribbean politics is at a crossroads: over the last ten to
fifteen years there has been a deterioration in the traditional structures
of political power in the region, seen in widespread disillusionment
with the role of traditional political parties and in the weakening of
the organized labor movement. The implementation of structural adjustment policies by the majority of governments in the region has also
produced its own economic and social crisis. The political dimensions
of the crisis of the late 1980s have yet to be fully played out or
recognized.

This chapter seeks to analyze the impact of the twofold economic and institutional crisis on the politics and social organization of Caribbean society. The inability of traditional organizations, such as political parties, trade unions, and to a certain extent, the institutionalized church, to identify, service, and satisfy the credible needs of the people has paved the way for new forms of organization and political participation at the local level. Our primary interest is in assessing the new forms of organization which have emerged, particularly community action or grassroots groups, local development organizations (LDOs), nongovernmental organizations (NGOs), and women's groups—to attempt to understand the extent to which they constitute new social movements which might engender a new direction to Caribbean politics.

We give special attention to the organization of women, who over the past decade have become increasingly active social actors. Our concern is with both the degree to which traditional organizations have been able to incorporate the alternative visions emerging from women and other traditionally disenfranchised groups, as well as with the new forms of women's organizations which are increasingly voicing the demand for equitable development across social groups, genders, and generations.

The Politics of Structural Adjustment

Throughout the region, the politics of the 1980s stand in sharp contrast to those of the 1970s. While the 1970s were a period of radicalization, both within established political parties and with the emergence of new organizations with socialist and nationalist visions, the 1980s were increasingly conservative. In the 1970s some Caribbean states attempted to redefine their external relationships away from the passive pro-Western attachment of the colonial period, toward policies of active nonalignment, pioneering a new and wider set of relationships in the world community. In the 1980s such adventurousness was quelled, and the "interests" of the United States acquired an increasing preponderance in the foreign relations of Caribbean states and in the organization of their economies.

The perception of the role of the state in development also changed substantially. While in the 1970s the main role in the organization and direction of production was seen as belonging to the state, in the conservative vision of the 1980s these tasks were increasingly shifted to the private sector.[2] The renewed focus on the private sector was accompanied by a renewed regard for the role of foreign capital in developing the economies of the region. Whereas the 1970s were characterized by nationalizations of foreign enterprises and a tendency toward joint ventures between foreign capital and the state, the agenda of the 1980s centered on privatization of state enterprises and incentive schemes to lure foreign investors. Many of the changes in state policy and concomitant reorganization and ideological redefinition of political institutions have been accomplished by and through the policies of structural adjustment advocated by the International Monetary Fund (IMF), the World Bank, and the U.S. Agency for International Development (AID). These policies need to be understood within the context of political and economic developments of the 1970s which formed the backdrop against which the policies of structural adjustment were advocated.

Lessons of the 1970s

New progressive parties and new political movements emerged everywhere in the Caribbean during the 1970s, including the New Jewel Movement in Grenada, the Workers' Party of Jamaica (WPJ), the Movement for the National Liberation of Barbados, the United Popular Movement of St. Vincent, the Dominican Liberation Movement, the St. Lucian Labour Party, the Antigua Caribbean Liberation Movement, and the Working People's Party of Guyana, all influenced by the wide-ranging popular discontent being voiced throughout the region.[3]

To be sure, although there was a general trend toward "radicalization" of political movements and state policies in the late 1970s, this process, inevitably, was uneven. At one extreme were Jamaica, Grenada, and Guyana, where the parties in power explicitly affirmed their socialist commitments—although with very different views and practices regarding popular participation. At the other extreme were Puerto Rico, where conservative pro-U.S. statehood forces were in the ascendancy, and the Dominican Republic, where the quest for democracy was being led by Joaquin Balaguer and other heirs of the thirty-one-year Trujillo dictatorship. In between, in places such as Trinidad-Tobago and Belize, governments tried to make a success of nationalist economic and social policies.

Sustaining the radical movements of the 1970s was disillusionment with the development models of the postwar period. These had been premised upon the sustained inflow of U.S. capital into the region, mainly into the mineral export sector of the larger territories of the region, and to a lesser extent into manufacturing and tourism (See Chapter 5). While external demand for Caribbean exports remained buoyant and investment flows were sustained, there was considerable economic growth in real terms. The benefits of this growth, however, were concentrated in a few social groups. A new class of entrepreneurs in manufacturing and tourism emerged and the growing number of professionals found employment in the expanding public sector. The bulk of the population—urban workers, new migrants to the cities, and small farmers—did not benefit to the same degree. Income inequalities widened and unemployment and underemployment mounted. The distributional consequences of the export model became even clearer once the growth of the world economy slowed down in the 1970s, precipitating the crisis in the colonial economy model of the Caribbean and widespread social discontent.

Radical political movements throughout the region sought alternative economic and political models aimed at achieving social and economic equality, national control of the economy, and popular participation or direct democracy in the political process. At the economic level, their demands centered upon: (1) the redistribution of income; (2) limiting the role of foreign enterprises through selective nationalization; (3) land reform; (4) an increasingly activist role for the state—as the crucial agent of change and development—in the organization of production, distribution, and external trade; and (5) an independent foreign policy.

The reorientation of economic policy was associated with efforts to develop new forms of popular participation and representation. Attempts to form community councils in Jamaica or the national budget planning discussions in Grenada, for example, were intended to introduce some elements of direct democracy into the parliamentary representational institutions which characterize the English-speaking Caribbean. Economic policy reorientation also entailed a new set of political alliances, involving militant sections of the middle classes, the working class, and the subproletarian urban and rural masses. The policies of the period also led to a reduced political and economic role for both international and domestic capital.

The policy experiments of the 1970s proved to be short lived for a number of reasons, not the least of which was the underestimation of the problems of carrying out such fundamental transformations of Caribbean economies.[4] The deepening crisis in the world economy reverberated throughout the Caribbean, aggravating the structural weaknesses of Caribbean economies and heightening domestic economic difficulties. The new economic program in Jamaica, for example, was met by deteriorating terms of trade, the growing burden of debt service, and escalating inflation. As economist Clive Thomas has argued, the deteriorating economic situation left extremely limited space for social reforms and contributed to a rapid erosion of the political support for the Manley government.[5] Guyana was similarly struck by serious balance of payments difficulties which led to stagnation and the generalized deterioration in the standards of living of population, further fueled by the government's authoritarian policies that left the people excluded from decision-making and thus disinclined to maintain production levels.

The unrelenting hostility of the U.S. government and the major aid donor agencies, over which the United States exercises predominant influence, was a second factor in the destabilization of the nationalist political and economic projects. The vast array of destabilizing mechanisms employed by the United States against the 1970s Manley government in Jamaica and the New Jewel Movement in Grenada included campaigns to discourage U.S. tourists from visiting the islands (tourism is one of the main sources of income in both countries), verbal attacks against the "Communist inclination" of these projects, trade boycotts, and the infiltration of local trade union and popular organizations, among others.

A third factor which made these strategies nonviable in the 1970s was the inability of the radical governments to reorganize and stimulate production. Vacillation, erratic nationalizations of foreign enterprises, and the uncoordinated expansion of the state sector contributed to diminished rates of growth. Efforts at income redistribution also faced a broad range of internal contradictions: short-run measures required to alleviate poverty used up resources needed for medium or long-term growth and development. The pressure to redistribute resources was enormous. Meeting the demands of the masses meant risking longer term development, but ignoring them meant losing political support. Relations with the middle and upper classes were even more difficult, and all three projects faced sabotage and capital flight.

Social class tensions were compounded by political errors and internal conflicts within the various progressive parties, the most spectacular of which was the debacle of the New Jewel Movement in Grenada in 1983 which ended with the assassination of Maurice Bishop and the U.S. invasion of the island. Bishop's assassination by the "ultra-left" wing of the New Jewel Movement reverberated across the region and set the stage for an all-out attack on progressive forces by conservative parties and governments. The U.S. invasion of Grenada also led to the consolidation of conservative and pro-U.S. governments throughout the region.[6]

The net effect of all of these factors was a political reversal of the radical trend across the region, a reversal which brought in its train a new set of policy orientations, namely, the policies of structural adjustment.

The Social Basis for Structural Adjustment

As discussed in previous chapters, the main elements of the structural adjustment programs implemented in the Caribbean have been austerity policies complemented by a reorientation of the economy toward the production of nontraditional exports in the context of trade liberalization. Tariffs that formerly protected domestic producers within the local and regional market have been reduced or removed. The role of the state in the economy has been curtailed, both through the privatization of state-owned enterprises and severe reductions in state expenditures. At the same time, the entrepreneurial class has been nurtured (in some cases created) to respond to the incentives for export production— mainly devaluation and the reduction of real wage levels.

Understandably, the social supports for such a program are weak. Insofar as devaluation, wage controls, the end of consumption subsidies, and systematic public sector layoffs negatively affect the broad mass of the population, they undermine possible popular support for these conservative regimes. At the same time, the main beneficiaries of structural adjustment, the local bourgeoisie, are divided about it. One fissure, for example, is between importers, who favor the relaxation of import and price controls, and manufacturers, many of whom have gone bankrupt as a result of the flood of foreign imports into domestic markets.

To some extent, governments pursuing structural adjustment policies have been able to mitigate the political effects of these policies by virtue of extensive foreign economic support, as seen in the case of U.S. and multilateral aid to Jamaica under the government of Edward Seaga and to postinvasion Grenada. These governments also maintain support on the basis of appeals to the conservative ideological inclinations which characterize wide sections of the region's population. The Seaga government in Jamaica, as well as those of Grenada and Dominica, rely on strong anticommunist rhetoric as a means of bolstering support. Overall, however, it is clear that structural adjustment policies have heightened governmental instability in the region, most clearly seen by the defeat of Seaga in 1989 and of the ruling Dominican Revolutionary Party in the Dominican Republic in 1986.

Structural adjustment policies, not accidentally, were accompanied by the heightened militarization of the region. U.S. military assistance under the Reagan administration increased significantly in the early 1980s, particularly to Jamaica and the Dominican Republic, in concert with the elaboration of new regional "security" institutions after the U.S. invasion of Grenada (see Chapter 6). Moreover, a number of Caribbean governments have increased military and security expenditures—which have risen as a share of current government expenditures—in a period when social services are being strongly curtailed (see Table 4.1). While some Caribbean nations have a stronger standing military presence than others (with Guyana, the Dominican Republic, and Barbados in the lead in the 1980s), government expenditures on

Table 4.1
Militarization of the Caribbean, 1975–85

	Military Expenditures (ME) (US\$ millions)[1]	ME/Central Government Expenditures	ME/GNP	Armed Forces per 1,000 People[2]
Barbados				
1975	1	0.4	0.1	0
1980	14	3.6	1.1	4.0
1981	13	3.4	1.1	3.8
1983	10	2.8	0.9	3.5
1985	9	2.3	0.8	3.3
Dominican Republic				
1975	121	8.6	1.6	3.6
1980	133	7.8	1.5	4.1
1981	149	8.9	1.6	4.0
1983	135	8.7	1.4	3.7
1985	138 [3]	11.7	1.4	3.3
Guyana				
1975	35	13.2	6.6	2.6
1980	20	5.7	4.0	9.4
1981	21	5.6	4.4	9.2
1983	20	5.9	5.3	9.2
1985	33	n.a.	8.9	9.1
Haiti				
1975	21	8.2	1.5	1.2
1980	31	9.3	1.6	1.3
1981	35	9.6	1.9	1.4
1983	28	8.9	1.6	1.4
1985	29	8.4	1.6	1.0
Jamaica				
1975	20	2.1	0.8	0.5
1980	19	1.8	0.9	0.9
1981	25	2.5	1.2	0.9
1983	28	3.0	1.2	1.3
1985	17	1.8	0.9	0.8
Trinidad-Tobago				
1975	14	1.1	0.2	1.0
1980	45	1.5	0.5	0.9
1981	56	1.5	0.6	1.9
1983	253 [3]	4.5	3.0	1.8
1985	n.a.	n.a.	n.a.	1.7

Source: U.S. Arms Control and Disarmament Agency, *World Military Expenditures and Arms Transfers, 1987* (Washington, D.C.: ACDA, 1988), table 1.

1) In constant 1984 US dollars
2) Soldiers only
3) Preliminary

security have been exceptionally high in Haiti as well as in the Dominican Republic, and have increased in this latter country, as well as in Trinidad-Tobago, in concert with growing popular discontent with structural adjustment policies. It is evident that the repressive arm of the state has been a critical element in containing the social dislocations and protests occasioned by structural adjustment policies.

The tendency toward the restriction of civil rights, the manipulation of the media, and so on, has not been as widespread as in other regions, such as the Southern Cone of Latin America during the military dictatorships. One factor limiting governments' freedom of action in this regard is the depth of traditions of liberal democracy within the political culture of the English-speaking Caribbean.[7] Coupled with this is the fact that in a number of countries, such as Jamaica, opposition parties have well-established political structures and influence across the whole spectrum of classes and social organizations, which effectively constitute an important veto power over "reckless" attempts to restrict the ambit of civil rights. In turn, this veto power constitutes an important platform from which to wage a struggle for reform and alternative development strategies.

At the same time, the progressive forces of the region were left without a political project after the collapse of the radical experiments, and for the most part, find themselves today still attempting to understand what happened. Nonetheless, as we will argue below, the results of structural adjustment policies are actually setting the stage for progressive alternative development strategies, strategies emerging out of the new organizations and movements that have emerged as a response to the economic crisis.

Cleavages in the Traditional Institutions of Political Power

Notwithstanding their lack of formal organization, poor women and men not only in the Dominican Republic, but also in Haiti and Jamaica, have taken to the streets to protest the rising cost of living and governments' acceptance of the terms of the IMF to meet debt repayments. In January 1985 a three-day protest broke out in Kingston, Montego Bay, Ochos Rios, and other Jamaican cities protesting price increases in foodstuffs and gasoline, the consequence of the government's following IMF recommendations to eliminate subsidies and to devalue the currency. The protest included street demonstrations by people from all sectors of Jamaican society, barricades and the looting of stores in the poorer neighborhoods, and a large protest march on Government House. The Seaga government contained the disorder but ten people were killed and twenty arrested. The government also held firm on the austerity measures.[8]

In Haiti, food riots and protests against austerity measures were an important contributing factor to the fall of "Baby Doc" Duvalier. The Haitian government had entered into a standby agreement with the IMF in 1981, implementing measures which required ending government employment-creation programs. Rising unemployment, combined with corruption in the distribution of donated food supplies and growing hunger, contributed to a series of food riots around the country in May 1984. In November of the next year, as austerity measures continued, the protest was rekindled on a much broader scale. Joining the urban poor were now students (several of whom were subsequently killed), teachers, shopkeepers, and many church and political opposition figures, united around an even broader demand: the removal of Duvalier. After three months of mayhem, Duvalier departed for exile in France in February 1986.[9]

In the Dominican Republic, the April 1984 protest had been preceded by a total of 1,423 protests of various types during the previous eleven months.[10] An analysis of these protests revealed that 386 corresponded to the labor movement, 375 to the peasant movement, 115 by workers in the health sector, 70 by women's organizations; 229 were community/ neighborhood actions demanding services such as electricity, roads, health care, education, and housing, as well as the reduction in the price of foodstuffs and higher wages. In the aftermath of the bloody 1984 protest, an organized one-day protest was led by church, business, and labor leaders in 1985, but spontaneous neighborhood protests continued, demonstrating the desperate situation of masses of the population. More recently, in 1987, 1988, and 1989, these popular protests have increasingly been coordinated with labor strikes, but have yet to coalesce in a coordinated political movement.

In Haiti, Mardi Gras 1989 served as an occasion to voice popular dissatisfaction against the continuing repressive measures of the new government of General Prosper Avril. Peasants and urban poor flooded the streets with chants against the regime and a general boycott was called to resist government attempts to control future elections.[11] Moreover, disillusionment with all of the political parties is strong and growing.

Throughout the region, existing political institutions have been shaken by these popular protests and, in many instances, have failed to find new ways to engage with the aspirations of the poorer sectors. Trade unions and political parties have not been able to channel popular unrest and propose a program for economic recovery and democratization of Caribbean societies. Moreover, these traditional institutions have, for the most part, failed to move into the new arenas where the responses to the crisis are being articulated—poor urban neighborhoods and rural communities—and to incorporate into the problem-solving efforts those groups most affected by the crisis, particularly poor women and those in the mushrooming informal sector. Not too surprisingly, political parties in many countries of the region have been losing credibility and legitimacy at the local level.

A further consequence of the implementation of structural and adjustment policies in this period has been the relative marginalization of trade union organizations within the political process. Government hostility to trade union representation in free-trade zones in Jamaica and the Dominican Republic, and the passage of anti-union legislation restricting the rights of public-sector employees to join unions in a number of countries, are important reflections of the effects of structural adjustment policies on working-class institutions.

Four factors have undermined the ability of organized labor to become effective mobilizers of popular discontent: the traditional umbilical cord between the unions and parties throughout much of the Caribbean; the effective penetration of much of the labor movement by pro-capital U.S. institutions; the lack of unions in sectors where the growing number of women workers are employed; and the inability to organize effectively in the informal sector.

Dating from the organization of the trade union movement in the 1930s, political parties in the Caribbean have tended to be wedded to specific trade unions.[12] This has meant that all too often the national party or government agenda supersedes the independent demands and needs of organized labor. Moreover, the umbilical cords between different parties and unions have split the labor movement, effectively preventing it from taking a unified autonomous stance.

For example, in the Dominican Republic, during the liberal PRD government of Antonio Guzmán, the trade union movement flourished, with some 350 new unions created by 1981. Two new labor confederations were formed, each appendaged to a political party. Because of this affiliation, rifts within the parties affected the unification of the labor movement and created divisions within the labor confederations as well, precisely at the time when labor unity was most needed to confront the policies of structural adjustment and to give direction to mass discontent.[13]

Another factor which has diluted organized working-class struggle over the years has been the international affiliation of most Caribbean trade unions with the U.S.-supported International Council of Free Trade Unions (ICFTU) and their links to the American Institute for Free Labor (AIFLD), the overseas arm of the AFL-CIO.[14] Since its organization in 1960, the Caribbean Congress of Labour (CCL) (which is largely funded by the ICFTU and AIFLD) has been an effective force against the development of a progressive labor movement in the Caribbean. The CCL is made up of unions in fourteen countries of the English-speaking Caribbean in addition to Suriname, Curaçao, and St. Maarten. Through AIFLD, the CCL also maintains close links with unions in the Dominican Republic, Haiti, and the French Antilles. Between 1962 and 1987 some 22,985 union members from the English-speaking Caribbean and 53,976 from the Dominican Republic attended AIFLD in-country seminars, to be trained in effective labor organizing and collective bargaining. Much of the training, however, centers on the dissemination of anticommunist and pro-capital ideology so, not surprisingly, union leaders trained by AIFLD often tend to be supportive of conservative governments.

Another implication of the interrelationship between trade unions and political parties is that the policies advocated by the regional trade union movement often have an effect on the policies of national governments, a connection which has been cultivated by AIFLD. According to noted author George Lamming, "the more receptive therefore Caribbean labour is to the presence of American investment and management patterns, the more so will be the regional politicians."[15] This interrelationship is clearly seen in current discussions regarding structural adjustment policies and the promotion of foreign investment in the free-trade or export-processing zones.

Trade unions with strong ties to the CCL have tended to give critical support to governments pursuing structural adjustment policies in the Caribbean. The CCL itself, in its analysis of the 1984 Nassau Understanding among CARICOM heads of government, accepted the premises behind structural adjustment policies, criticizing the Nassau Understanding only because the trade union movement was not consulted. According to the CCL, any program of structural transformation must involve the participation of unions, employers, and governments, or tripartism; they remain strangely silent about the participation of the majority of Caribbean populations.

To their credit, however, the CCL did call for a reexamination of IMF stabilization programs, noting their adverse effect on living conditions in the Caribbean, and argued that the external debt should be restructured so that debt service be reduced to a level compatible with fighting unemployment and poverty.[16]

A number of independent unions in the Caribbean, however, have been most outspoken in their criticisms of structural adjustment policies and of conservative Caribbean governments' pro-capital policies. The Oilfields Workers Trade Union of Trinidad-Tobago (OWTU), for example, has strongly condemned structural adjustment policies which it sees as favoring vested interests, notably foreign capital and local big business.[17] Moreover, it sees the privatization component of structural adjustment policies called for by the IMF and the World Bank as purely ideological and designed to undo what little national economic independence exists. And whereas the CCL calls for tripartism in order to implement structural adjustment policies, the Oilfields Workers Trade Union calls for a deeply democratic process of economic planning—at the level of both the workplace and community—to effect real transformation at both the economic and political levels.

The CCL and some of the independent unions, interestingly, do not differ significantly in their view of the role of foreign investment, seeing it as a necessary component for Caribbean growth. While the OWTU strongly opposes "freeing up" the conditions for foreign investment, they are not opposed to all foreign investment, just that which is predicated on extravagant incentive schemes. Both the CCL and OWTU call for national review boards to assure that foreign investment maximizes its contribution to employment generation and development.

The establishment of free-trade zones has led to a certain degree of tension between governments and trade unions across the region. The CCL, for example, is skeptical of the benefits of export-processing zones and has argued strongly that workers in such zones should not be deprived of their legal rights, such as the right to join and be represented by unions. Nonetheless, organized labor has been most timid in challenging what appears to be the unwritten understanding between governments and foreign capital that labor legislation will not be applicable in these zones.

Part of the explanation for the timidity on the part of unions in pressing for the right to organize and bargain collectively in the zones may be that the majority of workers in export processing are women. The recent record of Caribbean unions in organizing women workers in general has been poor. Moreover, sexism pervades at every level: between women workers and male management and between women workers and male labor organizers in unionized industries; and in union halls between male and female staff and among male and (the few) female labor leaders.[18] Nonetheless, the CCL has at least formally taken up the call for the need to increase women's access to education and training and to remove discrimination in employment; it also supports such measures as greater access to childcare at the workplace.[19]

The failure of Caribbean trade unions to organize women workers in the free-trade zones certainly has dampened the growth of union membership, since the zones have been the fastest growing sector of formal employment during the 1980s. The trade union movement has

also been weakened by rising rates of unemployment and the mushrooming of the informal sector during the economic crisis. Trade unions
have not adapted to this important change in the structure of the labor
market and have remained incapable, for the most part, of organizing
individuals in informal economic activities, again a large number of
whom are women.

While the growth of the informal sector has stymied traditional union
organization, it has led to new forms of organization and new organizations. Some of these new organizations have been fostered by
Caribbean states and international development agencies aiming to
strengthen the private sector through support for the creation of "microenterprises." Others of the new informal sector organizations have
arisen in opposition to state policies, often the result of the search for
collective solutions to the economic crisis.

An example of the former type is the Association for the Development
of Microenterprises, Inc. (ADEMI), a private voluntary organization in
the Dominican Republic. It was founded in 1983 by a group of influential
Dominican business leaders with financial support from the Dominican
government and AID to provide credit to small businesses. ADEMI
microenterprises are involved in a variety of manufacturing activities,
from making clothes, ceramics, and bread, to the repair of refrigerators
and mattresses. The ADEMI credit program initially supported, besides
relatively stable small firms, the organization of income-generating
projects by what were termed "solidarity groups," as a prelude to
microenterprise development; many of these groups were made up of
poor women. Unfortunately, once the economy began to erode, ADEMI
suspended credit to the solidarity groups, in the process eliminating
77 percent of the female beneficiaries.[20]

In the English-speaking Caribbean women and men in the informal
sector, particularly in the marketing trade, have been forming their
own organizations to confront state policies and the economic crisis.
In Jamaica, street vendors, largely women, organized to counter police
efforts to clear the streets of vendors and created the United Vendors
Association, based in the main food market of Kingston. Among its
aims and objectives is to protect the rights of vendors, to negotiate
with the authorities on all matters affecting them, and to foster a
cooperative movement for the export and import of foodstuffs.[21]

In Dominica, the Dominican Hucksters Association assists traders in
obtaining credit and with such problems as gaining access to foreign
exchange, helping in port procedures, and arranging travel accommodations. Similarly, in St. Vincent and the Grenadines 143 traders
formed the Traffickers Small Business Association in 1983; five years
later this association had more than 250 members, 77 percent of them

women. While the problems of aggressive, individualistic, and competitive behavior characteristic of the informal sector have yet to be conquered, and many of these new organizations are still quite weak, these new informal sector organizations are providing the means for new types of collective action and arresting the further fragmentation of Caribbean working people.

The Awakening at the Grassroots

Trade unions and political parties have for the most part failed to move into the arena of not only the informal sector, but also the community and the household, where responses to the crisis are increasingly being articulated. This vacuum is increasingly being filled by new grassroots groups, local development organizations (LDOs) such as cooperatives, and nongovernmental organizations (NGOs), all engaged in pragmatic actions to defend the rights of poor men and women—opposing the austerity and sometimes repressive measures of governments—and usually creating new modes of generating livelihoods and new visions of alternative modes of development.

In both cities and towns and rural areas, the pressing economic situation of Caribbean societies has mobilized activists to develop strategies to relieve the short-term impact of the crisis on the poor and working class, while engendering a longer range consciousness of the need for more profound social change.[22] In some cases, this work has been carried out strictly at the local level, and from the grassroots, has led to the development of new organizations which sometimes take the form of NGOs or, in other cases, interest-based national organizations or loosely coordinated social movements. In other instances, the organization of grassroots groups and LDOs has been the direct product of the work of NGOs, constituted as centers or institutes for research and action. By developing income-generating projects, production and marketing cooperatives, health and nutrition campaigns, and promoting popular education—linked to the development of community consciousness and self-empowerment—the NGOs have supported and engendered grassroots groups, which together are slowly altering the character of Caribbean politics and society.

The relative success of the NGO/LDO sector tends to rest on its ability to respond to the immediate socioeconomic needs of the people, with direct consequences for popular participation, improved economic conditions, and a heightened political awareness at the community level. The NGOs have also been critical actors in the emergence of new social movements in the Caribbean focused on the empowerment of women (discussed in the next section), the protection of civil and human rights, the pursuit of peace and anti-militarism, environmental causes, and cultural preservation. It is useful here to consider some illustrative examples of the kinds of groups and alliances that have emerged in the late 1970s and 1980s, while keeping in mind that in many instances, the new groups play multiple roles in addressing the pressing needs of their members and societies.

In the Dominican Republic, COPADEBA (Comité para la Defensa de los Derechos Barriales, or Committee for the Defense of Neighborhood Rights) has emerged as the main alliance of Christian base communities, trade unionists, displaced workers, and women in the northern barrios of Santo Domingo. Initially focusing on the defense of the standard of living of the poor, COPADEBA also sponsors projects ranging from skills training workshops to farm-to-market fairs. COPADEPA coordinates its work with NGOs focusing on popular education in urban and rural communities, such as CEDEE (Centro Dominicano de Estudios de la Educación, Dominican Center for Educational Studies) and the Centro Cultural Poveda (the Poveda Cultural Center).

Popular education is also the main focus of a number of NGOs in the English-speaking Caribbean. For example, in Belize SPEAR, the Society for the Promotion of Education and Research, is an NGO oriented toward the formation of a strong national consciousness through participatory research, popular education, community development, and social action. It also sponsors productive activities and programs to develop and strengthen cooperatives, trade unions, and youth and women's organizations.

In Jamaica, the Association of Development Agencies (ADA) coordinates a network of national development agencies in a forum of collective analysis, discussion, planning, and advocacy, supporting local development initiatives aimed at effective social change—defined as that which promotes the participation, power, and control of local communities and popular organizations. Among the NGOs which are members is the Institute of Hunger Affairs in West Kingston, which assists community groups with health and nutrition problems, adult literacy programs, and employment and skills training projects for the unemployed.

Religious organizations have taken the lead in Haiti in organizing local responses to the deterioration in living conditions while leading the struggle for the respect for civil and human rights and democracy. The Ecumenical Center for Human Rights is the main civil and human rights group, which is part of an extensive network of Christian base communities, peasant and small farmer organizations, and urban neighborhood groups pushing for democratization. GRIMPO (Groupes de Religious Immerse en Milieu Populaire, Groups of Religious Immersed in the Popular Sectors), an NGO, works directly with local communities throughout Haiti on local development projects, denouncing civil and human rights violations and promoting political participation.

In the islands of the Eastern Caribbean, where small farmers still produce a significant volume of export crops such as bananas and spices, NGOs and LDOs have led efforts both to organize producers to confront international marketing networks, and to promote alternative projects aimed at food self-sufficiency. The Dominican Farmers Union (DFU) is a national organization of small farmers and tenants, dedicated to farmer education and training regarding production and marketing cycles, crop diversification, and new technology. Through its network of farmers and cooperation with the Dominican Hucksters Association, it has developed a national farm-to-market program to form an integrated distribution network tied to markets within the Eastern Caribbean. The goal of the project is to promote greater consumption of local foods and to raise the nutritional content of local diets. A Dominican NGO, the Small Projects Assistance Team (SPAT) developed from the collective experiences of various self-help groups and community organizations to form local cooperatives. SPAT provides training in cooperative management, community organizing, and appropriate technology. It also promotes exchanges and networks among local development organizations.

There are now national-level farmer's unions in St. Lucia and St. Vincent, besides Dominica. The St. Vincent Farmer's Union coordinates the Windward Islands Farmers Union (WIFA) network, working closely with the various NGOs in the region. The largest national peasant organization in the region is in the Dominican Republic, the Movimiento Campesino Independiente (MCI, the Independent Peasant Movement), with over 35,000 members, the majority of them small farmers and landless workers. Founded in 1979, it has become an increasingly important social actor in that country.

CARIPEDA (Caribbean People's Development Agency) is a network of regional NGO/LDOs which covers the Eastern Caribbean, Trinidad, Puerto Rico, and Jamaica, which sponsors development work and links international agencies with regional organizations involved in building strategies for alternative economic and political empowerment in the Caribbean. It is at the center of the regional debate on such issues as export-processing zones and the CBI, structural adjustment policies and the payment of the debt, and militarization.

A number of other NGOs in the region have also focused their work on broader social issues, attempting to develop a regional peace and environmental movement, for example, through the creation of regional networks concerned with militarization, internal political repression and civil and human rights violations, and environmental degradation. On the environmental front, in Puerto Rico, Misión Industrial (Industrial Mission) focuses on education as the primary vehicle to promote popular activism regarding environmental threats, particularly those which accompany industrialization, such as toxic waste. It also strives to promote greater national awareness in Puerto Rico with regard to control over natural resources, linking environmental issues with awareness regarding the island's colonial status. The peace and anti-militarization movement in Puerto Rico is led by the Proyecto Caribeño de Justicia y Paz (Caribbean Project for Peace and Justice).

Among the new types of cultural organizations which have sprung up is the Movement for Cultural Awareness of Dominica and the Caribbean Media Workers Association of Barbados, a collective of television, radio and newspaper workers. They draw attention to the growing cultural saturation of the Caribbean by the U.S.-based electronic media and both organizations promote appreciation of and participation in Caribbean cultural expression.

Although there is a wide variation in the nature, purposes, and work styles of the NGOs and LDOs, their work is generally constructed on the basis of direct participation of the recipients in the process of design and administration of community programs. This has begun to yield many positive results including (1) a process of self-empowerment at the community level; (2) a reappraisal of the values of solidarity and mutual help which were once central in the culture of the Caribbean working class; (3) the opportunity to develop an analysis of the nature of their problems and to recognize the need for collective action; (4) the development of a collective consciousness about the limits and costs of the export-oriented economic model promoted by the IMF, the World Bank, and the U.S. government; and (5) the creation of a sense of regionalism and internationalism through the exchange of information and experiences between and among groups in different countries.

One of the most interesting features of the development of many of the grassroots groups, NGOs, LDOs, and social movements over the past decade, particularly in the Spanish-speaking Caribbean, is how they have taken on as their own the specific interests and aspirations of other groups. For example, the demand for gender, racial, and ethnic equality is becoming a widespread claim; community groups are increasingly supporting the demands of the environmentalists for a better management of natural resources; women's groups are endorsing the quest for peace and a nuclear-free Caribbean. In the Dominican Republic, Puerto Rico, Jamaica, and a number of the smaller islands, solidarity strikes, protests, and rallies increasingly involve a broad gamut of organizations, brought together under the banner of social change. The recognition of the need for reciprocity and complementarity is still at an embryonic stage, however, and the new and growing solidarity among these popular organizations has yet to coalesce as a political alternative.

Much—although by no means all—of the grassroots organizing, particularly in the Spanish-speaking Caribbean, has in one way or the other been connected to progressive elements within the various religious bodies, particularly those inspired by the theology of liberation within the Catholic church. Moreover, one of the few regional bodies which links the English-speaking with the non-English-speaking Caribbean is the Caribbean Conference of Churches (CCC), formed in 1973 as the first regional ecumenical association. The CCC has promoted the involvement of the churches in issues of regional economic development, peace activism, and political empowerment processes.

Nonetheless, there has always been a tension between the progressives within the regional body and the conservatives who now generally dominate the work of the National Council of Churches. This tension erupted in the wake of the invasion of Grenada in 1983 when the CCC was branded "communist" for its condemnation of the invasion, and the editor of the CCC newspaper, *Caribbean Contact* (a citizen of Guyana), was deprived of his work permit in Barbados, where the headquarters of the CCC is located. Also, since the invasion of Grenada, the Caribbean has been the site of numerous North American evangelist crusades, often intensely political, and as one study of these crusades observed, frequently "loaded with money and with anticommunist propaganda."[23] Such missionary work has served as another form of division, creating confusion as well as competition for the loyalty of the people, dissuading religious people, as well as the organizations with which they are affiliated, from speaking with a common voice.

Articulating the different aspirations and interests of the many grassroots groups, LDOs, NGOs, and other groups is not an easy task; neither is it easy to establish clear priorities when faced with scarce resources and extremely broad and heterogenous demands. Deciding upon a short-term versus a long-term plan of action to sustain alternative development can pose serious dilemmas. Moreover, the rejection of traditional work styles, such as charity, authoritarian decision-making, and elitism, requires more than commitment. Financing the work of grassroots groups, NGOs, and LDOs is both a challenge and a problem, as cooptation on the part of institutions (whether national or international) with political agendas is always a risk.[24]

It is also questionable whether the NGO/LDO network will have the capacity to integrate the issue of political power beyond the grassroots level to serve as a bridge between political parties and these emerging social movements. For the most part, political parties have ignored either the existence of these groups or the impact that they have had on the societies of the region. To the extent that parties have incorporated these new groups, they have restricted their roles in the political agenda. As a recent report on these organizations concludes, unless aspirations and activities are coordinated to formulate integrated social, economic, and political alternatives at both the national and regional level, very little structural change and empowerment will take place in the Caribbean.[25] In spite of the difficulties, the emerging grassroots groups, local development organizations, and social movements in the Caribbean constitute a ray of hope in an otherwise fragmented and deteriorating social and economic climate.

The Empowerment of Women

Women have been among the first to protest and organize in new ways in the 1980s, often being at the forefront of the emerging grassroots groups and social movements. This is perhaps not surprising, given the specific ways in which the crisis impinges upon women. Moreover, since the 1970s and in the context of the United Nations Decade for Women (1975–85), a number of new women's organizations have emerged which have as their explicit focus the empowerment of women. These organizations—some, sections within political parties, unions, and religious groups; most, autonomous and community based—differ from earlier Caribbean women's organizations in a number of ways, principally in their attempts to challenge traditional male-dominated structures and to articulate alternatives which focus on women's strengths, concerns, and perspectives.

Moreover, the new women's organizations are supported by a network of NGOs—some research centers dedicated to popular education, others development institutes or agencies—which have an explicitly feminist focus. The feminist NGOs have attempted to integrate gender and class analysis while linking research with policy recommendations, popular education, and action—that is, mobilizing to meet practical and strategic gender interests. Through the use of more holistic approaches to research and practice, these centers are attempting to bridge the gap between the personal and the political, between the private and public domains, between the household and the economy. As a result, the analysis of the emerging women's movement in the region is perhaps the most comprehensive and compelling of all current attempts to articulate an alternative analysis and agenda for the future.

Here it is useful to examine in more detail how the feminist agenda has gradually taken root in the region, influencing state policy and political party programs, as well as spurring the organization of women at the local, national, and regional levels.

The Legacy of the UN Decade for Women

There is little question that the UN Decade for Women boosted awareness of gender issues throughout the Caribbean. Most governments were forced to incorporate some structure to address the position of women. The Manley government in Jamaica was the first to appoint an advisor on women's affairs in early 1974 and a Women's Desk was established later that year. Subsequently, the desk was upgraded into a Women's Bureau in the Office of the Prime Minister. By 1980 all the CARICOM governments had established similar structures, located in different departments and sections of the bureaucracy.[26]

The performance and fortunes of these national machineries has been at best mixed, but on the whole disappointing.[27] Women's national apparatuses have lacked both status and financial and human resources and often their agendas have been unclear, which is not surprising since many were established in response to the international call for action without first defining clear goals.

Furthermore, many governments have been unwilling to implement the policies proposed by these women's departments. Sometimes the issue—such as demands for legislation concerning rape or incest—has been considered a personal or family matter and not a governmental issue. Or in regard to maternity leave with pay, custody of children, or continuing education for teenaged mothers, requests for legislation have met with puritan ethical retorts or have been dismissed under the guise of being too costly for the national economy to support.

The UN Decade for Women also activated many traditional social welfare organizations in the region, such as the Soroptimists and the Young Women's Christian Association (YWCA), to begin making demands upon the state to enhance the welfare of women. They called on governments to revise social legislation dealing with such matters as divorce, child custody, maternity leave, to establish family courts, and to increase women's access to training, employment, and health care.

In concert with the international call to incorporate women into development, a number of NGOs were established with the explicit goal of promoting women and development programs, enhancing women's job skills and training, and organizing income-generating projects for women. In the Extra-Mural Department of the University of the West Indies in Barbados, the Women and Development Unit (WAND) was created in order to stimulate and support women and development programs in the region. WAND's primary objectives were to build the capacity of women's programs, to increase awareness of women and development issues, and to build linkages between and among related programs in the Caribbean.

Another type of NGO is MUDE (Mujer y Desarrollo or Women in Development) in the Dominican Republic which was founded by a group of influential businessmen with support from AID. MUDE began organizing small groups of women throughout the country, most of them focused on handicraft and other small income-generating projects. Church groups also began organizing income-generating projects for women throughout the region, such as the Program for Better Nutrition in Dominica and Grenfruit Women's Cooperative in Grenada. On another front, women's NGOs have formed to focus on the rights and working conditions of women in the export-processing zones. One of these is the Centre de Promocion des Femmes Ouvrières (Center for the Promotion of Working Women) in Port-au-Prince. It serves as a support institution for women workers, providing legal defense and training in skills, literacy, and worker rights.

Other NGOs founded in the mid-1970s began working with an explicit feminist and multipurpose agenda. An example is CIPAF (Centro de Investigación para la Acción Femenina, Center for Research for Feminine Action) in the Dominican Republic. Dedicated both to carrying out research on women and translating the results of research into political action, it has provided crucial support services, training, and educational materials to women's groups throughout the country. Both through its monthly newsletter, *Quehaceres*, and through close work with the media, CIPAF has also brought the broad range of women's issues—from domestic violence and rape to the plight of women workers in the free-trade zones and the need for child care—to the national arena.

The growing gender consciousness of the Decade for Women also led to the formation of the first feminist support groups—sometimes formed around the need for battered women's shelters or rape crisis centers—and feminist activist groups in the Caribbean. Of the latter, the SISTREN Collective of Jamaica, an independent women's cultural organization, is perhaps the best known. Dedicated to advancing gender awareness and the empowerment of women, SISTREN, through the use of theater, seeks to channel and stimulate women into purposeful action to deal with the reality of their own lives. The SISTREN Collective has become an important regional resource, providing the methodology for other women's groups to follow for their own process of consciousness-raising and self-assessment.

Feature

Grenfruit Women's Cooperative, Grenada

The story of Grenfruit is one of a decade of struggle to integrate poor rural women into the economic and social development of their country. The Grenfruit cooperative is committed to empowerment—economic, political, and psychological—of people whose history is marked almost exclusively by powerlessness.

The women at Grenfruit are poor, unskilled, and, in most cases, single mothers. Grenfruit not only trains and employs them, it also gets involved in their daily lives—their day-to-day concerns of food, childcare, housing, and health care. Beyond this, the coop confronts the immense difficulties of a poor, technologically backward agricultural community embedded in an underdeveloped national economy—in a nation that has endured U.S. political, economic, and cultural occupation since 1983.

A 1978 study in one rural community found that a shocking 90 percent of all school leavers were unemployed. Most of these were young women, many of whom had migrated to the capital, St. George's, to find work. After working a few months as low-paid domestics, shop clerks, or prostitutes, they returned home, without a job, and many of them pregnant. It was for these women that the Education and Skills Training Project was started in 1978 with the assistance of the Pope Paul Center of the St. John Catholic church.

The project set up its first factory in an unused church building in the rural parish of St. John. The first Grenfruit women numbered twenty-five, and ranged in age from 16 to 24; eighteen of them were mothers. Judy Williams, Grenfruit's director, explains that the first task was to give the women a more positive image of themselves, as people with "worth and value [who] can try for alternatives for their living." They then received training in food preservation and later experimented with canning.

By 1982, when Grenfruit registered as a cooperative, only eight of the original women remained. While the tasks of image building and skills training remained paramount, an immediate concern was earning money, since most of the women by then had two children, and no paid work. In fact, many of those who had started the program had dropped out for this reason. Even so, nine women registered in 1982.

Grenfruit immediately faced the problem of competing with the practice of making jams, jellies and cakes at home. Grenadan women preserved their own guava jelly and other fruits, and made their own guava cheese, when the fruit was in season. Recognizing this, Grenfruit focused on

(continues)

candied fruits—condicion, paw paw, damsel, and french cashew—to offer housewives a cheaper and local substitute for imported currants and raisins. In 1981 someone realized that the secret to success lay in storing the fruit in season and processing it for sale when it was out of season.

The women had just begun to do this—experimenting with guava halves to replace the costly imported peach and pear halves—when the traumatic events culminating in the U.S. invasion of 1983 put a halt to all of Grenfruit's operations. U.S. Marines occupied their factory and immediately evicted the women, destroying all of the coop's documents and records since its inception. Then the Catholic church, which had allowed them free use of their land, decided to reclaim the land.

By summer 1987 Grenfruit had relocated, with fourteen members and five trainees. In addition to producing candied fruits they process and package the local spices—nutmeg, cinnamon, mace, clove, and saffron—for which Grenada is famous, as well as mauby syrup, a bittersweet syrup made from bark, and pepper sauce. In 1987, when the price for cloves plummeted on the international market, all the clove farmers turned to Grenfruit to sell their produce. Grenfruit also maintains links with other cooperatives, such as a mechanics coop that helps with transportation, and has begun selling plants to farmers so they will grow the fruits it needs.

But the coop faces new problems. Under the Peoples Revolutionary Government, cooperatives were actively supported, and avocadoes, mangoes, yams, and pepper sauce were shipped to Grenadan communities in England and the United States. Today, these exports have been cut back, and many coops have been forced to disband because of a lack of financial and/or managerial resources. Grenfruit has to pay a new value-added tax on the bottles and jars it imports. Even so, the coop not only survives, but has managed to grow and diversify. Part of the reason lies in its commitment to its members.

The women at Grenfruit receive EC$15.50 per day, higher than the average wage (1987), as well as hospital insurance for themselves and their children. The women pay $1 each month into a pension scheme, which the cooperative matches at the end of the year. Perhaps most innovative is the $5,000 revolving loan fund, begun in 1984. Women can borrow money from the fund for "essential things"—to repair a leaking roof, put in a glass window, or buy school books and uniforms for their children. Sister Judy points out that when you are working all day and taking care of kids, essential things mount up:

If the woman must come to work on time, if she must have her children to school before she gets to work, if she must work hard in the factory, and then go home and prepare her child's lunch and her children's clothes for school the next day, it is important for her to have some basics. Like be able to cook in a decent kitchen without having to go and look for

(continues)

firewood, having water that she can bathe and bathe her children and wash their clothes and clean her house, having electricity.

Members meet each month to discuss coop problems as well as women's problems—a child needing hospitalization, or a woman who lived a long way away and could not get to work on time. And every quarter all members meet with their parent organization, the Grenada Community Development Agency (GRENCODA). A committee meets on a rotational basis to construct the agendas, and each member takes a turn, so that everyone gets a chance at leadership.

Aware of the always precarious situation the coop faces, given the uncertainty of the markets for its products, Sister Judy says: "When I consider the fact that Grenfruit can grow and expand out of that situation . . . it means that what you're saying to farmers is that you're creating an alternative for farmers to produce things that do not have to be exported . . . they have an alternative to foreign exchange, with money being put directly into the pockets of very small farmers in this country."

Sister Judy believes "that rural communities can make it if they organize," especially rural women. She speaks for them all when she says: "You don't have to walk into a rural community and put down a massive industrial plant and bring the women in there to work. . . . You can develop small-scale things . . . allow the people to take decisions and make decisions and discuss their own problems and find solutions." Such priorities explain how Grenfruit has survived in spite of the obstacles, and why it serves an example of grassroots solutions to Caribbean problems.

Source: Interview by Betsy Oakes with Judy Williams, director of GRENCODA, 1987.

Growing Gender Awareness

While in the early years of the UN Decade for Women there was often considerable strife between women's organizations dedicated to integrating women into development and those groups and organizations which defined themselves explicitly as feminist, increasingly, women's organizations of all types have joined in the mission of empowering women. WAND, for example, has consciously shifted its orientation from the "integrationist" approach with which it started, to one which is now concerned with working toward alternative concepts and structures, challenging women's subordination at all levels of society, and empowering women at the local level.

The growth of women's consciousness groups also has begun to change the nature of women's participation in political parties. In

Jamaica, the women's arm of the People's National Party (PNP) is an interesting example of the evolution of a traditional women's political "auxiliary"—which provided unquestioned support for the male leadership of the party—toward a feminist position on issues of concern to women, reflected in its change of name from "Women's Auxiliary" to "Women's Movement" (PNPWM).[28] Within the Workers' Party of Jamaica (WPJ), the Committee of Women for Progress (CWP) was formed, explicitly concerned with developing the links of gender, race, and class.[29] During the late 1970s the women of the PNPWM developed a special working alliance with those of the CWP, sometimes in defiance of both sets of male party leadership. Their joint action focused on such issues as "maternity leave despite the IMF."[30]

The new feminist thinking has also begun to characterize women trade unionists in the mainstream labor movement. Hundreds of women, including the rank and file in addition to those in leadership positions, from throughout the English- and Dutch-speaking Caribbean have participated in the Development of Women in the Trade Unions project. The project is designed to develop the women's organizing skills and raise their consciousness as women, as citizens, as workers, and as trade unionists.

Throughout the 1980s the number of national and regional level women's forums and conferences in the Caribbean grew significantly, aiding to build alliances of women focused on issues of poverty and social change, and transcending the usual boundaries of class, race, and political affiliation. This process has been aided by the international work of a group of third world feminists who met in preparation for the end of the UN Decade for Women meetings in Nairobi in 1985, forming DAWN, Development Alternatives with Women for a New Era. Their argument—that it is the perspective of poor and oppressed women that provides a unique and powerful vantage point from which to examine the effects of development programs and strategies—and their agenda—to analyze the impact on women of the interlocking global crises of debt, food insecurity, environmental degradation, demographic pressures, religious fundamentalism, and increasing militarism—has increasingly formed the framework for research and political action in the region.[31]

The building of a Caribbean women's movement has also received momentum from the growing tendency for local women's organizations to join together in national-level organizations, as seen in the case of CONAMUCA, the Peasant Women's Confederation of the Dominican Republic, with a membership of over 8,000. Consisting of twenty-one regional rural women's federations which had formed in the early 1980s, CONAMUCA held its first national conference on rural women's issues

Feature

Training Women Trade Unionists

Throughout the English-speaking Caribbean, women participate actively in the trade union movement, for the most part as shop stewards, organizers, or low level administrators. They have continued this active participation for nearly five decades, despite a general failure to rise to decision-making positions.

In 1979 the International Labour Organization (ILO) reported that "executive positions in the trade unions in the Caribbean are still held largely by men, by a ratio of 75 percent men to 25 percent women," confirming what women had known for a long time. At a regional seminar for women trade unionists that same year, co-sponsored by the ILO, the Danish International Development Agency (DANIDA), Scandinavian development agencies, and the Caribbean Congress of Labour, participants concluded that the Caribbean trade union movement badly needed trained women leaders. Thus was born the Project for the Development of Caribbean Women in the Trade Unions, funded by the InterAmerican Foundation and administered by the University of the West Indies in Jamaica, with a steering committee representing Jamaica, Trinidad-Tobago, Barbados, the Bahamas, and St. Kitts-Nevis.

From 1982 to 1985, the Project helped develop skills in management, organization, planning and consciousness-raising for both men and women. Participants studied trade unionism and theories of socioeconomic and political development. They also focused on factors which promote or hinder women's personal development as women, workers, and citizens. By the end of the Project, about 4,000 women had taken part. While benefits from the project are still coming forth, with women running for—and sometimes winning—high-ranking union positions, women face enormous hostility from their male peers. While once this would have silenced or controlled the more ambitious women, more women leaders are holding their ground. Although few would identify themselves as such, the collective activities of the female trade unionists are feminist: as women workers and as citizens they are indeed part of a movement which seeks to erase gender inequality from society, though they do so within the confines of their institutions, quietly boring from within.

Lynn Bolles, in collaboration with some members of the Project, conducted interviews with women trade unionists in six countries—Antigua, Barbados, Guyana, Jamaica, Montserrat, and Trinidad-Tobago—

(continues)

across three generations—from the beginning of organized labor in the 1930s, to the independence era activists of the 1960s and 1970s, to the future leaders of the movement. The women engaged in "participant participation," which meant that former project members identified prospective interviewees, and in some cases interviewed these women themselves, becoming part of a research team with their North American collaborator. In answer to a question regarding opportunity for advancement, and what kinds of discrimination women experienced, women recognized the limitations both in society and in themselves:

> "Not many women were interested in advancing. They avoided the hard work that was associated with the leadership position."

> "There are a number of women who are showing that they can separate, but I think that somewhere along the line there is still this traditional feeling that men must operate more readily in the positions. . . . I think women have to prove too much that they have a super ability to be given the post first off-hand. . . . You will not be given it as readily as if a man had come in and showing the kind of ability."

> "You must . . . fight very hard and be very well educated if you are to attain these positions and men in the unions have not been superbly educated in terms of academic ability."

> "There is room for advancement and opportunity for both genders. But as we know in the trade union world many of the members are men and they can't but to work with men, so we the women in the organization have to speak out and show where we also need opportunities to advance our knowledge, our abilities."

> "Very often men did not support me because I was a woman. They felt I was playing a man because it was felt that trade unionism is for men."

> "The discrimination within the trade union is just like within any other organization . . . because the men and women—sometimes I would even say more so the women—feel that men can handle the situation better than the women."

> "I know that . . . they look at you as an upstart, a strife-maker and an aggressive woman who wants to be put in her place, at the right time. . . . Why pay her sufficient attention that she'll think she's important, that is how I feel . . . "

These deep-seated inequalities informed the women's beliefs about the future of the trade union movement. Asked if Caribbean trade unionism would be different with more women in leadership, for example, the conclusions ranged widely—yes, no, better, worse—but the reasons for these conclusions sounded very similar.

(continues)

"I believe that women would make it much better, because women together with men would make it much better. . . . You would have a more balanced situation where both sides might be able to look at what's happening to them. . . . I can see an improvement in a different thrust, a different thrust to the whole approach of trade unionism."

"Yes! Unity between women is not strong enough. Men tend to stick together more. The trade union movement would therefore be weaker."

"I don't think so because I feel that the men would have been still seeing themselves as superior."

"It would be different, but different positively or negatively it is a bit difficult to identify given the socialization of women. Women tend to rely on men a lot. I find that very few women are able to make certain decisions on their own. . . . Times are changing now but this . . . has only begun for us."

"It would have to depend on the women and then it depends on the support she gets from both women and the men working under her."

Because gender inequality is so deeply embedded in the nature of capitalist production, women involved in this project believe that if action is taken to countermand gender inequality in the labor movement, then it also attempts to forge a new vision for workers and fights the status quo. A Barbadian woman trade union leader expressed what is needed in this fight:

"You cannot be satisfied, you have to keep educating the women, keep getting behind the women to do things for themselves and then break them out of that whole pattern, that whole traditional role if possible. . . . There will always be some women who will not change, but those of us who recognize that what benefits can be derived on a personal level from breaking away from the past in terms of what we are accustomed to, what are expected of us, what we have to do is to work on our children and work on other women where possible to get them to break out of the tradition, to take up things that are not necessarily seen as 'women things,' get into areas which are not seen to have traditional women areas, . . . see themselves as individuals and try to improve themselves as a person and try to take up more, be more ambitious in their goals, in their careers, take up more challenging roles. . . . I would like to see women being recognized . . . as proper equals . . . not behind men nor out in front of men. . . . Equality will preserve all through life."

Source: Lynn Bolles, "The New Challenge: Gender and Equality in Trade Unions in the English-speaking Caribbean," paper presented at the Caribbean Studies Association meetings, Guadeloupe, 1988.

in 1986. Moreover, on International Women's Day in 1988 in Jamaica, the Association of Women's Organizations in Jamaica (AWOJA) was launched as that country's first umbrella organization for women's groups. It constitutes the widest cross-section of women's organizations in the English-speaking Caribbean. Its aims and objectives make it clear that it intends to pursue an activist role in promoting the process of social change.

At the regional level, the Caribbean Association for Feminist Research and Action (CAFRA) was founded in 1985 at a meeting to mark the end of the UN Decade for Women. Consisting of women activists and researchers from throughout the Caribbean (including the French overseas departments, Curaçao, Puerto Rico, Cuba, and the Dominican Republic, in addition to the English-speaking Caribbean), CAFRA's aims include: (1) developing an approach to women's problems from the perspectives of race, class, and gender, to show how the exploitative relationship between men and women facilitates the continuation, maintenance, and reproduction of exploitative capitalist relations, and how the capitalist system benefits from this situation; (2) developing the feminist movement in the entire Caribbean region; and (3) promoting the interrelationship between research and action.[32]

CAFRA members have been instrumental in conducting research on working conditions in the export-processing zones and in translating their research into policy demands. In Jamaica, they have challenged both government and trade unions to correct the inhospitable working conditions under which the majority of women factory workers in these zones labor. They called for the implementation of a government policy that would force factories to guarantee certain health and safety conditions prior to their establishment in these zones.[33] Drawing on the Jamaican experience, in Trinidad-Tobago CAFRA members helped organize the Women Against Free Trade Zones to protest the extension of export-processing zones to that country.

CAFRA is also beginning to play an important role in bringing together women researchers from different parts of the Caribbean to share their experiences and expertise. For example, CAFRA's "Women in Caribbean Agriculture" research project in St. Vincent-Grenadines and Dominica was a collaborative effort involving the Committee for the Development of Women in St. Vincent, the Women's Programme of the Small Projects' Assistance Team in Dominica and researchers from CIPAF in the Dominican Republic.[34]

CAFRA as well as WAND have also played crucial roles in bringing together feminist researchers and activists, grassroots women's organizations and groups, and women activists in trade unions, NGOs, political parties and national governments, sowing the seeds for a truly

regional and united women's movement. WAND's Tenth Anniversary
Consultation brought together fifty-seven women from dozens of groups
who for three days analyzed the forms, strategies, programs, and
structural relationships of the organizations working with women. Then,
in a two-day symposium, they shared their findings with regional and
international institutions and development agencies.[35]

As the participants in the WAND Consultation concluded: "Ten years
ago we were seeking recognition and integration. Today, we are seeking
transformation and emancipation. . . . We, the women of the region
will continue to work towards a just and human society in which the
potential of all our people can be realized, and in which we as women
will achieve full emancipation. We believe that we have to take a
central role in the shaping of this process. We declare triumphantly
that we have collective strength to roll away the great stone and be
shapers of our own destiny."[36]

In sum, individually, in communities, and in regional networks,
Caribbean women are beginning to transform traditional roles and
relationships of nurturance and support into a movement for personal,
social, and political change. With this growing new vision, diversity
of skills, and experience, they can perhaps give hope to all Caribbean
people who see in the continuing crises the opportunity for social
transformation. The emerging solidarity of the new organizations and
movements of the 1980s is gradually constructing the bases of a new
Caribbean politics.

Notes

1. Our translation of the leaflet distributed during the strike. This account
of the 1984 events in the Dominican Republic is drawn from a background
paper prepared for PACCA by Fafa Taveras, "Abril, Una Insurrección Sin Armas,"
July 1988 (Santo Domingo).

2. See Trevor Farrell, "The Caribbean State and its Role," in Omar Davies,
ed., *The State in Caribbean Society* (Kingston: University of the West Indies,
1986) and Neville Duncan, "El Rol del Estado y los Sistemas Políticos del
Caribe," in CLACSO, ed., *¿Hacia un Nuevo Orden Estatal en América Latina?*,
Vol. 2 (Buenos Aires: Biblioteca de Ciencias Sociales, 1988).

3. Ilya Villar, "Opciones del Movimiento Obrero y Popular en el Caribe,"
Cuadernos de Nuestra América, 5, no. 11, (1988).

4. An excellent discussion of the problems faced by these experiments and
the lessons of the 1970s is found in the collection edited by George Beckford
and Norman Girvan, *Development in Suspense: Selected Papers and Proceedings
of the First Conference of Caribbean Economists* (Kingston: University of the
West Indies, 1989).

5. Clive Thomas, "The Next Time Around: Radical Options and the Caribbean Economy," in Beckford and Girvan, *Development in Suspense*, pp. 290–313.

6. See Catherine Sunshine, *The Caribbean: Survival, Struggle and Sovereignty*, 2nd ed. (Washington, D.C.: EPICA, 1988), pp. 131–37.

7. The exception is perhaps Guyana where authoritarian structures have been made possible partly by historical (although diminishing) racial divisions and by the support of foreign powers for the ruling party.

8. John Walton, "Debt, Protest, and the State in Latin America," in Susan Eckstein, ed., *Power and Popular Protest: Latin American Social Movements* (Berkeley: University of California Press, 1989), table 10.2.

9. Ibid., p. 321.

10. This analysis is drawn from Taveras, "Abril."

11. *Haiti Solidarité Internationale* 34, 30 January–13 February 1989.

12. The exception to this historic trend is Trinidad-Tobago. However, recently the Oilfield Workers Trade Union of Trinidad-Tobago has formed a political party.

13. Centro Dominicano de Estudios de la Educación, *Balance de una Huelga, 1988* (Santo Domingo: CDEE, 1988).

14. This section draws heavily on Sunshine, *The Caribbean*, pp. 106–11. See her excellent discussion of the role of the U.S. government in undermining the development of an autonomous trade union movement in the region. Also see Jeffrey Harrod, *Trade Union Foreign Policy: a Study of British and American Trade Union Activities in Jamaica* (London: Macmillan, 1972) and Susanne Jonas, "Trade Union Imperialism in the Dominican Republic," *NACLA's Latin America and Empire Report*, 9, no. 3 (1975), pp. 13–30.

15. Earl Bousquet, "C'Bean Recolonized: George Lamming Identifies Three Forces," *Caribbean Contact* 15, no. 6 (1987), p. 1.

16. International Council of Free Trade Unions (ICFTU) and Caribbean Congress of Labour (CCL), *A Trade Union Programme for the Structural Transformation of the Caribbean* (Barbados: ICFTU/CCL, 1986), ch. 4.

17. Oilfields Workers Trade Union (OWTU), *Memorandum to the Government of Trinidad and Tobago* (Port of Spain: OWTU, 1987).

18. Lynn Bolles, "The New Challenge: Women Trade Union Members in the English-Speaking Caribbean," paper presented at the Caribbean Studies Association meetings, Guadeloupe, May 1988.

19. ICFTU/CCL, *A Trade Union Programme*, ch. 4.

20. See Rae Blumberg, "A Walk on the WID Side: Summary of Field Research on Women in Development in the Dominican Republic and Guatemala," report prepared for the Agency for International Development (Washington, D.C.), 1985.

21. See United Nations Economic Commission for Latin America and the Caribbean (ECLAC), *Women in the Inter-Island Trade in Agricultural Produce in the Eastern Caribbean* (Trinidad: ECLAC, 1988).

22. Much of this section is drawn from Coordinador Regional de Investigaciones Económicas y Sociales (CRIES), "The Contemporary Caribbean Economic Crisis, Social Movements, and Alternative Development Strategies," report

to OXFAM-America, 1988. David Lewis, the author of this report, also provided considerable assistance to the authors in formulating and refining many of the ideas in this chapter.

23. Leslie Lett, "The Church and Caribbean Identity," paper presented to the Second Caribbean Conference of Intellectual Workers, Trinidad, January 1984, p. 4.

24. See the excellent analysis by David Lewis, "Non-Governmental Organizations and Alternative Development Strategies in Central America and the Caribbean," paper presented to the Caribbean Studies Association meetings, Barbados, May 1989.

25. CRIES, "The Contemporary Caribbean Economic Crisis," p. 26. However, it should be noted that a number of groups are aware of the need for new regional organizations representing the grassroots and that at least one group, the Oilfields Workers Trade Union of Trinidad-Tobago, has called for the formation of a Caribbean Workers and People Congress (CWPC). This Congress would bring together representatives of the "progressive democratic forces committed to the independence and sovereignty of the region and to the perspective of one Caribbean" to develop a "working people's agenda." The trade unionists envisage the CWPC involving political parties, trade unions, religious bodies and churches, cultural organizations, and organizations of farmers, youth and students, the unemployed, women, intellectuals, cultural activists, human rights organizations, and others from the English, French, Dutch and Spanish-speaking Caribbean. Reported in *Caribbean Contact*, 1984.

26. Peggy Antrobus, "Gender Implications of the Debt Crisis," in Beckford and Girvan, eds., *Development in Suspense*, pp. 145–60.

27. The notable exception was the Ministry of Women's Affairs established by the revolutionary government of Grenada.

28. Maxine Henry-Wilson, "Pilot Study on Women Politicians in Jamaica," paper presented to the Caribbean Studies Association meetings, Belize, May 1987.

29. In 1984 the CWP became the Organization of Women for Progress (OWP).

30. It is important to note that in the conservative context of the 1980s, there was somewhat of a reversal in the semi-autonomous role of the PNPWM. By its own admission, the PNPWM has been weakened by too closely following the party agenda when it conflicted with the interest of women.

31. See Gita Sen and Caren Grown, *Development, Crises, and Alternative Visions: Third World Women's Perspectives* (N.Y.: Monthly Review Press, 1987).

32. See *CAFRA News*, 2, no. 3, (September 1988).

33. Ibid. pp. 15–16.

34. Ibid., p. 4.

35. Andaiye and Joan French, *Report of the Women and Development Unit 10th Anniversary Consultation and Symposium, "Crisis and Challenges" November 7–11, 1988* (Barbados: WAND, 1988), pp. 48–50.

36. Ibid., pp. 48–50.

CHAPTER 5

The Historical Legacy: U.S.-Caribbean Relations

U.S. POLICY INITIATIVES toward the Caribbean region are, we believe, ill-suited to the region's needs. To understand them, we begin with an historical overview of U.S.-Caribbean relations in the twentieth century as well as of previous regional development policies initiated both by the United States and by Caribbean governments. Three distinct periods in U.S.-Caribbean relations, differentiated by the changing role of the United States in the world economy, can be identified: a period of U.S. expansionism, 1898 to World War II; the period of U.S. hegemony, World War II to the 1960s; and the current period of challenge to U.S. dominance, the 1970s to the present.[1] During each period a distinct development model emerged in the Caribbean, each linked to the way in which the region was inserted in the international economy as well as to specific U.S. policy initiatives.

The Period of Expansionism

The Spanish-American War of 1898 heralded a new era in the Caribbean Basin, with the United States emerging from the war as unquestionably a major power in the region. Over subsequent decades the United States strove to define the Caribbean as its privileged sphere of influence through formal and direct methods of rule, military intervention, and the growing economic links of trade and foreign investment. The U.S. victory over Spain resulted in formal colonial rule in Puerto Rico, while Cuba became an official United States protectorate under the infamous Platt Amendment, which made the exercise of Cuban sovereignty subject to the will of the U.S. Congress. In the name of peace and stability the United States intervened militarily in the

Caribbean and Central America thirty-three times between 1898 and 1926, including prolonged periods in Haiti (1915–34), the Dominican Republic (1916–24), and Cuba (1917–33).[2]

The justification for the growing U.S. role in the region centered on protecting vital strategic interests, first among these the building of the Panama Canal. A second was to secure the region against further European encroachments, with Germany the principal concern on the eve of World War I. A third concern was economic: to make the Caribbean a privileged zone for U.S. exports and investment, thereby challenging the previous economic dominance of Great Britain in the region.

By 1929 the United States was the main source of foreign investment in the Caribbean and nearly rivaled the United Kingdom with respect to investment in Latin America and the Caribbean as a whole (see Table 5.1). The growth in U.S. investment between 1913 and 1929 was indeed spectacular, increasing at least fivefold in Cuba, the Dominican Republic, and Haiti. Cuba was the hub of the growing U.S. economic presence in the region, accounting for over one-quarter of total U.S. investment in Latin America. By the late 1920s U.S. investments in the sugar industry of Puerto Rico alone had reached $45 million, followed by total investments of $30 million in Haiti, $25 million in Jamaica, $24 million in the Dominican Republic, and $4 million in Trinidad.[3]

Increased trade followed the U.S. flag, with the growth of U.S. exports far exceeding those of Great Britain between 1913 and 1926. In the latter year the United States was supplying some 61 percent of the imports of Cuba and the Dominican Republic, 75 percent of those of Haiti, and 90 percent of those of Puerto Rico. The United States also had made significant inroads into British Caribbean markets by 1929, particularly those of Jamaica and Trinidad.[4]

U.S. investment in this period was largely in the form of direct investments in agriculture, mining, and public utilities. The structure of investment together with increased trade largely shaped the form of insertion of the Caribbean into the world economy; these countries became modern agroexport or enclave economies, with one or two agricultural products or raw materials contributing the overwhelming share of their export earnings while manufactured products and capital goods were imported from the advanced economies. Sugar was the leading export of Cuba, the Dominican Republic, and Puerto Rico, accounting for between 60 and 80 percent of the total exports of these countries in the late 1920s. Coffee accounted for 80 percent of Haiti's exports, while bananas and sugar were the main exports of Jamaica, and petroleum products dominated Trinidad's exports.[5]

Table 5.1
U.S. and UK Investment and Trade with Latin America and the Caribbean, 1913 and 1929

	Investment (millions of $)				% Increase in Investment	% Increase in Trade
	1913	% of total	1929	% of total	1913–29	1913–27
United States						
Cuba	220	} (18)	1,526	} (28)	594	104
Dominican Republic	4		24		500	149
Haiti	4		30		650	79
Mexico	800	(65)	1,550	(28)	94	51
Central America and Panama	41	(3)	163	(3)	298	—
South America	173	(14)	2,294	(41)	1,226	160
Total	1,242	(100)	5,587	(100)	350	118
United Kingdom						
Cuba	222	(5)	238	(4)	7	21
Dominican Republic	—		—		—	1,050
Haiti	—		—		—	13
Mexico	807	(16)	1,035	(18)	28	20
Central America and Panama	119	(2)	131	(2)	10	—
South America	3,835	(77)	4,485	(76)	17	25
Total	4,983	(100)	5,889	(100)	18	26

Source: Compiled from Max Winkler, *Investments of United States Capital in Latin America* (Boston: World Peace Foundation, 1929), tables XI and XII.

Foreign investment also led to a reorganization of the productive process—the modern plantation economy—and to significant dislocation of rural populations. Through purchase, force, bribes, and the indebtedness of peasants, foreign corporations came to own massive tracts of land, particularly in Cuba and Puerto Rico, while dispossessing thousands.[6] The standard of living in the region remained notoriously low, with the per capita consumption of Cuba, for example—the pearl of the Caribbean—less than one-fifth of the level of the United States.[7] The low standard of living was a product of the region's distorted economic structures, in which domestic output and resource use were divorced from local consumption and the basic needs of the population.[8]

The new structure of investment and trade also structured labor flows in the region. Cuba, the main focus of U.S. investment, became the main pole of attraction for the growing number of landless in the region. Between 1902 and 1932 some 311,000 Jamaicans and Haitians migrated to the Cuban sugar fields.[9] The building of the Panama Canal served as another stimulus to intraregional migration; thousands of Jamaicans, Barbadans, and other Caribbean migrants worked, and many died, on that endeavor. The United States itself accommodated 230,972 Caribbean immigrants between 1901 and 1920.[10]

The tensions brought on by the changes in the rural economy, exacerbated by the Great Depression, resulted in an important wave of social protest movements in the mid-1930s. General strikes in Cuba and anti-colonial rebellions throughout the English-speaking Caribbean were among the factors that propelled Roosevelt's Good Neighbor Policy, which ended the U.S. occupation of the Dominican Republic and Haiti and rescinded the Platt Amendment in Cuba. In the British Caribbean, the struggles of the 1930s became the basis for a change in British policy, which came to support moves toward greater self-government in the region, leading to independence in subsequent decades.

World War II to the 1960s:
The Structure of U.S. Hegemony

The United States emerged from World War II not only victorious but strong enough, economically, politically, and militarily, to structure and stabilize capital accumulation on a world scale through international agreements in the areas of trade, finance, and defense. The Bretton Woods Agreement—which established the dollar as the international currency—and the 1948 General Agreement on Tariffs and Trade (GATT)—which minimized international trade barriers—laid the foundation of the institutional framework within which the international division of labor would be structured.[11]

The progressive elimination of barriers to trade and investment resulted in a massive increase in world trade, fueled by the growth in U.S. foreign investment, which doubled in the decade of the 1950s. The structure of foreign investment changed considerably in this period, becoming increasingly concentrated in the advanced capitalist countries and in the manufacturing sector.

During this period the United States maintained its military superiority through its dominance of international military defense agreements and through its own military aid and assistance programs.[12] Military superiority had three foundations: superior technological capability (which depended on a strong defense industry and research and development sector); dominance in world market shares of arms sales; and the capacity to establish military bases and to enforce military agreements. Military superiority in turn protected capital accumulation on a world scale by guaranteeing access to raw materials, to markets, and to sea lanes, and by protecting U.S. investments abroad.

U.S. military influence started to challenge British dominion in the Caribbean in the 1940s. The United States first gained access to air and sea facilities in Barbados, Jamaica, St. Lucia, and Trinidad-Tobago in 1940, when Britain granted ninety-nine year leases for these bases in exchange for fifty U.S. destroyers. In the 1960s, as these territories became independent, new military agreements were signed between the United States and these countries, plus Antigua, expanding the number and quality of U.S. bases.[13]

The Spanish-speaking Caribbean Basin countries were signatories of the 1947 Río Treaty, the first of the mutual defense agreements that the United States crafted in the early years of the Cold War. The Río Treaty committed each signatory to come to the defense of any other signatory in the event of an attack by an outside force. Puerto Rico became the center of U.S. military operations in the Caribbean; it was the site of several important U.S. military bases and served as a training and maneuvering area for the U.S. army and navy as well as for the NATO Atlantic Fleet.

Besides revitalized trade, aid, and investment flows and an enhanced military-security framework, U.S.-Caribbean relations, as redefined in the post World War II period, were mediated by an extended set of multilateral institutions. Multilateralism gradually replaced bilateralism in interstate dealings as the main European colonial structures were dismantled and the U.S. economic presence strengthened and extended. U.S. policy in the Americas began to depend less on open intervention, and more on multilateral and interamerican institutions such as the Organization of American States (OAS), founded in 1947. The exceptions, of course, were the failed Bay of Pigs invasion of Cuba in 1961 and the successful U.S. invasion of the Dominican Republic in 1965.

The Cuban Revolution

As noted earlier, up until 1959 Cuba had been the center of U.S. investments in the region. The largest of the islands in physical size and population, it was also the best endowed and the wealthiest. Sugar, the leading sector of its agroexport economy, was largely controlled by U.S. interests, which had been well accommodated by the island's dictator, Fulgencio Batista. It is not too surprising then that the United States was hostile to Batista's overthrow and the triumph of the revolutionary forces led by Fidel Castro's July 26th Movement in January 1959.

The economic goals of the July 26th Movement have been summarized as follows: "increase the rate of growth, reduce dependence on sugar, diversify agriculture, develop the industrial sector, diversify trade relations, and increase the standard of living of the population through the expansion of health, education and welfare programs."[14] The collision course with the United States began when the revolutionary government began to implement the policies to meet these goals, specifically, an agrarian reform and the nationalization of U.S. companies.

The initial agrarian reform law passed in 1959 was rather mild by the standards of the 1980s. Only those properties in excess of 400 hectares were to be expropriated, but properties of this size included a number owned by U.S. investors. Just as troubling to the U.S. administration was the fact that as Cuba attempted to diversify its trade, it took advantage of a Soviet offer to import cheaper Soviet oil. The United States demanded that Cuba cease doing so and ordered U.S.-owned refineries to refuse to refine the oil. Cuba responded by nationalizing these refineries. In retaliation, the United States reduced Cuba's sugar quota in the protected U.S. market. Cuba then nationalized all sugar mills and oil refineries as well as U.S.-owned banks and manufacturing plants. The United States responded by placing a trade embargo on Cuba, and Cuba nationalized the remaining U.S. properties.[15]

As a result of these escalating reprisals, by 1961 some 75 percent of Cuban industry and 30 percent of its farmland had been nationalized. Moreover, as internal political polarization increased, the Cubans further expropriated, nationalized, and redistributed. Consequently, in a rather short period of time, the Cubans had broken with the preexisting structures of accumulation and had established the base for an alternative development model, one that was centered on the leading role of the state and state enterprises.

Breaking with the structures which had previously integrated Cuba into the capitalist world economy was not without cost. U.S. policy obliged Cuba to pay the highest possible price, not only closing the principal market for its main export and blocking access to spare parts to maintain its U.S.-oriented industrial base, but also requiring that the island remain in a state of military preparedness against invasion and attack throughout much of the 1960s. Shortly after its defeat of the U.S.-sponsored Bay of Pigs invasion by Cuban exiles, Cuba announced to the world its socialist path and subsequently established increasingly strong ties with the Soviet Union and other socialist countries. The United States drew on its new multilateral agreements, successfully calling on the OAS to expel Cuba from its membership, and pressuring member countries to participate in the trade embargo.

The Alliance for Progress

The Cuban revolution provoked a fundamental revision of U.S. policy toward Latin America. Henceforth this would promote a strategy of combining limited social and economic reform with harsh counter-insurgency measures. The new policy was encompassed in the Alliance for Progress, signed in 1961 at Punta del Este, Uruguay. The reforms promoted in Latin America aimed at broadening internal markets and securing the conditions for successful capitalist development. These were encouraged by increased U.S. development assistance—channeled through two new institutions, the Inter-American Development Bank (IDB) and the U.S. Agency for International Development (AID)—and backed up with increased military assistance to bolster counterinsurgency forces—just in case the reforms failed.

In part, the Alliance for Progress was also a U.S. response to Latin American demands for economic betterment. Resentful of being left out of the postwar Marshall Plan after supporting the United States in the war effort, these countries had begun demanding increased financial assistance on good terms. There was a growing consensus that import-substitution industrialization had to replace the previous economic model centered on primary export production to foster Latin American economic development, an analysis promoted by the Economic Commission on Latin America (ECLA) in the late 1950s.

The economic and social reforms promoted by the Alliance for Progress (agrarian, fiscal, and educational) reflected Latin American economists' understanding that self-sustaining growth on the basis of an expanding internal market required the strengthening of backward and forward linkages within the economy, and particularly the removal of those structural limitations which hindered industrialization. These reforms also reflected the class interests of the emerging national bourgeoisies bent on undermining the economic, social, and political power of traditional oligarchies.

Only two Caribbean countries—the Dominican Republic and Haiti—were among the beneficiaries of the Alliance for Progress, since it was not until the decade of the 1960s and 1970s that a significant number of the other islands began to achieve independence. Between 1962 and 1982, a total of $12.7 billion in development assistance was channeled to Latin America. The Caribbean and Central American countries included under the Alliance for Progress received a total of $3.8 billion. One of the major regional beneficiaries was the Dominican Republic—particularly after the fall of dictator Rafael Trujillo and the 1965 U.S. invasion—which received 21 percent ($795 million) of the total credit allotted to nine Caribbean Basin countries.[16] Along with reform, the

Alliance for Progress provided increased funding for military training, particularly in counterinsurgency warfare. While the use of national armies was to be the preferred policy in meeting guerrilla threats, the United States also signaled its continued readiness to use direct military intervention to prevent the rise to power of any nationalist revolutionary movement.

The history of Juan Bosch and his party in the Dominican Republic served as an early indicator of the U.S. response to Caribbean political experiments after the Cuban revolution. Bosch, an energetic and charismatic leader of the Dominican Revolutionary Party (PRD), was elected president in 1962 on a platform which promised land reform, increased access to education and a more autonomous model of development as part of a democratic socialist revolution. But the PRD faced fierce opposition from the country's traditional ruling class and after only seven months in office, the military staged a coup in September 1963, overthrowing Bosch. The subsequent military junta was unpopular and ineffective and corruption and repression increased.

In April 1965 a group of progressive military officers seized power and restored constitutional government. But the takeover was not met by enthusiasm by conservatives, the military, or the U.S. embassy, and heavy fighting began between the pro-Bosch factions and the military. Just as the civilian forces appeared to be winning, President Lyndon Johnson ordered U.S. military forces to Santo Domingo, ostensibly to protect U.S. property and citizens. Approximately 30,000 U.S. troops were sent to the Dominican Republic in order to prevent a "second Cuba" in the Caribbean.[17]

Regional Development Models

During the 1950s and 1960s two quite different industrialization policies—export oriented vs. import substitution—were pursued in the different Caribbean islands. Their contrasting experiences point up the limitations of either one within the current structure of the international economy.

Puerto Rico's Operation Bootstrap. Up to the 1950s, Puerto Rico's economy had centered on its agricultural sector. Sugarcane and tobacco plantations—mostly owned by absentee U.S. corporations—produced for U.S. consumption, at the growing expense of local food crop production and agricultural employment. Due to its territorial status, Puerto Rico was unable to impose tariffs to protect potential local industries from U.S. competition, and the overwhelming share of consumption items and capital goods was imported from the United States. In the late 1940s, lacking the political power to design inward-looking import-substitution development strategies in a period of growing social and political tensions, Puerto Rico's government chose an industrialization strategy explicitly designed to integrate Puerto Rico more closely to the U.S. market. Known as "Operation Bootstrap," the strategy consisted of attracting U.S. investors through tax incentive schemes to establish manufacturing plants on the island geared to the U.S. market.

The foundations of the model rested on the structural advantages Puerto Rico could offer to U.S. manufacturing industries. These included low wages (Puerto Rican wages were 27 percent of average U.S. manufacturing wages in the 1950s); selective minimum-wage exemption; generous tax exemptions, including exemptions on U.S. and local corporate income taxes, income taxes on dividends distributed to individuals, municipal taxes, license fees, and property taxes; duty-free access to the U.S. market; geographical proximity to the United States; and a governmental infrastructure which enforced and managed the development model.[18]

In the initial decade of Operation Bootstrap, Puerto Rico experienced an invasion of textile and apparel, electrical machinery, and leather goods industries, and later of pharmaceutical, petrochemical, electronic, and chemical industries. Between 1951 and 1960 Gross National Product (GNP) grew by an annual real rate of 5.3 percent as a result of the new investment in the manufacturing sector.[19] Up through the 1970s, manufacturing, commerce, services, construction, and government sector activities continued to grow appreciably; the agricultural sector, however, witnessed a spiraling decline.

The relative success of Operation Bootstrap in this period with respect to growth rates was more tempered with respect to employment generation, since the growth in manufacturing employment did not keep up with the rate of agricultural labor-force displacement. Moreover, the manufacturing sector which developed in the 1960s was increasingly characterized by capital-intensive technologies, reducing the demand for labor. As a result, other measures had to be adopted to maintain the model of capital accumulation: along with the introduction of population control and sterilization programs, migration to the United States became virtually institutionalized. It is estimated that between 1940 and 1969, 700,000 Puerto Ricans migrated to the United States, accounting for 48 percent of those of working age in 1970.[20]

The massive injection of U.S. capital into export-oriented manufacturing also did little to foster domestic capital formation. Rather, the island came to depend on U.S. capital for 90 percent of manufacturing investment.[21] The new manufacturing sector had few backward and forward linkages with the local industrial sector, depending upon imports of raw materials and capital goods from the United States. Thus the strategy did little to foster a sustained development process.

Since the island's government chose not to tax the U.S. corporations, the Puerto Rican model depended financially on public debt issue and on access to U.S. fiscal expenditures through transfer payments and grants. Puerto Rico's public debt mushroomed from $41.5 million in 1954 to $801.8 million in 1964.[22] External borrowing was necessary to finance the public services and infrastructure for the new industries which would only stay in Puerto Rico if tax holidays were continually extended, thus deepening the debt spiral.

Industrialization by Invitation. In the 1950s, Puerto Rico's economic growth rates appeared dazzling in the rest of the region and Operation Bootstrap became the model for the industrialization strategies pursued in the English-speaking Caribbean known as "industrialization by invitation."[23] Trinidad passed its Aid to Pioneer Industries Ordinance in 1950 and Jamaica's Industrial Development Corporation set up shop in 1952. By the end of the decade most of the countries that were to later form the Caribbean Community and Common Market (CARICOM) had put in place the requisite legal and infrastructural framework by which "industrialization by invitation" was to function.

The similarity of these programs with Operation Bootstrap was that the expansion of manufacturing took place with the assistance of government subsidies, tax benefits, and government provision of infrastructure; that is, industrialization required active government intervention in the economy.[24] As in the Puerto Rican case, the new manufacturing sector was dominated by foreign, principally U.S., capital and faced similar structural constraints, such as a high import content, including raw materials, even for the food-processing sector. And many companies simply carried out the final assembly of components made abroad.

In contrast to Puerto Rico, however, import substitution for the local market far outweighed export-oriented industrialization. In fact, most industries were quite insular, not even taking advantage of the regional market. The larger countries succeeded in producing the entire array of consumer items with a ready regional market (textiles and garments, footwear, toiletries, cement, beverages, etc.) But a regional market of any significance never developed, much less an extra-regional export sector. Thus, even in Jamaica, where an Export Industry Encouragement Law was promulgated as far back as 1956, only 40 of the 130 firms established between 1950 and 1964 were net exporters.[25] This was basically true for the entire region, as reflected in the fact that in 1970 exports of manufactured goods constituted only 4.4 percent of total manufacturing output in the Commonwealth Caribbean.[26]

High import-intensity with few local linkages, a high degree of foreign capital ownership, an emphasis on insular import-substitution rather than regional export promotion, and reliance on the capital-intensive techniques truncated the transformative potential of the new industrial sector. The distortions were apparent in the fact that more and more public resources were channeled into the industrial sector at the expense of all other sectors, especially agriculture. In Jamaica, as in Puerto Rico, agricultural decline created a relative surplus population which could not be absorbed by the increasingly capital-intensive industrial sector, and migration to the United States, Britain, and other Caribbean islands became part of the local industrialization by invitation model. It was partly in response to the flaws of postwar industrialization that regional economic integration under the Caribbean Free Trade Association (CARIFTA) and then CARICOM took shape.

Regional Integration. The Caribbean Free Trade Association was founded in 1968 by the newly independent Caribbean states associated with the British Commonwealth.[27] It sought, as its name suggests, to create a free-trade zone in the Commonwealth Caribbean by systematically eliminating most tariff barriers constraining inter-island trade. The aim was to expand market size in hopes that new large-scale industries would be encouraged to service the regional market while excess capacity that came with insular import-substitution industrialization would be eliminated.[28]

In the pre-CARIFTA inter-island trade regime, products traded were mainly petrochemicals (from Trinidad); fertilizers, chemicals and cement (from Trinidad and Jamaica); rice (from Guyana) and root crops from the less developed Leeward and Windward Islands. With the advent of CARIFTA, manufactured goods came to dominate and between 1967 and 1971, intra-CARIFTA trade in manufactured goods grew at twice the rate of growth of all other items.[29] But because of the particular type of industrialization on which this trade was based, value-added in production was rather small. Indeed, under the CARIFTA agreement to define rules for area tariff treatment, goods that were not manufactured in the region, but which were deemed necessary inputs for already-established manufacturing industries, were given local-origin status. Thus much manufactured output did little to enhance local economic performance, providing few benefits for the economies of the region. By the early 1970s it was quite clear that the type of industrialization taking place, even under free trade, posed severe limitations on the long-term objectives of the integration movement and that integration had to be shifted to a deeper and more effective level. A series of negotiations led to the formation of CARICOM in July 1973.

Notwithstanding the disappointment with CARIFTA, the period of U.S. hegemony was a period of growth and diversification for the Caribbean islands. By 1960 the manufacturing sector contributed 15 percent of GDP in the Dominican Republic, 17 percent in Jamaica and 26 percent in Trinidad-Tobago.[30] During the 1960s growth in manufacturing was a healthy 5 percent per annum in these countries.[31] In the 1960s average annual growth rates of GDP per capita were above 3 percent in Barbados, the Dominican Republic, and Jamaica, and over 2 percent in Trinidad-Tobago (see Table 2.1).

There was also a significant diversification of the primary export sector during this period. During the decade of the 1950s the bauxite industry was developed in Jamaica, as it was in the next decade in Haiti, the Dominican Republic, and Guyana. Trinidad-Tobago became an important center of oil refining. In addition, a number of the islands became tourist meccas for Europeans and Americans, particularly after the Cuban revolution. The U.S. embargo on Cuba effectively closed down what had been previously the undisputed center of Caribbean tourism.

U.S. corporations responded to local industrialization strategies, investing in Caribbean countries for local manufacturing production, and increasing their exports of capital goods and manufactured inputs to the islands. By the mid-1960s the United States was replacing Great Britain as the primary trading partner of the newly independent countries of the English-speaking Caribbean. For example, in the mid-1960s, 38 percent of Jamaica's and 28 percent of Trinidad-Tobago's exports were to the U.S. market, compared with 27 percent and 22 percent to the United Kingdom. With respect to imports, the United States had increased its share from 8 percent and 14 percent of total Trinidadian and Jamaican imports in the early 1950s, to 14 percent and 31 percent, respectively, in the mid-1960s.[32]

While growth in per capita income was healthy for most of the islands in the decades of the 1950s and 1960s, income distribution became even more skewed within each of, as well as among, the Caribbean islands. At one pole was the Bahamas, with the highest per capita income in the region ($3,362 in 1974), followed by Puerto Rico ($2,465), Cuba ($2,142), and Trinidad-Tobago ($1,778). At the other end was Haiti, with the lowest per capita income in the hemisphere ($125), followed by St. Vincent ($310), and Grenada ($346).[33]

While most islands continued to emphasize agroexport production, they all tended to neglect food production. Over this period, most Caribbean islands became increasingly dependent on imported foodstuffs, although the majority of their populations in many cases were still rural and employed in the agricultural sector. By 1970 over 50 percent of the food consumed in the region was being imported; food imports in 1972 constituted approximately one-quarter of total imports in Barbados, Belize, Dominica, Grenada, St. Kitts-Nevis, and St. Vincent.[34] The consolidation of export agriculture and the decline of basic food production, combined with the pull of urban industrialization, also stimulated rural-urban and international migration.

Caribbean migration to the United States became significant in the decade of the 1940s, accelerating in the late 1960s (see Table 3.7). In the late 1960s, the Caribbean islands contributed 20 percent of the legal migrants to the United States compared with only 5 percent in the decade of the 1950s and 9 percent in the early 1960s. In the 1960s, Cubans represented the majority of Caribbean migrants, followed by Dominicans and Haitians; in the latter half of the 1960s migration by Jamaicans increased significantly. In the early 1970s migration from Cuba was surpassed by that from the English-speaking Caribbean—Jamaica, Trinidad-Tobago, Barbados, and Guyana—a trend repeated in the 1980s.

The 1970s to the Present:
The Challenge to U.S. Hegemony

By the end of the decade of the 1960s the recovery and subsequent restructuring of the economies of Western Europe and Japan had led to a deterioration in the U.S. competitive position abroad. This trend was aggravated by the inflationary pressures built into the U.S. economy by the Vietnam war, which led to U.S. balance of payments deficits and eventually to the abandonment of the Bretton Woods agreement and the dollar as the basis of the postwar financial system.

Significant changes had also taken place in the structural framework within which previous patterns of international integration had been shaped. In the area of trade, the GATT had not been designed to regulate those areas of trade that gained in relative importance in the decade of the 1970s, such as trade in services and intra-firm transactions among multinational corporations and their subsidiaries. The uncertainty generated by the GATT's inability to regulate an increasing share of world trade—within the context of the contraction of economic growth and exports brought about by the global recession of the late 1970s—generated fierce competition among the principal trading blocs to maintain overseas markets while protecting domestic ones. Fierce competition led, in turn, to trade disputes, protectionist sentiments, and to the formulation of alternative international trade strategies. Meanwhile, growth in world production and trade declined precipitously.

With the collapse of Bretton Woods, the foundations upon which U.S. balance of payments' stability and financial capacity rested eroded. Flexible exchange rates and variable international interest rates then became important instruments to manage fiscal and balance of trade deficits. But high interest rates in the early 1980s, designed to attract capital inflows into the United States, enormously aggravated balance of payments problems for third world nations, including those of the Caribbean. Indebtedness escalated as countries were unable to service debt commitments in the face of decreased export earnings (as a result of the recession in the advanced countries) and high interest rates on new lending. These problems finally exploded in the debt crisis of the 1980s.

In the late 1970s, U.S. military superiority also eroded, U.S. world market shares in arms sales shrank, and the USSR and Europe achieved parity in military technological capability, including the nuclear arms race. The Vietnam war had also created a crisis of legitimacy for the U.S. military establishment and U.S. foreign policy generally, which led to the abandonment of the "global interventionism" policy of the Kennedy, Johnson, and Nixon administrations in favor of one of military retreat and expenditure cuts.

In the post-Vietnam period, therefore, the United States reduced its military presence in the Caribbean and the considerable regional infrastructure of bases and military installations was partly dismantled. In 1966 the naval base of Chaguaramas in Trinidad was transferred to the government of Eric Williams and several small U.S. army installations were closed in Puerto Rico, joined in 1973 by an important air base, Ramey Field. U.S. military activities for the most part were concentrated in the Roosevelt Roads navy base in Puerto Rico.[35]

Congressional action and budget restrictions also limited the traditional instruments of influence over the military and police forces of the region—military aid, training, and the sale of arms. But the reduction in the U.S. military presence and influence was not a source of concern to U.S. policy elites so long as other instruments of foreign policy seemed adequate to control regional developments.

Alternative Development Strategies of the 1970s

The failure of the economic development strategies of the 1950s and 1960s formed the basis for a wave of social and political activism which swept the region toward the end of the decade of the 1960s. New social movements emerged (students, women, labor, culture), new ideologies developed, and political turmoil surfaced in many countries. The 1970s were, indeed, a period of renaissance and experimentation, of constructing new utopias, and of rethinking development policy in different terms.

While the particular mix of policy initiatives pursued during the decade varied across territories, and the reorganization of policy was more comprehensive in some countries than in others, a common tendency was nonetheless evident. There was a steady expansion in the economic role of the state, a deepened commitment to, and reevaluation of the importance of, Caribbean regionalism, and a general diversification of international relations. These changes are best illus-trated by the policies of the first Michael Manley government in Jamaica, the development of CARICOM, and the experience of the New Jewel Movement in Grenada.

Jamaica Under Manley. Jamaica under Michael Manley exemplifies the dilemmas that confront a less developed country when it chooses an alternative development path without breaking its ties to the capitalist world economy. The Manley government's goals upon assuming office in 1972 included bettering the distribution of income and ending the economic stagnation which characterized Jamaica in the late 1960s. These policies in turn were tied to the growth of public expenditure and of the public sector.[36] Food subsidies on various staples were introduced and free education was guaranteed to all. Public work programs were created to generate employment, and equal pay for equal work was legislated. In addition, the government pegged the Jamaican dollar to the U.S. dollar (it had previously floated relative to the British pound) in an attempt to control imports and increase exports and foreign exchange. In 1973 the government introduced Operation GROW (Growing and Reaping Our Wealth), a broad, long-term project for the rural areas focusing on building micro-dams for irrigation, new roads, rural electrification, and food-processing plants. Lastly, under the slogan "put idle lands into idle hands," the government redistributed land and formed sugar cooperatives.

These policies triggered some basic social contradictions. In order to finance the growing activity of the public sector, the government had to augment its revenues, and the most likely source was the export sector, particularly bauxite production. In an attempt to stabilize this source of revenue, the government helped found the International Bauxite Association (in hopes of stabilizing prices) and introduced a production levy on bauxite production. In reaction, the bauxite com-panies started pulling out of the island and production of bauxite fell by 26 percent in 1975.[37] The state also purchased bauxite lands and leased these to the bauxite companies for thirty to forty years, while acquiring 51 percent ownership in others. Furthermore, in order to implement the policy changes, the Manley government had to further tighten foreign exchange controls, shift tax burdens to high-income groups and property owners, raise consumption duties, and establish income policies.

These moves greatly aggravated class conflict as well as the balance of payments. As violence escalated, tourism slumped and sabotage and industrial cutbacks multiplied. The economy was also destabilized through illegal capital flight, hoarding, and speculation.[38] Hard-pressed to keep the economy running, Manley was then forced to expand nationalizations to include banking, communications, key public utilities (telephone, electricity, public transportation), and cement production.

Social polarization was inevitable. Community councils, community enterprise organizations, rent tribunals, voluntary price inspectors, women's organizations, sugar cooperatives, all mobilized and coordinated, constituted an alternative power in opposition to the capitalists, the middle classes, sectors of the army, and other groups. Edward Seaga's Jamaican Labour Party allied itself with these latter groups in opposition to the Manley regime. Notwithstanding the economic and social turmoil, however, the People's National Party (PNP) was reelected in 1976.

In foreign policy, Manley's aim was "to construct economic alliances that give us the greatest chance to underwrite our economic independence; . . . it is our purpose to make common cause with all developing nations of the world who share our fate."[39] This implied taking a stand within the Non-Aligned Movement, and in other international forums and organizations in favor of third world interests and of a New International Economic Order. Foreign policy changes also included engaging in dialogue and trade with Cuba and exchanging technical, scientific, and managerial assistance on matters ranging from agriculture and education to security and international trade. Lastly, economic independence implied taking a stand against foreign capital and its alliances with Jamaica's capitalist classes to protect the people's interests. All three of these positions incurred the wrath of the United States, but particularly, the opening toward Cuba.

The concrete government response to the increasing polarization of Jamaican society was the elaboration of the "Emergency Production Plan," a strategy based on self-reliance and popular mobilization. The Emergency Production Plan consisted of three elements: (1) achieving self-reliance by reducing the country's dependency on foreign sources of raw materials and consumer and capital goods; (2) diversifying economic relations; and (3) changing the structure of the economy so that the production of goods and services would use only small quantities of foreign exchange, have a high employment content, and be oriented toward the provision of the basic needs of the mass of the population.[40]

In order to meet the goals of the plan it was envisioned that the state would have to expand its ownership and control of the banking and insurance sector, the oil refinery, and factories producing basic necessities such as flour and cement. The state was also to monopolize foreign trade, although local commerce was to remain private. The plan also envisioned support to cooperatives and community-owned enterprises.

The plan, however, was rejected by the Jamaican cabinet, who opted instead to turn to the International Monetary Fund (IMF) to seek balance of payments support. In so doing, they compromised the concept of self-reliance and the possibilities for inward-oriented development in favor of IMF stabilization policies. The subsequent story is now well known: the stabilization agreement focused on dismantling the bulk of Manley's programs in a tight austerity program; when the government was unable to meet the stringent conditions imposed by the IMF, the IMF aided in discrediting the Manley administration. Subsequently, the opposition led by Seaga was elected into office and the new government obediently accepted the IMF's conditions. The Jamaican case clearly illustrates the structural constraints facing attempts to construct alternative paths of development.

CARICOM. The political effect of the international crisis which began in the 1970s in the Caribbean was to trigger a resurgent nationalism centered on the terms of the region's integration into the world economy, and the goal of active nonalignment. Michael Manley took the lead in broadening the region's relationships in the world economy as well as in the Caribbean. In 1973, Jamaica, Barbados, Trinidad-Tobago, and Guyana jointly decided to reestablish diplomatic relations with Cuba, in defiance of U.S. policy. The chords the Non-Aligned Movement struck in the region in turn reinvigorated regional cooperation.

CARICOM, which was formed in 1973, includes the former CARIFTA members in addition to the Bahamas and Belize. CARICOM includes three clearly defined areas of cooperation that did not exist under CARIFTA. The first is the creation of a common market for the purposes of trade and general cooperative economic enhancement. Where CARIFTA stipulated only tariff-free trading among members, CARICOM goes further in requiring a common external tariff, the phasing out of nontariff trade barriers, coordinated fiscal stabilization policies, and the unhindered movement of capital within the region (though no parallel provision for the movement of labor was made). The second is the institutionalization, through various interministerial committees, of "functional cooperation" in the areas of health, education, transport and communications, labor, finance, energy, meteorology, mining, science and technology, and agriculture. Ad hoc cooperation in information, law, and women's affairs are also provided for. The third is the coordination of foreign policy, a unique provision in the history of international integration. CARICOM is thus a very ambitious project; that it has not had uniform success in all areas is therefore not unexpected.

Intraregional trade among the CARICOM countries grew significantly in absolute terms, with intraregional imports rising from $47 million in 1962 to $330 million in 1984. In relative terms, however, intraregional trade is still only about 10 percent of the region's total trade volume. In the period 1967–84, intraregional imports never exceeded 10 percent of the total value of imports while exports peaked at 13 percent.[41]

The volume and structure of trade reflects regional resource endowments and distributions, and is skewed heavily in favor of member countries with strategic resources. Thus Trinidad-Tobago's oil accounts for 40 percent of intra-CARICOM trade and 75 percent of that country's exports to its neighbors. Trinidad-Tobago dominates regional imports as well, accounting for 33 percent of the total in the 1980s. Just three countries—Barbados, Jamaica, and Trinidad-Tobago, the most industrialized members—account for 80 percent of intraregional trade in manufactures. The countries that make up the Organization of Eastern Caribbean States (OECS), however, have been able to boost the share of manufacturing in their exports from 11 percent in the early 1970s to 40 percent in 1984.[42] Encouraging as these figures seem, there is still a marked asymmetry between the region's trade with the outside and that with member countries. Thus Trinidad-Tobago exported only 7–11 percent of its gross exports to other CARICOM countries between 1973 and 1985, and Jamaica managed only 4–7 percent from 1973 to 1981 (rising to 12 percent in 1981–82). On the other hand, 24–28 percent of Barbados' export trade was with its neighbors over the same period, reaching a high of 31 percent in 1981–82.[43]

CARICOM at its very formation had to contend with the international economic crises precipitated by the first oil-price shock of 1973. Barely two years after its formation, in April 1975, the first signs of structural and personal conflict broke into the open regarding certain bilateral economic arrangements that some of the weakest CARICOM nations had entered into with wealthier Latin American neighbors. The dissension appeared to reach crisis proportions when in 1977 Jamaica and Guyana restricted their overall imports—even those from CARICOM nations—in response to domestic fiscal difficulties. This severely undermined the free-trade regime that underlies the regional integration effort and exposed the structural weak points that could cause regional disintegration.

Perhaps more significantly, the most important regional project of "production integration" was put on the back burner. In response to the criticisms leveled at CARIFTA—that regional free trade merely expanded the field of operation for multinational corporations, thus deepening, rather than alleviating, the Caribbean's dependent position in the international economy—a commitment to build production capacity to ensure regional economic self-sufficiency had been incorporated in CARICOM's statutes.[44] Production integration was to occur through the establishment of regional agricultural and industrial projects which utilized locally available inputs, the products of which were geared toward satisfying local demand.

The first such project, announced in 1974, consisted of two aluminum smelters to be located in Guyana and Trinidad-Tobago and owned by the governments of Guyana, Jamaica, and Trinidad-Tobago. The importance of this scheme was that it would have advanced the cause of "production integration" tremendously by utilizing some of the region's most valuable raw materials: hydroelectric power from Guyana, bauxite from Guyana and Jamaica, and natural gas from Trinidad-Tobago. In the wake of the optimism generated by this announcement, plans were soon afoot to build a cement plant in Barbados to be owned jointly with Guyana, Guyana to do the final processing on the cement-clinker produced in the Barbadan plant. Some thirty-five new industries in all were also slated for the smaller countries of the Organization of Eastern Caribbean States (OECS).[45]

A number of events dashed the high expectations these projects generated. The smelter plant fell victim to a dispute between Jamaica and Trinidad-Tobago over the role of outside forces in the regional economy, and the government of Trinidad decided to construct the smelter alone. The cement project suffered a similar fate, mainly due to technical problems, with the result that it has become a Barbadan project only. This left the minor industrial allocation within the OECS as the only fruits of a once-promising regional program. Even here, only eight of the thirty-five ventures initially visualized have been realized.

In March of 1980 a team of regional experts were empaneled to conduct a review of the integration project with a view to mapping out new goals and directions for the region. The major "innovation" in their 1981 recommendations was an unmistakable emphasis on production integration.[46] Even though this report provides a renewed basis for regional industrialization, CARICOM is faced today with the task of surviving in a regional and international setting markedly different from what prevailed at its inception. For one, over the 1970s and early 1980s a wide economic gap opened between Trinidad-Tobago and the rest of CARICOM. Secondly, the regional consensus upon which the movement was erected in 1973 has given way to an "ideological pluralism" of the 1980s that has brought divergent views on the very meaning of economic development, much less how to achieve it. And third, protectionist sentiments have grown throughout the CARICOM community.

Between 1981 and 1984 there was a drastic and disturbing 25 percent drop in intraregional trade, partly due to significant currency devaluations in Jamaica and Guyana. Moreover, in a reflection of their domestic economic crises, both countries heavily curtailed all their imports, including those from CARICOM. In the case of Jamaica, this was particularly due to its reorientation toward the U.S. economy. Barbados and Trinidad-Tobago then retaliated in kind against Jamaica. Also, in 1983 the only trade-facilitating instrument in the Community, the Community Multilateral Clearing Facility (CMCF), reached its $100 million credit-granting limit and collapsed. Much of that money, $96 million, was owed by Guyana alone, so that CARICOM members decided to trade on a purely balanced basis, especially with Guyana. The overall effect has been a depression of intra-CARICOM trade to this date.

The Grenadan Revolution. The vanguard of social change in the Caribbean in the early 1980s was the small island of Grenada under the New Jewel Movement (NJM). The People's Revolutionary Government (PRG), formed in 1979 and headed by Maurice Bishop, attempted to implement an autonomous, inward-looking model of economic development. Traditionally an agroexport economy, Grenada's insertion into the international division of labor was tied fundamentally to the production of nutmeg, cocoa, and bananas. The revolutionary government's objectives were to (1) lay the foundations to restructure the economy; (2) establish linkages among the different economic sectors "putting idle hands to work resources;" (3) put an end to speculation and corruption; and (4) stimulate investment in those sectors which would generate growth, employment, and foreign exchange.[47]

The Grenadan government planned to achieve these objectives by strengthening the public sector, creating a new cooperative sector, and preserving the private sector. It also focused on food production and tourism to reactivate the economy. The state sector came to encompass about 30 percent of the economy and consisted of twenty-three enterprises, ranging from utilities to new investments in an agroindustrial plant which made juices from locally grown fruits and a fish processing plant which produced salted fish (a West Indian dietary staple). The PRG nationalized only a few hotels and nightclubs which were the property of the former dictator, Eric Gairy.

In 1981, the PRG implemented a mild land reform law calling for the compulsory lease of unused tracts over 100 acres in size. Considering the wastage associated with idle lands on a small island, this was not an unexpected act and was not openly resisted by landowners.[48] The private sector consisted primarily of peasant farmers and fishermen and was therefore not for the most part antagonistic to the revolution's programs; this sector accounted for 60 percent of agricultural production. The agrarian reform established a cooperative sector as an alternative strategy of restructuring production within the agricultural sector, fundamentally oriented toward creating linkages between agricultural production, processing, and marketing.

The PRG also launched a broad program of social services, including free education through the high school level; free, high-quality medical and dental care; hot school lunches and distribution of milk to mothers and infants; a revolving loan program to help poor families repair their houses; and a voluntary literacy program which enabled illiterate adults to learn to read and write.[49] The PRG soon established two state-owned banks to extend credit to small producers, enabling them to expand or diversify their production. A marketing board purchased fruits and vegetables from farmers and sold them throughout the island. This assistance encouraged farmers to diversify and helped to reduce the country's dependence on imported food.

In order to implement their alternative economic development model, the government needed control over trade and access to international financial credit. Therefore, the government placed some curbs on the commercial sector by increasing taxes on imports and by giving the state a monopoly to import certain basic goods such as rice, sugar, flour, and fertilizer. In order to protect itself from international price fluctuations of agricultural goods and from unforeseen natural climatic changes, it focused on tourism as an alternative source of foreign exchange. The development of this sector was to be designed so that it would have strong linkages with the local agricultural sector. A prerequisite for the expansion of tourism on the island was the building of an international airport, which the Cubans agreed to finance and build.

Access to international financial credit and technical assistance was obtained, notwithstanding U.S. pressures to obstruct it, from various multilateral organizations including the OAS, the UN Children's Fund (UNICEF), the UN Food and Agriculture Organization (FAO), and others. The European Economic Community (EEC) and numerous countries besides Cuba (Canada, Venezuela, Libya, Syria, Algeria) also extended such assistance. These funds were channeled to construct infrastructure, to invest in agriculture and agroindustry, and to finance housing, education, and health-care services.[50]

In 1981, a three-year balance of payments loan which the IMF had promised Grenada was reduced, following U.S. pressure, to a one-year loan and to one-third of the original sum. U.S. Secretary of State Alexander Haig had recently declared that the socialist government of Grenada would not receive a penny of indirect aid from the United States, asserting that Grenada was building an airport which could be used as a stopover point for the transport of Cuban troops to Angola. The U.S. executive director of the IMF immediately objected to the planned loan, arguing that excessive expenditure on the airport was the main reason for the country's economic difficulties and that this had not been sufficiently taken into account in the stabilization agreement.[51] Ironically, the members of a Caribbean Basin Initiative Hotel Development Mission to Grenada recently concluded that "Grenada has potentially one of the best airport facilities in the region," noting that the airport is within a twenty-minute drive of most of the existing and potential hotel sites on the island.[52]

The reasons for the economic difficulties the country was experiencing lay elsewhere and included low prices for Grenada's export crops on the international market; weather disasters; U.S. propaganda campaigns which scared away tourists; U.S. pressures to block economic aid to the island; a shortage of trained personnel to carry out government programs; and internal divisions within the New Jewel Movement. The NJM's autonomously designed and inward-looking experiment ended tragically when these internal party divisions and disputes culminated in the assassination of the country's prime minister, Maurice Bishop. The Reagan administration, seeing the opportunity to reduce Cuban influence in the Eastern Caribbean, subsequently invaded the island in the fall of 1983, ostensibly to "protect U.S. lives and property."

Changes in the Region's Insertion
in the International Economy

One of the most interesting aspects of the decade of the 1970s was that while progressive experiments—the majority aimed at securing self-sufficiency to meet the basic needs of the population—were taking place throughout the Caribbean, important changes were taking place in the world economy which would integrate the region more closely to the United States in the subsequent decade. These changes centered on the promotion of export-oriented manufacturing industries in the Caribbean. Moreover, U.S. investment shifted in content and locale from its previous concentration in oil and bauxite production (Netherlands Antilles, Trinidad-Tobago, and Jamaica) toward the booming financial centers of the region (the Bahamas and Bermuda) as well as the export-processing zones of Barbados, the Dominican Republic, and Haiti, all of which registered significant increases in the rate of growth of U.S. investment (see Table 2.7).

The emerging new international division of labor is spreading the different phases of manufacturing production across the globe, partially transferring the production of labor-intensive consumer goods for export to certain third world countries along with the assembling or processing of components or parts for export. Here it is useful to examine the specific model of industrial organization which is becoming generalized in the region, the *maquiladora*.

Between 1956 and 1963 the United States amended its tariff schedules to incorporate provisions appropriate to the restructuring of the international division of labor. Faced with increasing competition from Japan and Western Europe, the United States sought changes in tariff stipulations to favor relocating labor-intensive phases of manufacturing operations abroad. Two new items in the U.S. Tariff Code—806.30 and 807—reduced duties on imports with U.S. components assembled or processed abroad. This benefited U.S. multinational corporations because, as explained by U.S. industry representatives before the U.S. Tariff Commission Hearings on May 5, 1970, "[these items] improve the competitive position of the American industry by allowing a more efficient combination of factors of production through joint utilization of American capital and advanced skills with lesser skilled labor from less developed countries. . . . They preserve jobs in the U.S. in those very industries that otherwise would be even harder hit by foreign competition, thus allowing a more gradual adjustment to future trade patterns by industries that couldn't otherwise survive."[53]

The *maquiladora* model of industrial organization—assembly plants producing for export which operate as subsidiaries of multinational corporations under sections 806.30 and 807 of the U.S. Tariff Code— was institutionalized as a policy initiative under the Mexican Border Industrialization Program launched in 1965. The program was first proposed as a "twin plant" co-production system: U.S. firms would establish two plants under a single management, one on each side of the border. The U.S. plant would perform the capital-intensive operations and the factory on the Mexican side would take on the labor-intensive processes. The strategy targeted some of the industries where the United States was experiencing the toughest competition, such as semiconductors and textiles/apparel.

While the *maquiladora* model is closely identified with Mexican export-oriented industrialization and U.S. tariff concessions, in the decade of the 1970s an increasing number of Caribbean countries encouraged U.S. corporations to establish Caribbean subsidiaries, which consisted of assembly plants geared to the export market. As a model of industrial organization, this outward looking development strategy favors U.S. interests by facilitating the location of U.S. multinational corporations' processing facilities in low-wage areas, allowing them to maintain the competitive edge. Under such an arrangement there are no foreign aid obligations, as in the Alliance for Progress, or public transfer of funds, as in Operation Bootstrap.

In order to attract foreign investment, the countries of the Caribbean have had to provide extremely favorable conditions to U.S. capital, including, for example, exemption from local taxes for at least eight years (see Table 5.2). Most countries allow unrestricted profit repatriation and exempt imports from duties. In addition, most of the Caribbean countries vying for investment in new manufacturing industries have had to construct industrial parks that provide the complete infrastructure for manufacturing operations. Among those countries for which data is available, the Dominican Republic—which appears to have been the most successful in attracting foreign investment—offers the most favorable conditions.

Besides government incentives, the other major factor attracting new industries to the region are the low labor costs. For example, garment workers in the Dominican Free Trade Zones earn 47 cents an hour compared to $3.35 for their U.S. counterparts.[54] Once fringe benefits are taken into account, the wage gap between the Dominican Republic and Haiti—which have the lowest wages in the region—and Puerto Rico is on the order of seven to one (see Table 5.3). The high-wage countries of the region also include the Bahamas, Barbados, the Netherlands Antilles, and Trinidad-Tobago, the countries which have the higher per capita GDPs in the region.

As a result of low wages, government incentives, and the special tax treatment for U.S. assembly operations overseas, manufacturing exports from the Caribbean grew rapidly throughout the decade of the 1960s and 1970s. To take the example of Haiti, the number of companies engaged in assembly operations increased from 13 in 1966 to 154 in 1981. In the decade of the 1970s the total number of workers employed in this sector increased from 10,000 to 40,000.[55] Whereas in 1960 primary commodities constituted 100 percent of Haitian exports, by 1979 manufactured exports constituted 39 percent of the total. Similarly, in Jamaica manufactured exports increased from 5 percent of total exports in 1960 to 52 percent in 1979; in the Dominican Republic, they increased from 2 percent to 26 percent over this same period.[56] But the growth of this export-oriented manufacturing sector did little to assuage the high rates of unemployment in the region since the export-processing zones account for such a minimal proportion (less than 1 percent in Jamaica and 3 percent in the Dominican Republic)

Table 5.2
Investment Incentives in the Caribbean, 1986

	Free Trade Zones	Tax Holiday	Import Duty Exemption	Profit Repatriation	Double Tax Relief
Antigua-Barbuda	—	10–15 yrs.	on raw materials & machines	no restrictions	—
Aruba	1	10–11 yrs.	granted	—	granted
Belize	1 industrial park, another under construction	10–15 yrs.	on raw materials & machines for export production	no restrictions	granted
British Virgin Islands	—	10 yrs.	granted	no restrictions	granted
Dominica	planning export processing zone	10–15 yrs.	on raw materials & machines for export production	almost no restrictions	granted
Dominican Republic	4 export processing zones; 2 industrial parks under construction	8–20 yrs.	granted	no restrictions	granted
Grenada	industrial park under construction	10–15 yrs.	no restrictions if from CARICOM sources	no restrictions	granted
Haiti	yes[1]	5–20 yrs.	some restrictions	no restrictions	granted
Jamaica	2 export processing zones; 1 to begin operations	5–10 yrs.	granted	no restrictions	granted
Montserrat	—	10–15 yrs.	—	no restrictions	granted
St. Lucia	yes[1]	10–15 yrs.	—	some restrictions on nonresidents	granted
St. Vincent-Grenadines	1 industrial park, another planned	10–15 yrs.	granted	no restrictions	granted
Trinidad-Tobago	—	—	granted	no restrictions	granted

Source: Caribbean/Central American Action, Country Profiles (Washington, D.C.: C/CAA, 1986).

1) Number of free trade zones or export processing zones not reported
— Information not reported

Feature

Roselía

Roselía and her husband Lucien own a two-room apartment in Cité Soleil, a sprawling urban neighborhood in Port-au-Prince close to the industrial park. The two rooms are separated by a blanket hung between the walls. Beds in each of the rooms take up much of the available space. The front porch has been enclosed so it forms a room where food is stored, meals are cooked, and where Roselía sometimes works at her sewing machine. Their electricity comes from tapping into a neighbor's hookup. Appliances are turned on by connecting them to bare wires hanging from the ceiling.

The apartment, in a housing project built by the Catholic church, is also home to Roselía's two sisters, Delisme and Myrta. Roselía, Lucien, and Delisme all work in garment assembly factories. Myrta stays at home most of the day and does chores for Roselía.

Roselía was twelve years old when she left her parents' home in the mountains above Port-au-Prince and came to live with an aunt who owned a sewing school. She attended her aunt's school for free and helped with cleaning the house, doing laundry on Saturdays, and cooking the Sunday meal. Once she became competent at sewing she made clothes for her family and for her aunt's clients. For four years she worked for her aunt without pay because she was too young: "I was called a *ti moun*, I didn't need any money." The phrase *ti moun* means small child, but it also refers to child servants living in their relatives' households.

Roselía later took a free training course for industrial-type sewing offered by the Catholic Church's vocational center. The director of the center often tries to find jobs for graduates in the factories. Roselía did not finish the course and instead asked Lucien to "present" her at the place where he worked. Despite her skill in designing and making clothes, the factory job she got was low-skilled and required sewing the pockets and seams on pants.

Roselía continued to live with her aunt until 1983, when she married Lucien and they moved into the housing project. Roselía had a baby a year later, and at the time there were two of Lucien's cousins living in the house. She said the three men were of no help to her and she relied on a neighbor to take her to the hospital and help her with her chores after the baby was born. Roselía later asked her sister Delisme, who was still living at home, to come to Port-au-Prince and help with the baby.

(continues)

Soon after she arrived, Delisme started a sewing course in the evenings and began looking for work in the factories. She eventually bribed a guard to gain entrance into a job, obliging Rosella to hire a maid to help watch the baby. During the first year the baby became seriously ill and when he recovered, Rosella decided that he would be better off living in the mountains with her parents. Rosella now sees her son only on weekends when she makes the five-hour trip home. Some weekends she gives her parents money or brings clothes for the baby. Rosella says she will bring her son back to the city when he is old enough to go to school.

In 1984 Lucien got laid off from his job at the factory and did not work for almost a year. Rosella continued to work until 1985 when the factory where she worked temporarily closed. She received US$187 in severance pay, but it did not last very long; she had debts to pay off at the pawnshop and she bought some things for her son and gave some to Lucien for his expenses, though he had found another job by this time. Once the severance pay ran out, Rosella had to borrow money from the workers' retirement fund and she did a little marketing of food. She bought large quantities of rice or beans at the downtown market and resold it in her neighborhood at a higher price. She also sold fried food on the street.

To find another job, Rosella stood outside the gates at the industrial park, where there were always lots of people waiting for a job. After about two months a manager came to the gate and asked her if she could use a sewing machine. She passed a test and began sewing pants seams, at a wage of US$3 a day. Later she got paid by the piece, and now can make up to US$4 a day, but work has not been steady in recent years.

A typical day starts at 4:30 a.m., as she has to leave the house by 5:00. If she does not have the 15 cents for the bus, she might walk an hour to get to the factory. She starts work at 6:30 and gets a break at 11:30. Often she buys a small breakfast of corn meal or plantains for about 30 cents; for lunch she spends about 60 cents for beans and rice and a small piece of meat. She goes back to work at 12:00 and sews until 3:00, arriving back home at 4:00 p.m.

When Rosella gets home she starts preparing dinner, sometimes with the help of her sisters. Food is often shared, either with the next door neighbors or with the children who run in and out of the door. The woman who lives across the street reciprocates every so often by sending over plates of food large enough for Rosella's whole household. After everyone has eaten, Rosella cleans up and gets ready for her nightly literacy course at the vocational school. She is learning to read and write in Creole.

(continues)

On Saturdays, if the factory has an order, Rosella may go in for a half day, returning home in time to do the laundry. Saturday is a big laundry day, especially for women who work all week. The public water fountains in Cité Soleil are crowded on Saturdays and the wait can be twenty minutes or more. If Myrta is present, she will help get the water by waiting in line. Water is paid for at the fountain, about two cents a bucket for public water or more if drinking water is brought in by truck.

Saturday is also a market day, especially if Rosella has been paid. She takes the bus to the downtown market and buys beans and rice and cornmeal by the pound. On Sundays she goes to church in the morning and spends the afternoon preparing a large meal.

Rosella is lucky in many ways: she has a job and she does not have to support her family by herself. Still, her life is very hard, with little room for anything but work. Part of her literacy course includes discussions about family relations and Rosella openly talks about her subordinate position in the household:

Many young girls are like mules, they don't have a day of rest. I myself never get a day of rest. When my sister is not staying here, I must do everything, sweeping in the morning, getting water, going to market, cooking. I work like an animal, like a slave. A man, when he leaves work, he comes home, bathes, eats dinner, and then goes out. It is the system here. . . .
A house that doesn't have a woman is missing something. Little boys cannot do anything, if there is a little girl, they let the boy do what he wants, to go play with his friends. The little girl washes dishes, cleans the floor, makes the bed, dusts . . . it's housework they give to the girl.
A girl grows up the way you want them to, liking work in the home.

Source: Paul Monaghan, Center for Latin American Studies, University of Florida, based on interviews conducted in February 1987.

of the labor force. It has also done little to stem the tide of Caribbean-U.S. migration (see Table 3.7).

In sum, by the end of the 1970s the Caribbean was already well integrated into the new international division of labor which favored export-oriented industrialization at the behest of U.S. capital. This new international division of labor is based on the comparative advantage of cheaper labor in the Caribbean as compared to the United States, and is intimately tied to the industrial restructuring required by the U.S. economy in this period.

Notes

1. The analysis of U.S.-Caribbean relations draws on Peter Phillips, "US-Caribbean Relations in Historical Perspective," paper presented to the Caribbean

Table 5.3
Hourly Wages in the Caribbean, 1988 (in US$)[1]

Dominican Republic	.55
Haiti	.58
Grenada	.75
St. Lucia	.75
Dominica	.83
Belize	.85
Jamaica	.88
St. Kitts	.90
Montserrat	.92
St. Vincent	1.15
Antigua	1.25
Trinidad-Tobago	1.80
Netherlands Antilles	1.80
Bahamas	2.10
Barbados	2.10
Puerto Rico	4.28
U.S. Virgin Islands	4.50

Source: The Bobbin Consulting Group (Columbia, S.C.), 1988, pamphlet.

1) Hourly wages include fringe benefits; the data are for semi-skilled labor in export processing industries

Studies Association, May 1988, Guadaloupe. Maribel Aponte and Nikoi Kote-Nikoi also made substantial contributions to this chapter.

2. Kathy Sunshine, *The Caribbean: Survival, Struggle and Sovereignty* (Washington, D.C.: EPICA, 1985), pp. 31–32.

3. See Max Winkler, *Investments of United States Capital in Latin America* (Boston: World Peace Foundation, 1929), pp. 265, 222, and 271.

4. Ibid., pp. 3 and 264; Phillips, "U.S.-Caribbean Relations," p. 13.

5. Winkler, *Investments of U.S. Capital*, pp. 182, 196, 217, 264.

6. Sunshine, *The Caribbean*, p. 32.

7. Winkler, *Investments of U.S. Capital*, table XIII.

8. Clive Thomas, *The Poor and the Powerless: Economic Policy and Change in the Caribbean* (New York: Monthly Review Press, 1986), p. 40.

9. Phillips, "U.S.-Caribbean Relations," p. 16.

10. Robert Pastor, "Introduction, the Policy Challenge," in Robert Pastor, ed., *Migration and Development in the Caribbean* (Boulder: Westview Press, 1985), table 1.2.

11. GATT was based on two principles: (1) trade was to be organized on a multilateral basis rather than on regions or currency blocs (typically during the interwar period these had tied a colony or neo-colony to the 'mother country') and (2) tariffs, quotas, and other direct barriers to trade were to be minimized. The leading effort in the area of international finance was the Bretton Woods Agreement, which established the dollar as the key international currency and created the complementary financial institutions of the IMF and the World Bank. The IMF was to deal with short-term balance of payments

assistance, and the World Bank was charged with long-term development aid. Both helped channel credit to nations which complied with free-trade policies.

12. The most important of these were the Foreign Military Sales Program (FMS) and the Military Assistance Program (MAP). Whereas the MAP consisted of grants of military equipment and services to friendly nations, the FMS comprised sales of major military equipment and services by the U.S. government for cash or credit. In addition, tens of thousands of Latin American officers and enlisted personnel were trained under various programs, and the U.S. established the practice of conducting joint training exercises with Latin American militaries.

13. See Lars Schoultz, *National Security and U.S. Policy in Latin America* (Princeton, NJ: Princeton University Press, 1987), pp. 163–79; NACLA, *Report on the Americas* (July/August 1985).

14. Claes Brundenius, *Revolutionary Cuba: the Challenge of Economic Growth with Equity* (Boulder: Westview Press, 1984), p. 41.

15. See Center for Cuban Studies, *Cuba in Focus: the U.S. Blockage—a Documentary History* (New York: Center for Cuban Studies, 1979), p. 312.

16. Agency for International Development, *U.S. Overseas Loans and Grants and Assistance from International Organizations, Obligations and Loan Authorizations, July 1, 1945–September 30, 1986* (Washington D.C.: AID, 1982), various tables.

17. José A. Moreno, *El Pueblo en Armas* (Madrid: Ed. Tecnos, 1973), p. 40.

18. James L. Dietz, *Economic History of Puerto Rico* (Princeton, NJ: Princeton University Press, 1986), p. 301.

19. Emilio Pantojas-García, "The U.S. Caribbean Basin Initiative and the Puerto Rican Experience," *Latin American Perspectives* 12, no. 4 (1985), p. 117.

20. Carmen Gautier Mayoral, "La Economía Puertorriqueña en los 1990: Modelo para el Caribe?" paper presented to the Caribbean Studies Association Meetings, Guadaloupe, May 1988, p. 3.

21. Pantojas-García, "The U.S. Caribbean Basin Initiation," p. 118.

22. Ibid., p. 119.

23. W. Arthur Lewis is usually credited with having convinced West Indian planners to adopt "industrialization by invitation" policies. His proposal, as laid out in "The Industrialization of the British West Indies," *Caribbean Economic Review* 11 (1950), was quite different, however, than the model of import-substitution industrialization which subsequently resulted. For one, he envisioned industrialization to be based on the natural resources of the islands, thus fostering linkages with the rest of the economy, particularly agriculture, and based on labor-intensive production processes, given the abundance of low-waged labor. He also considered that import-substitution could proceed only on a regional basis, given small market size, and that export-promotion would have to be the mainstay of the program.

24. See Michael Kaufman, *Jamaica Under Manley, Dilemmas of Socialism and Democracy* (London: Zed Books, 1985), p. 15, and Thomas, *The Poor and the Powerless*, ch. 5.

25. S. de Castro, "Tax Holidays for Industry: Why we have to abolish them and how to do it," *New World Pamphlet*, no. 8 (Kingston), 1973, p. 5.

26. Sidney E. Chernick, *The Commonwealth Caribbean: the Integration Experience* (Baltimore: The Johns Hopkins Press for the World Bank, 1978), p. 181.

27. Following the short-lived attempt at a West Indies Federation, Antigua, Barbados, and Guyana created the Caribbean Free Trade Association (CARIFTA) in 1965; it was subsequently joined by eight more members of the English-speaking Caribbean in 1968. In the same year, Dominica, Grenada, Montserrat and St. Lucia formed the Eastern Caribbean Common Market (ECM) in which they were later joined by St. Vincent (1979), St. Kitts-Nevis (1980), and Antigua (1981). The ECM became the Organization of Eastern Caribbean States (OECS) in 1981. CARIFTA was replaced in 1973 by the CARICOM which Belize and the Bahamas also joined.

28. See William G. Demas, *The Economics of Development in Small Countries with Special Reference to the Caribbean* (Montreal: McGill University Press, 1965) for the arguments supporting regional integration and a regional strategy of import substitution industrialization.

29. ECLA, "The Impact of the Caribbean Free Trade Association (CARIFTA)," *Economic Bulletin of Latin America* 18 (1973), p. 144.

30. Inter-American Development Bank, *Economic and Social Progress in Latin America, 1980–1981* (Washington, DC: IDB, 1981).

31. World Bank, *World Development Report 1982* (New York: Oxford University Press, 1982), tables 2 and 3.

32. Phillips, "U.S. Caribbean Relations," p. 23.

33. Drawn from Trevor Harker, "Caribbean Economic Performance: an overview," paper presented to the Second Conference of Caribbean Economists, Barbados, May 1989, table 2.

34. Clive Thomas, *The Poor and the Powerless*, pp. 127–28.

35. Jorge Rodríguez Beruff, *Política militár y dominación: Puerto Rico en el Contexto Latinoamericano* (Rio Piedras: Ed. Huracán, 1988).

36. Michael Kaufman, *Jamaica Under Manley*, p. 76.

37. Ibid., p. 106.

38. Ibid., p. 119.

39. Ibid., p. 87.

40. Ibid., pp.135–36.

41. Thomas, *The Poor and the Powerless*, pp. 310–11.

42. Ibid., pp. 311–12.

43. Ibid., p. 312.

44. The most influential of the critiques of the integration movement was Havelock Brewster and Clive Thomas, *The Dynamics of West Indian Integration* (Kingston: University of the West Indies, 1967).

45. Caribbean Development Bank, *Annual Report, 1975* (Bridgetown, Barbados: CDB, 1976), p. 16.

46. CARICOM, *The Caribbean Community in the 1980s*, Report of the Group of Experts (Guyana: CARICOM Secretariat, 1981).

47. Sunshine, *The Caribbean*, p. 96.

48. Ibid., p. 97.

49. Ibid., p. 98.

50. See Marcia Rivera, *DOSSIER Granada*, no. 2 (San Juan: Proyecto Caribeño de Justicia y Paz, 1984), p. 2.

51. P. Korner, et. al., *The IMF and the Debt Crisis: A Guide to the Third World's Dilemmas* (London: Zed Books, 1986).

52. *CBI Business Bulletin* (July 1989), p. 2.

53. June Nash, and Maria Patricia Fernandez Kelly, *Women, Men and the International Division of Labor* (New York: SUNY Press, 1983), p. 241.

54. CIPAF, *Quehaceres*, no. 5 (May 1988), p. 2.

55. Josh DeWind and David Kinley III, *Aiding Migration: the Impact of International Development Assistance on Haiti* (Boulder: Westview Press, 1988), pp. 108–9.

56. World Bank, *World Development Report 1982*, tables 2, 3, and 9.

CHAPTER 6

The Caribbean Basin Initiative

THE CARIBBEAN BASIN INITIATIVE (CBI) was first unveiled by President Reagan on February 24, 1982, in an address before the Organization of American States (OAS). Pledging that the United States would do whatever is necessary to prevent the overthrow of the region's governments, Reagan proposed a broad plan of trade and investment incentives designed to "improve the economic well being of the Caribbean area."[1] This plan represented the economic component of U.S. policy toward the region and would later be signed into law as the Caribbean Basin Economic Recovery Act (CBERA).

President Reagan's proposal was met by diverging reactions among different labor organizations, corporate groups, and government institutions. After a prolonged consultative process, and a heated debate in Congress, a scaled down version of the initial proposal was signed into law on August 5, 1983. As originally proposed by the administration, the CBI had three components—trade, development assistance, and investment incentives. More specifically, the CBI would (1) allow the president to proclaim duty-free treatment for eligible items from designated beneficiary countries of the Caribbean Basin (i.e., the Caribbean and Central America) for a twelve-year period; (2) provide $350 million in supplemental developmental assistance to key countries in the region to meet balance of payments shortfalls or as emergency aid; and (3) create an investment tax credit of 10 percent for U.S. businesses investing in the Caribbean Basin.

The investment tax credit was never seriously considered in Congress since it was unpopular with labor groups as well as Members of Congress who feared job flight from their districts. Moreover, many expressed concern about reducing federal tax revenue in a period of growing

U.S. fiscal deficits.[2] As a result, the administration instead proposed a relatively insignificant tax deduction for business conventions held in the Caribbean. The CBERA legislation which took effect on January 1, 1984, thus focused on duty-free access for selected Caribbean exports and a once and for all increase in development aid.

The Reagan and Bush administrations both tend to use the term "CBI" to encompass a much broader range of programs which operate in the Caribbean Basin, including on-going bilateral and multilateral aid programs, Export-Import Bank and Private Investment Corporation loans, loan guarantees and insurance, and services of the U.S. Departments of Agriculture and Commerce that promote trade and investment. In addition, many of the numerous proposals that grew out of the 1984 Kissinger Commission study on Central America were incorporated in the Reagan administration's initiatives toward the Basin.[3] The CBI is thus a constantly evolving package of programs intended to augment trade and capital flows between the United States and the Caribbean Basin. Most people, however, equate the CBI with the CBERA, because it was for the trade and aid aspects of the initiative that the Reagan administration had to request legislative approval. Much more than a single piece of legislation, the CBI is a broad policy directive which is bringing to bear the weight of the U.S. government on the economies of the region.[4]

Strategies Behind the CBI

Most observers agree that the Caribbean Basin Initiative was designed to implement the Reagan administration's strategy of ensuring "security through development" in what it considered to be its private sea. U.S. policy-makers began to focus attention on the Caribbean Basin with the success of the Sandinista revolution in Nicaragua and that of the New Jewel Movement in Grenada, both in 1979. The subsequent growth of the revolutionary movements in El Salvador and Guatemala, combined with the collapse in economic growth rates throughout the region, made it increasingly apparent that defusing the perceived security threat had to be tied to improvements in the region's economic situation.[5]

Critics, however, initially saw the economically oriented CBI as a smokescreen for U.S. military escalation in the region, serving to divert attention from the primary goals of "containing communism" and maintaining U.S. allies in power.[6] They asked how $350 million and the mere opening of the U.S. market were to solve the economic problems of the region. Furthermore, the lion's share of the economic assistance was targeted to Central America, particularly El Salvador.[7]

The premise behind the economic components of the CBI is the alleged promise of laissez faire, that more open economies and increased trade will spur economic growth in the region. The strategy assumed that the opening up of the U.S. market would spur investment in the region, generating more employment and higher incomes while expanding trade. Increased trade, it was hoped, would enhance foreign exchange generation, allowing those countries in the region facing an external debt crisis to meet their debt-service commitments.

Whether this laissez-faire model has the potential for economic development in the Caribbean, and is one which will solve the economic crisis, has been the source of considerable controversy. Critics contend that rather than promoting Caribbean development, the CBI is geared toward restructuring U.S.-Caribbean economic relations, integrating the region more closely to the United States, while improving the international competitive position of U.S. industries facing deteriorating world market shares.

Regardless of how one answers the question of to what extent a strategy focused on export diversification can solve the region's economic problems (a question we will examine below), it is undeniably true that the strategy is premised on considerable benefits to U.S. capital. The CBERA attempts both to stimulate exports in Caribbean Basin countries, thus generating foreign exchange to meet debt-service payments, and encourage greater imports from the United States, thus ensuring sales in an era when the United States no longer dominates world markets or holds merchandise trade surpluses. The decision to confront the debt crisis with a strategy linked to new trade agreements came from an understanding that not only borrowers but also creditors were caught in the debt trap.

As a trade strategy, the CBI offers U.S. multinationals several advantages over the special tariff programs already in existence, namely, the Generalized System of Preferences (GSP), which authorizes the president to grant duty-free treatment to eligible products from third world countries for a period of ten years, and sections 806.3 and 807 of the Special Tariff Provisions, which provide special duty treatment for imports containing U.S. components. The rules of origin provisions are more flexible under the CBERA. While the CBERA, like the GSP, requires that the sum of the cost or value of materials produced in beneficiary countries, plus the direct costs of processing operations performed in beneficiary countries, be not less than 35 percent of the appraised value of the article, unlike the GSP, it stipulates that up to 15 percent of these requirements can also come from U.S. materials. This in effect lowers the real requirements to only 20 percent of the appraised value of the article.

Also, to satisfy the 35 percent requirement, CBERA rules permit the cumulation of materials and direct costs of processing from any combination of beneficiary countries and from Puerto Rico and the Virgin Islands; the GSP allows cumulation only among an association of countries that qualify either as a free-trade area or as a customs union. Under the CBERA, an article is allowed to pass through other beneficiary countries without losing its status of origin denomination.

In addition, those 806.30 and 807 articles which became eligible under the CBERA, and which meet value-added requirements, now enter duty free under the CBERA, instead of having to pay duties upon the value of the processing done abroad. This benefits U.S. assembly operations in the Caribbean (electronics, pharmaceuticals, and hospital equipment in particular) by giving them cost advantages over Asian producers who compete in the U.S. market. It also makes Caribbean assembly operations more profitable than those carried out in Mexico or elsewhere in Latin America.

The eligibility criteria to qualify as a CBI beneficiary are also designed to create privileged access for U.S. capital to the markets of the Caribbean. By law, a country is excluded from beneficiary status if it provides preferential treatment to products of other developed countries that are likely to have a significant adverse effect on U.S. trade; if it has nationalized, expropriated, or otherwise seized U.S.-owned property; and if it fails to cooperate with the U.S. government in narcotics control. Other beneficiary criteria, left to presidential discretion, include whether a country agrees to provide equitable and reasonable access to its markets and basic resources to the United States; the degree to which a beneficiary country uses export subsidies or imposes export performance requirements or local content requirements that could distort international trade; and the degree to which workers' rights are protected.[8]

Of the twenty-eight potentially eligible countries in the area designated as the Caribbean Basin—which explicitly excludes Cuba—five remain classified as "nondesignated": Nicaragua, Suriname, the Cayman Islands, the Turks and Caicos Islands, and Anguilla. During 1988 Panama became the first country to lose beneficiary status because of its failure to cooperate with U.S. drug control efforts (a status it regained after the U.S. invasion in December 1989), and Guyana was granted CBI beneficiary status because of a shift toward more conservative policies by a new government.[9]

Trade, investment, and financial assistance under the CBI should be viewed as a complement to a broader set of macroeconomic and financial strategies implemented by an array of U.S. and international agencies, including the Agency for International Development (AID), the International Monetary Fund (IMF), and the World Bank. CBI policies are explicitly or implicitly designed to support and promote other U.S. policy goals in the region. One of the most important goals under both the Reagan and Bush administrations has been to shift AID's funding from public-sector projects to the promotion of private-sector or "market" activity. Financial assistance has been linked to compliance with IMF stabilization policies and structural adjustment reform efforts geared to repay the external debt. Thus, to impose an export-oriented growth model in the region, the United States has conditioned direct or indirect financial assistance to comply with a reform package that includes exchange rate adjustment, privatization of government services, wage controls, elimination of energy or food subsidies, and rescheduling of the debt, among other conditions. In order to impose a broader set of policy objectives on Caribbean countries, the United States has shifted from channeling aid through regional organizations to bilateral agreements.[10]

The CBI may also be viewed as part of the U.S. government's strategy to restore the military and economic foundations of U.S. superiority which eroded in the 1970s by incorporating the Caribbean Basin countries into the U.S. military-industrial complex. It is hoped that the CBI will improve the competitive position of the U.S. defense industry by encouraging U.S. contractors to take advantage of lower labor costs in the Caribbean. In sum, the CBI incarnates a strategy to attain U.S. economic and military superiority within the new set of circumstances which have characterized the 1980s, and are expected to continue in the 1990s.

Before analyzing the accomplishments of the Caribbean Basin Initiative, it is useful to consider its potential scope and benefit to the region. Both are quite limited, in part because the CBERA legislation was diluted considerably by Congress. As already mentioned, the investment tax incentive was eliminated, leaving no direct mechanism to stimulate investment in the region. And perhaps more importantly, a number of trade exclusions were included in or added to the legislation, thereby excluding some of the more important Caribbean export products from the potential benefits of free trade.

The product exclusions in the legislation include textiles and apparel (which since 1975 are subject to quotas), selected leather products and footwear, canned tuna, and petroleum and petroleum derivatives. In 1983 crude petroleum and petroleum products were the leading export from the Caribbean Basin to the U.S. market, while textiles and apparel were the second leading manufactured item (see Table 6.1).

The potential for new export promotion was also limited by the fact that the CBERA overlapped with a number of already existing programs

Table 6.1
Leading U.S. Imports from CBERA-Designated Countries, 1983–88[1] (in US$)

	1983	1984	1985	1986	1987	1988	1983–88, %
Agricultural							
Coffee & Cocoa	574,303	671,241	706,350	1,066,839	669,881	456,080	
Sugar, Syrup & Molasses	400,490	426,763	262,994	205,591	113,834	150,348	
Bananas	361,749	368,033	423,483	398,819	467,723	467,990	
Beef & Veal	105,770	90,053	105,926	128,488	124,979	133,748	
Shellfish	170,496	195,997	206,799	251,683	253,520	249,772	
Subtotal	1,612,808	1,752,087	1,705,552	2,051,420	1,629,937	1,457,938	(−9.6)
Annual Percent Growth		(8.6)	(−2.7)	(20.8)	(−20.5)	(−10.6)	
Minerals & Derivatives							
Petroleum & Petroleum Products	4,453,147	3,900,048	2,252,238	1,354,854	1,348,859	1,038,034	
Bauxite & Alumina	97,413	277,785	117,347	103,955	124,156	150,564	
Ferronickel	—[2]	36,444	40,292	21,433	32,390	59,938	
Silver & Gold	118,982	182,931	128,752	116,193	117,515	98,819	
Subtotal	4,669,542	4,397,208	2,538,629	1,596,435	1,622,920	1,347,355	(−71.1)
Annual Percent Growth		(−5.8)	(−42.3)	(−37.1)	(1.6)	(−17.0)	

Manufactures

Garments	100,048 [3]	95,311 [3]	204,099	470,485	639,176	821,684	
Electrical Machinery	79,318	94,026	66,194	67,666	89,729	114,793	
Chemicals & Pharmaceuticals	168,554	181,498	149,553	176,815	134,937	122,633	
Leather Products	27,433	41,332	39,771	35,098	55,682	63,096	
Methyl Alcohol	—[2]	5,241	19,145	10,208	15,892	41,188	
US Goods Returned	183,053	114,816	106,330	95,844	85,217	108,960	
Subtotal	558,406	532,224	585,092	856,116	1,020,633	1,272,354	
Annual Percent Growth		(-4.7)	(9.9)	(46.3)	(19.2)	(24.7)	(127.9)
Total, Items Shown	6,840,756	6,681,519	4,829,273	4,503,971	4,273,490	4,077,647	
Annual Percent Growth		(-2.3)	(-27.7)	(-6.7)	(-5.1)	(-4.6)	(-40.4)
Total, All Commodities	8,763,900	8,649,235	6,687,226	6,064,745	6,039,030	6,061,054	
Annual Percent Growth		(-0.1)	(-22.7)	(-9.3)	(-0.4)	(0.4)	(-30.8)

Sources: U.S. International Trade Commission, *Annual Report on the Impact of the Caribbean Basin Recovery Act on U.S. Industries and Consumers, Fourth Report, 1988* (Washington, D.C.: USITC, 1989), table 1-5; data for 1983 are drawn from the *Second Report* (1986), table 7.

1) Based on thirty leading TSUS items only, in 1988
2) Not reported in top thirty in 1983
3) The TSUS numbers for apparel were revised in September 1985. Comparable data for 1983–84 are not available.

which provided duty-free treatment, such as the GSP and tariff provisions under sections 806.3 and 807. Moreover, a number of other Caribbean products enter the United States duty free because they do not compete with U.S. industries. Of the fifteen leading product categories from the region, accounting for over 70 percent of trade with the United States, only four categories were awarded some new exception from tariffs and only one, beef, was granted full duty-free access.[11]

The level of existing tariffs on these products had been quite low, on the order of 2.6 percent in 1983, making the potential benefit from the duty-free provisions also quite low. Nonetheless, several items became duty free under the CBERA which had tariffs of over 20 percent: ethanol, avocados, fruit juice, melons, rum, strap tobacco, and glassware.[12]

Estimates of the share of the region's exports which were granted *new* duty-free access through CBERA range from 7 percent to 10 percent.[13] The direct beneficiaries of this modest increase in trade will be U.S. multinational corporations operating in the Caribbean, for seven of the twelve leading products on which tariffs are eliminated are ones where U.S. offshore producers supply the bulk of the category to U.S. markets.[14]

The main reason that the potential benefits of the CBERA are limited is that those Caribbean export products with the greatest potential for growth were excluded under the legislation. Had textiles and apparel, for example, been included in the CBERA, it is estimated that the trade-related benefits to the region would have increased by 285 percent.[15] The forgone benefits are of this magnitude primarily because these industries are subject to relatively high tariffs (around 25 percent) as well as quotas. Thus the value of these exclusions is approximately comparable to all nonsugar trade eligible for the free-trade privileges of the CBI (around $400 million).

In partial recognition of the export potential of the Caribbean garment industry, President Reagan, during his visit to Grenada in February 1986, announced a "special access program" which increased quotas for certain apparel imports from CBI-designated countries. The program, referred to as 807-A, is applicable only to garment items assembled in the region which are cut in the United States from the U.S.-formed fabric. Bilateral agreements will determine the guaranteed access levels (GALS) which CBI beneficiaries can aspire to, independent of the normal quotas applicable to other textiles and garments under section 807 of the Special Tariff Provisions.[16] Products entering the United States under 807-A, just as under 807, continue to pay duty on the Caribbean value-added component. As of 1989 only five Caribbean Basin countries had signed bilateral agreements to take advantage of this benefit: the Dominican Republic, Haiti, Jamaica, Trinidad-Tobago, and Costa Rica.[17]

Perhaps most damaging for the potential developmental impact of the CBERA have been recent changes in U.S. sugar policy. Between 1934 and 1974 the United States set quotas on sugar imports to protect the domestic industry; these had been discontinued in the 1975–81 period due to the high prices prevailing in the international market. The Agriculture and Food Act of 1981 mandated that sugar prices be supported each year at minimum specified levels. As a result, when sugar prices started to plummet, the Reagan administration reimposed an import quota system in May of 1982 to maintain domestic prices high. Subsequently, the 1985 Food Security Act required the sugar program to be administered at no cost to the U.S. Treasury.[18] U.S. imports of sugar have been reduced from approximately 5 million short tons in 1980–81 to 1 million tons in 1987.[19]

The sugar import quota for all Caribbean Basin countries was reduced from an average annual 1.6 million tons in 1979–81 to 268,000 tons in December 1987. Quota reductions of 78 percent since the CBERA went into effect have cut potential sugar export earnings of the Caribbean Basin in the 1984–88 period by approximately $500 million.[20] The Dominican Republic, which accounts for 46 percent of the quota allotted to CBI countries, lost $210 million in potential earnings between 1984 and 1987.[21] Six sugar mills have been closed, contributing to growing unemployment on the island. Guyana, Trinidad-Tobago, Barbados, and Belize are among the other Caribbean countries particularly suffering from the changes in U.S. sugar policy. By 1990 it is estimated that 120,000 jobs will be lost in the Caribbean Basin as a result of diminishing U.S. sugar import quotas.

It is projected that by 1991—when the current U.S. farm bill expires—the United States could eliminate imports of sugar altogether and become a net exporter; currently, sugar imports constitute less than 5 percent of the U.S. market as a result of the steady expansion of domestic production in response to sugar price supports and the restricted market.

The Impact of CBERA

According to the Fourth Annual Report on the Impact of the Caribbean Basin Economic Recovery Act, the Caribbean Basin in 1983 accounted for 3.5 percent of U.S. imports from the rest of the world; by 1988 this figure had declined to 1.4 percent.[22] U.S. imports from CBERA-designated beneficiaries declined 31 percent between 1983 and 1988, from $8.8 billion to $6.1 billion (see Table 6.1).[23] The value of imports from the

162

Feature

Lomé, CARIBCAN, and CBI Compared

Europe's Lomé Convention and Canada's CARIBCAN program are two trade packages that, like the CBERA legislation of the Caribbean Basin Initiative, promise to spur economic development in the region by fostering increased economic integration of the Caribbean to larger and more industrialized economies. The Lomé Convention preceded both the CBI and CARIBCAN. It originated in the late 1950s as many of the colonies of the European Economic Community (EEC) achieved independence; when Britain joined the EEC, its former colonies joined in forming the African, Caribbean, and Pacific (ACP) country-grouping, which now includes sixty-six countries. Conventions have been signed in 1975, in 1980, and, what is known as Lomé III, in 1985.

The main trade provision of Lomé III is for duty-free access of ACP exports to European markets, covering 99.5 percent of ACP exports. About three-quarters of ACP exports would enter the EEC duty free anyway under Most Favored Nation terms. Where Lomé offers Caribbean producers an important degree of preference over other potential suppliers is with respect to exports of bananas, sugar, and coffee. The banana market, for example, is organized on a national basis, following colonial patterns; some 99 percent of the exports of the Caribbean Community and Common Market (CARICOM) countries go to the United Kingdom, which can only grant import licenses for non-Caribbean fruit if national demand exceeds the supply from this area. The sugar protocol provides a global quota of 1.3 million tons at guaranteed prices (the equivalent of the average price paid to European sugar beet producers), which is subsequently divided among beneficiary states. Among the CARICOM countries benefiting from this provision are Barbados, Belize, Guyana, Jamaica, St. Kitts, and Trinidad-Tobago. Finally, Lomé provides favorable treatment for Caribbean apparel exports, which are not subject to the Multifiber Arrangement, the understanding under the General Agreement on Tariffs and Trade (GATT) which allows the advanced, industrialized nations to use quotas to regulate the level of their imports of textiles and apparel. Thus, with respect to both traditional agricultural exports and new manufacturing exports, the terms granted by the EEC to the English-speaking Caribbean countries are more favorable than the limited duty-free provisions of the U.S.-CBERA.

Perhaps the most novel aspects of the Lomé Convention are the trade and aid arrangements known as Stabex and Sysmin. Stabex provides partial compensation for shortfalls in export earnings for certain commodities: the product must represent 6 percent of a country's exports to the EEC and their earnings from a given export must fall by at least

(continues)

6 percent before compensation is paid. In recent years, drawings on Stabex have been made by Jamaica, St. Lucia, and St. Vincent for bananas, and by Grenada for nutmeg, cocoa, and banana production.

Sysmin provides assistance to ACP countries when there has been a sharp drop in the capacity to export "hard" commodities, such as bauxite, tin, and other minerals. Unlike Stabex, funds are not made available automatically when earnings fall below historic levels, but rather, a country must apply for assistance. The aid provided is to be used to diversify exports or to rehabilitate the afflicted sector. Although Stabex and Sysmin have been criticized as being of limited impact in cushioning third world export earnings against the vacillations of the international market, they are certainly an important step in the right direction, a direction which the U.S. government has refused to even discuss.

CARIBCAN was initiated by Canada in 1986 and provides for one-way duty-free trade for many products from the English-speaking Caribbean for an unlimited period of time. As is the case with the U.S. CBERA, a certain number of key products (textiles and apparel, footwear, leather) are exempted from duty-free trade. Before CARIBCAN came into existence it was estimated that 93 percent of the Commonwealth Caribbean's exports to Canada entered duty free; with CARIBCAN this figure has risen to 99.7 percent. Canadian trade policy and CARIBCAN thus appear to be more favorable to Caribbean exports than U.S. trade policy and the CBERA. CARIBCAN also provided for increased development assistance to the region, with total Canadian aid doubling from $28.5 million in 1982 to $57 million in 1987; even at this higher level Canadian assistance is only about one-quarter of the level of U.S. development assistance to the Caribbean islands.

Between 1980 and 1986, nonfuel imports by the United States, the EEC, and Canada grew by an average 5.2 percent per year. Although imports from all less-developed countries to these three areas grew by 6 percent, those from the fifteen Caribbean countries grouped in the Caribbean Group for Cooperation in Economic Development (CGCED) grew by only 1.4 percent. Only in the case of Canada did the growth of imports from the Caribbean (9.6 percent annually) exceed the growth of imports from all countries. Most of this growth in imports is attributable to the expansion of alumina exports from Jamaica. Overall, primary exports from the Caribbean to the United States, the EEC, and Canada decreased by 4.5 percent a year, while manufacturing exports grew by 11.1 percent annually. As a result, there was a significant change in the composition of Caribbean exports to these three areas, with manufacturing increasing from 22 percent of total exports in 1983 to 40 percent in 1986.

(continues)

Between 1983 and 1986 the Canadian and EEC markets became more important to the Caribbean, although the United States continues to be the primary market for Caribbean exports. In 1983, the United States imported 79 percent of total Caribbean (CGCED) exports, the EEC imported 18 percent, and Canada imported 3 percent. By 1986 the U.S. share had fallen to 73 percent, while that of the EEC increased to 23 percent and that of Canada to 5 percent. Caribbean exports of manufacturing goods are even more concentrated on the U.S. market, with the United States importing 84 percent of Caribbean manufacturing exports in 1983 and 85 percent in 1986.

In the 1980s most Caribbean economies are more highly integrated to the U.S. economy than in the 1960s (see Table 6.6). The most drastic change was in the trading pattern of Barbados, which had directed only 7 percent of its exports to the U.S. market in the early 1960s compared with 53 percent two decades later; similar growth took place in terms of Barbadan imports from the United States. Overall, however, Caribbean exports rather than imports tend to be more closely tied to the U.S. economy.

Sources: World Bank, *Caribbean Exports: Preferential Markets and Performance* (Washington, D.C.: IBRD, 1988); and Clive Thomas, *The Poor and the Powerless* (New York: Monthly Review Press, 1988), pp. 341–42.

region only increased slightly in 1988 because an additional country (Guyana) is now included among the beneficiaries.

The sharp decline in U.S. imports from the region largely reflects the fate of two product categories: petroleum and its derivatives and sugar. Between 1983 and 1986 the value of imports of crude petroleum and petroleum products decreased by 70 percent, and sugar, syrups, and molasses by 49 percent. The value of imported petroleum from the Caribbean stabilized between 1986 and 1987, in turn stabilizing total imports from CBERA beneficiaries, given the weight of petroleum imports in the total import package. During 1988, however, petroleum imports again fell, by 23 percent. Sugar imports have declined precipitously, by 63 percent between 1983 and 1988.[24]

Significant changes have taken place among CBERA beneficiaries with respect to their share of exports to the U.S. market (see Tables 6.2 and 6.3). Hardest hit have been the oil-refining countries—the Netherlands Antilles, Trinidad-Tobago, and the Bahamas—with their share of exports dropping from 60 percent of the total in 1983 to 23 percent in 1988. In relative terms, the Central Caribbean countries (Belize, the Dominican Republic, Jamaica, Haiti) have gained the most, followed by Central America. The CBERA has had a negligible effect on the share of trade from the Eastern Caribbean. In absolute terms,

Table 6.2
U.S. Imports from CBERA-Designated Countries, 1983–88 (in US$ thousands)

	1983	1984	1985	1986	1987	1988
Antigua	8,809	7,898	24,695	11,849	8,621	6,893
Aruba[1]	—	—	—	1,797	2,452	647
Bahamas	1,676,394	1,154,282	626,084	440,985	377,881	268,328
Barbados	202,047	252,598	202,194	108,991	59,110	51,413
Belize	27,315	42,843	46,951	50,181	42,906	52,049
British Virgin Islands	880	1,335	11,902	5,904	11,162	684
Costa Rica	86,520	468,633	489,294	646,508	670,953	777,797
Dominica	242	86	14,161	15,185	10,307	8,530
Dominican Republic	806,520	994,427	965,847	1,058,927	1,144,211	1,425,371
El Salvador	58,898	381,391	395,658	371,761	272,881	282,584
Grenada	211	766	1,309	2,987	3,632	7,349
Guatemala	74,692	446,267	399,617	614,708	487,308	436,979
Guyana[2]	—	—	—	—	—	50,432
Haiti	337,483	377,413	386,697	368,369	393,660	382,466
Honduras	364,742	393,769	370,219	430,906	483,096	439,504
Jamaica	262,360	396,949	267,016	297,891	393,912	440,934
Montserrat	924	989	3,620	3,472	2,413	2,393
Netherlands Antilles[1]	2,274,510	2,024,367	793,162	453,330	478,836	408,100
Panama[3]	336,086	311,627	393,605	352,206	342,700	256,046
St. Kitts-Nevis[4]	18,758	23,135	16,258	22,278	23,793	20,822
St. Lucia	4,700	7,397	13,796	12,269	17,866	26,044
St. Vincent-Grenadines	4,276	2,958	9,643	7,836	8,493	13,950
Trinidad-Tobago	1,317,534	1,360,106	1,255,498	786,405	802,838	701,738
Total	8,763,900	8,649,235	6,687,226	6,064,745	6,039,030	6,061,054

Source: U.S. International Trade Commission, Annual Report on the Impact of the Caribbean Basin Economic Recovery Act on U.S. Industries and Consumers, Fourth Report, 1988 (Washington, D.C.: USTIC, 1989), table 1.3.

1) Aruba's designation as a CBERA beneficiary became effective on January 1, 1986. For statistical purposes, Aruba had been treated as part of the Netherlands Antilles until separate data became available.
2) Guyana was not designated a beneficiary until November 24, 1988.
3) Panama lost its designation as a beneficiary on April 19, 1988, but then regained it in December 1989.
4) Anguilla, which has not been designated as a beneficiary country, had been included with the data for St. Kitts-Nevis through 1985.

Table 6.3
U.S. Imports from CBERA-Designated Countries by Subregional Groups, 1983–88
(percentages)

	1983	1984	1985	1986	1987	1988
Eastern Caribbean	2.7	3.4	4.5	3.2	2.4	3.1
Central Caribbean[1]	16.4	21.0	24.9	29.3	32.7	38.0
Oil-Refining Countries[2]	60.1	52.5	40.0	27.7	27.5	22.8
Central America	20.8	23.1	30.6	39.8	37.4	36.2
Total	100.0	100.0	100.0	100.0	100.0	100.0

Source: Calculated form U.S. International Trade Commission, Annual Report on the Impact of the Caribbean Basin Economic Recovery Act on U.S. Industries and Consumers, Third Report 1987 (Washington, D.C.: USTIC, 1988), table 1.5, and for 1988, derived from data in Table 6.2.

1) Central Caribbean here includes Belize, Dominican Republic, Haiti and Jamaica
2) Oil-refining countries include Aruba, the Bahamas, the Netherlands Antilles, and Trinidad-Tobago

however, the growth in trade for a number of the Eastern Caribbean Islands has been impressive, more than doubling for Dominica, Grenada, Montserrat, St. Lucia, and St. Vincent (see Table 6.2). But the magnitude of exports from these islands is dwarfed by the magnitude of trade from the Central Caribbean, particularly the Dominican Republic, where exports also grew healthily, by 12.8 percent a year between 1983 and 1988. In Haiti and Jamaica, the growth in trade was more modest and fluctuated greatly, while Barbados suffered a significant reduction in trade due to the decline of its electronics industry.

An approximation of the degree of economic restructuring which has been induced under the CBI can be gleaned from Table 6.1. The data show that traditional agricultural exports are on the decline, falling 10 percent between 1983 and 1988. Only coffee demonstrated consistent growth until 1986; in 1987 and 1988, however, the value of coffee exports fell precipitously due to a decline in prices. Beef and veal are the only traditional agricultural products to be granted new duty-free treatment under CBERA, and since 1985 are one of the leading Caribbean exports under CBERA provisions.[25] But the growth of beef exports, as well as shellfish and bananas, has not compensated for the fall in the value of sugar exports. The fastest and most stable growth has been in nontraditional agroindustrial exports, particularly seafood, melons, pineapples, peppers, green peas, cauliflower, broccoli, and orange juice concentrate.[26] All except shellfish benefited from new CBERA duty-free status.

Traditional mineral exports, and their derivatives, are also on the decline, falling 71 percent between 1983 and 1988. Along with petroleum, exports of bauxite and alumina are down, while the behavior of ferronickel and precious metal exports has been erratic.

The greatest growth, 128 percent between 1983 and 1988, has been in manufacturing exports, led by two product categories excluded from CBERA provisions—garments and leather products. The export performance of electronics, chemicals and pharmaceuticals, methyl and ethyl alcohol, and sporting goods has been rather erratic.

The most spectacular gain in manufacturing exports has been in textiles and apparel, a sector excluded from CBERA benefits, but which benefits from section 807 of the tariff code. Between 1983 and 1986 textile and apparel imports into the United States from the region grew by an average annual 28 percent, increasing to 39 percent in 1987. Textile and apparel imports from the region, which accounted for only 4.5 percent of total U.S. imports from the Caribbean in 1983, now account for 25 percent of the total. This impressive increase is only partly due to the Guaranteed Access Levels (GALS) program. Special-access apparel imports (under 807A) amounted to $162 million in 1988, slightly less than 11 percent of total imports of textiles and apparels.[27]

Because of the growth in textile and apparel exports, imports to the United States under section 807, rather than under new CBERA eligibility for duty-free treatment, appear to be the fastest growing category of Caribbean exports. In 1986, total 807 exports accounted for 39 percent of the manufacturing exports of the fifteen countries in the Caribbean Group for Cooperation in Economic Development (CGCED).[28] The share of 807 exports in total manufacturing exports was far greater for the Caribbean than for other less-developed countries, including the Asian countries. The major 807 exporters in the region are Barbados, Belize, the Dominican Republic, Haiti, and Jamaica; the exports of the latter three have increased by more than 20 percent annually during the 1980s. Most of these exports are clothing, cut and sewn from U.S. cloth; the share of clothing and footwear in total 807 exports is between 80 percent and 100 percent for the Dominican Republic and Jamaica.[29]

Exports from the Caribbean islands under section 807 have consistently exceeded exports eligible under the CBERA. In 1985, 807 exports accounted for 11.5 percent of total exports from the region; in 1986, this figure was 14.2 percent, and in 1987, 17.7 percent. In contrast, exports under the CBERA accounted for 7.3 percent of total regional exports in 1985, 11.2 percent in 1986, and 14.7 percent in 1987. Exports under the CBERA appear to have displaced exports to the United States under the General System of Preferences; these declined from 7.9 percent in 1985 and 1986 to 5.2 percent of total exports from the Caribbean CGCED countries in 1987.[30]

All told, Caribbean Basin exports to the United States of CBERA-eligible, nontraditional products grew by an annual average 3.6 percent between 1983 and 1987.[31] Only seven items make up more than 90 percent of the products exported to the United States under CBERA provisions: beef and veal, rum, tobacco, analgesics, ethanol, steel and iron wire and bars, and electrical capacitors. The export value and share of the U.S. market of these products doubled between 1983 and 1986.[32]

While the CBERA has played a modest role in slowing down the rate of decline of U.S. imports from the Caribbean Basin—itself due to U.S. sugar and energy policy—the U.S. economy has benefited from freer trade. U.S. exports to the Caribbean Basin increased by 18 percent between 1983 and 1987, leading to a modest trade surplus. Moreover, the U.S. trade balance surplus with the Caribbean doubled between 1987 and 1988, increasing from $763 million to $1.5 billion.[33] The Caribbean Basin has thus become one of the few areas of the world to register a trade deficit with the United States, now, for two years in a row.

Investment

In its August 1985 issue of the *CBI Business Bulletin*, the Department of Commerce claimed that the CBI in its initial fifteen months or so of operation had generated 285 new investment projects, valued at $208.5 million and generating 35,891 jobs.[34] A detailed analysis of this survey by the U.S. General Accounting Office (GAO) revealed that these data were highly suspect. They found that about half of the 285 projects were not related to CBERA trade provisions, many of these firms either not exporting to the United States, producing goods not eligible for CBERA trade benefits, or exporting to the United States under trade provisions other than CBERA. A significant number never opened or subsequently closed down, were double counted, or were located in non-CBI beneficiary countries.[35]

The House Ways and Means Committee subsequently requested that the U.S. Department of Commerce carry out a more reliable CBI investment survey. The survey results, announced in November 1988, revealed that between 1984 and 1987 some 670 new investments and/or expansions had been undertaken in the region, valued at over $1.6 billion. Based on the total value of investment, 48 percent were attributed to the production of nonagricultural goods eligible under CBERA, 29 percent were in the textile and apparel industry, 13 percent in tourism, and 5 percent in the information services industry.[36] Start-ups accounted for $1 billion, or two-thirds of total investment. However, as noted in a subsequent report by the U.S. International Trade Commission, the survey data do not identify products by specific category, making it difficult to discern which investments have been directed to products which are receiving *new* duty-free treatment under the CBERA.[37] As a result, it is unclear what share of the reported $1 billion constitutes new investment induced by the CBERA duty-free provisions.

Among eligible items, investment has been concentrated in winter fruits and vegetables, pineapple and citrus, cut flowers, ethanol, and electrical and electronic assembly products. Investment in the latter three categories, however, was decreasing in 1987. The major growth sector in the Caribbean appears to be tourism, with new investment on the order of $637 million, about two-thirds of this registered in 1987.

According to the survey results and including minor investments in early 1988, the leading countries in terms of reported investments were the Dominican Republic, with 134 projects, Jamaica with 100, and Costa Rica with 81. The Dominican Republic also led in terms of the value of reported investments ($323 million), followed by the Bahamas ($223 million), Trinidad-Tobago ($207 million) and Jamaica ($159 million). Whereas the Dominican Republic led with respect to investments in the tourist sector, Jamaica was first with respect to the value of textile and apparel investments.

According to the survey, 54 percent of the value of new investments in the Caribbean Basin was of U.S. origin, with 24 percent of Caribbean origin. The remainder increasingly corresponds to Asian investment in the region. The Dominican Republic has attracted fifteen Korean and nine Taiwanese firms to its industrial parks while those in Jamaica have attracted capital from Hong Kong.[38] Asian investments have been concentrated in the garment sector. The incentives for Asian firms to invest in the Caribbean Basin stem from rising costs of production at home and the fact that South Korea, Singapore, Taiwan and Hong Kong "graduated" from the GSP program on January 1, 1989, losing privileged access to the U.S. market.

Comparative data on U.S. direct investments abroad suggests that between 1977 and 1982 U.S. investments in the Caribbean Basin were growing at a faster rate than in any other world region; the Caribbean Basin also offered the highest rate of return—17.4 percent—of all regions, considerably above the mean rate of 10.3 percent.[39] Since 1983, however, the only Caribbean countries favored by a steady growth in U.S. investment have been the financial centers of the Bahamas, Bermuda, and the other UK islands, along with Barbados (see Table 2.7). Total disinvestment has been most acute in the Netherlands Antilles, and investment has fallen precipitously since 1980 in Belize, the Dominican

Republic, Jamaica, and Trinidad-Tobago. If the Netherlands Antilles and the financial centers are excluded, U.S. investment in the Caribbean peaked in 1980 (at $1.8 billion) and fell throughout the years of the CBI to a low of $874 million in 1987. Whether the gain reported in 1988 is part of a recovery remains to be seen.

The only new source of investment financing forthcoming under the CBI has been the result of an initiative by the government of Puerto Rico, signed into law in November 1986 as a revision to section 936 of the U.S. Internal Revenue Code. Section 936 funds can finance investment projects in the Caribbean directly, through commercial financial institutions, or indirectly through Puerto Rico's twin plant program.

Finding itself initially excluded from the CBI, and afraid of losing its privileged status with respect to U.S. investment and the U.S. market, Puerto Rico launched what is known as the twin plant program. In return for retaining the tax privileges made available to U.S. corporations investing in Puerto Rico under section 936 of the Internal Revenue Code, the Puerto Rican government offered to provide low-cost financing to 936 corporations which invest in CBI beneficiary countries.[40] The idea is that U.S. corporations will set up intermediate industrial processing plants in the CBI countries and then export the product to Puerto Rico to be finished and then reexported to the United States. The benefit to U.S. corporations is that besides low interest loans, they will be able to repatriate their profits free of local and federal taxes. The projected benefit to Puerto Rico is that they will be able to retain 936 corporations operating on the island and not lose jobs to the lower wage countries of the Caribbean Basin.

The 936 initiative created great expectations in the Caribbean, since there was a vast amount of capital readily available for investment (as of the end of 1988 the total pool of profits not repatriated to the United States was $14.5 billion) and the government of Puerto Rico initially claimed that the provisions of 936 could result in a flow of $100 million annually to the region.[41] But the proposal took several years to implement, since Congress had to approve various of the regulations. In the process, some of the initial regulations were diluted, for example, one that required the borrowing firm to open or expand a Puerto Rican plant in order to borrow 936 funds. Moreover, for a project to qualify for 936 funding provided directly by a commercial financial institution, the CBI beneficiary country where it plans to invest must sign a Tax Information Exchange Agreement (TIEA) with the United States. Only six countries (Grenada, Jamaica, Barbados, Dominica, and recently, the Dominican Republic, and Trinidad-Tobago) have signed the agreement to date.[42] Some Caribbean countries see the TIEA as an infringement on their sovereignty, so it is doubtful that 936 funds will become a primary source of investment finance for all countries of the region. Other problems are that 936 loans are made by private banks and these have been reluctant to risk CBI loans, and the mismatch of short-term 936 deposits with the long-term financing needs of CBI projects. As a result of all of these factors, by the end of 1988 only three investment projects in the Caribbean, generating fifty jobs, actually had been funded out of 936 funds.[43]

Much more successful has been another related effort, by the Puerto Rican development agency, Fomento, to encourage the setting up of twin plants and other complementary projects in CBI countries regardless of their source of finance. Fomento has engaged in a major public relations effort to persuade 936 companies to invest in new projects in Puerto Rico and the Caribbean. Twin plant investments are eligible for subsidized credit provided by the Puerto Rican Development Bank.

According to Fomento's September 1988 report to the U.S. Congress, fifty twin plant investments were either underway or in operation in eleven CBI countries. By January 1989 the number of projects had increased to sixty, valued at $165.3 million. It is estimated that these investments will generate 10,327 jobs in the CBI countries as well as 3,805 jobs in Puerto Rico. Twenty-nine of the twin plants are located in the Dominican Republic, with the remainder scattered throughout the English-speaking Caribbean and Central America.[44] It is unknown, however, whether these investments will produce exports eligible for duty-free treatment under the CBERA, and thus whether these new investments should be attributed to the CBERA.

Employment

The lack of precise data on new investments directly related to the duty-free provisions of the CBERA makes it difficult to analyze the direct employment and income generating effects of the Caribbean Basin Initiative for the countries of the region. According to the survey findings of the Department of Commerce, between 1984 and 1987, new investments and expansions in the Caribbean Basin had generated approximately 100,000 new jobs. Nonagricultural, CBERA-eligible product investments accounted for 15 percent of the total (or 15,391 new jobs, of which 10,543 were generated in start-up projects and 4,848 in expansions). The textile and apparel industry (which accounted for 29 percent of the projects but only 10 percent of the value of investments) accounted for over 50 percent of the new jobs.[45]

Data on the free-trade zones in the Dominican Republic, the leading exporter to the United States among CBI countries, does allow analysis of some of the new trends. Since the CBI was implemented, both the number of firms and the number of workers employed in free-trade zones in the Dominican Republic have increased steadily. In 1983 there were only 22,272 workers employed by free-trade zone firms; by 1988 the number employed had jumped to 85,000 workers, equivalent to 3 percent of the economically active population of the country.[46]

A 1986 study of the free trade zones found that almost two-thirds of the free-trade zone labor force is employed in the apparel industry, an industry excluded from CBERA benefits but which since 1986 has benefited from larger quotas to the U.S. market under the GALS (807-A) program. Of the other leading sectors of employment—shoes, jewelry, tobacco, and electronics—only the latter two products are eligible for duty-free treatment under the CBERA.[47] The employment data thus suggest that rather than the free-trade provisions of the CBERA, a greater stimulus to investment and employment generation are the conditions offered by the free-trade zones themselves: cheap and docile female labor and attractive government policies.

U.S. Economic and Military Assistance

If the trade component of the CBI was limited in scope, diminishing its potential benefit for the region, what about U.S. aid? As noted previously, the bulk of the supplemental aid package included in the CBERA legislation was destined for war-torn Central America. While total U.S. appropriations for the Caribbean islands and Belize and Guyana more than doubled between 1981 and 1982, from that year on funding has fluctuated, averaging $247 million annually between 1982 and 1987; since then funding has dropped substantially (see Table 6.4). Central America has absorbed an increasing share of the funds destined for the Caribbean Basin, from a low of 55 percent of the total in 1982, to 83 percent in 1987, a trend that has continued. Among the Caribbean islands, two countries whose governments were strongly allied with the United States, Jamaica under the Seaga government and the Dominican Republic, have received the lion's share of the funds.

The bulk of assistance to the Caribbean as well as to Central America has consisted of balance of payments support (Economic Support Funds), rather than project-oriented developmental assistance. In most cases, U.S. balance of payments assistance has been conditioned on changes in internal economic policy prescribed by the IMF.[48] The aim of such assistance is structural adjustment or economic stabilization designed to allow these countries to service their foreign debt. The strategy thus centers on improving a country's export performance, and particularly,

Table 6.4

U.S. Economic Assistance to the Caribbean Basin, 1980–89[1] (in US$ millions)

	1980	1981	1982	1983	1984	1985	1986	1987	1988	1989
Belize	0	0	0	17	4	22	9	13	7	8
Dominican Republic	35	17	60	35	64	125	66	20	32	20
Haiti	11	9	12	27	26	31	46	74	31	28
Jamaica	3	54	119	82	88	115	83	42	19	77
Regional	45	27	50	58	105	58	49	51	33	29
Subtotal—Caribbean	94	107	241	219	287	350	253	200	122	162
Costa Rica	14	11	32	184	145	181	131	160	102	100
El Salvador	52	78	155	199	161	373	261	364	266	253
Guatemala	8	9	8	22	5	71	85	150	110	114
Honduras	46	26	68	87	71	199	105	173	130	53
Nicaragua	19	58	6	0	0	0	0	0	0	5
Panama	1	9	12	6	11	69	24	8	1	0
Regional Programs[2]	4	11	13	19	15	160	72	20	54	61
Subtotal—Central America	144	202	294	517	408	1057	678	875	663	586
Total Caribbean Basin	238	309	535	736	695	1402	931	1075	785	748

Source: Agency for International Development, Congressional Presentation Fiscal Year 1985, Annex III, pp. 2–3; Congressional Presentation Fiscal Year 1987, Main Volume, pp. 438–40, 479–81; Congressional Presentation Fiscal Year 1988, Main Volume, pp. 509, 512, 517; Congressional Presentation Fiscal Year 1989 and 1990, Summary Tables.

1) Development Assistance and Economic Support Funds only
2) Includes ROCAP

encouraging the development of nontraditional exports eligible for duty-free treatment under the CBERA.

U.S. aid strategy under the Reagan administration, which has continued under President Bush, represented a significant change from the aim of foreign assistance in the 1970s. In that period bilateral assistance was to be directed to the "poorest of the poor" and focused on meeting basic human needs: food and nutrition, health, education and human resource development. Since 1980, U.S. bilateral assistance has focused on the following components: (1) economic policy reform in beneficiary countries; (2) institution building; (3) technology transfer; and (4) increased involvement by the private sector.

The U.S. administration regards economic policy reform as the key to effective use of external resources. Among the major targets are the following: (1) changes in interest rates that may discourage savings and result in the misallocation of scarce credit; (2) divestiture of state-owned enterprises to encourage private-sector initiative and competition, improve efficiency, and thereby lessen demands on public resources; (3) exchange rate policy reforms to encourage exports, eliminate

Feature

The Implications of an Export-Led Development Strategy: Haiti

In the mid-1980s television viewers in the United States became accustomed to the sight of Haitian boat people capsized at sea or of those who had reached shore rounded up for deportation—penned behind high barbed wire fences while they awaited their return journey. Yet during the 1980s Haitians braved the dangers in record numbers to come to an unwelcoming United States. Since 1981, when the U.S. government agreed to deport all so-called economic refugees, some 21,000 have been turned back; only six have been allowed to stay. Yet each year more people try—the inevitable result of the export-led development strategies promoted throughout the Caribbean.

During 1981–82, U.S. AID and the World Bank devised a development strategy for Haiti, centered on agroindustrial and assembly exports. Agricultural exports were to be promoted both by planting tree crops such as coffee or cacao on marginal hillside lands—thereby reducing soil erosion and increasing export revenues—and by reorienting production on flat and productive lands toward fruits and vegetables for the winter market or for industrial processing for export. The development of these new agroindustries, which was to be accomplished through the provision of cheap credit to the private sector, implied shifting 30 percent of all cultivated land from the production of food for local consumption to the production of export crops.

AID advisors recognized that the strategy could cause a decline in income and nutrition among small farmers—who might also lose their land—but they argued that growing export revenues would pay for the import of foods not produced in Haiti and in the long run raise the standard of living in rural areas. In the short term, the strategy was expected to spur rural-urban migration, however, necessitating growth of an assembly industry to absorb the displaced rural population. The assembly industry, now consisting largely of garment and apparel operations, was also expected to generate foreign exchange for the import of food. According to AID, "the result will be an historic change toward deeper market interdependence with the United States" and provide the preconditions for Haiti to become the "Taiwan of the Caribbean."

The nature and condition of Haiti's economy at the time the plan was devised should have sounded a number of alarm bells concerning its success. For one thing, the strategy accepted and even encouraged the displacement of farmers who produce for the local market and the creation of dependency on imported food. However, by the late 1970s, *(continues)* food imports already frequently equaled the value of all agricultural exports in Haiti. Thus it was not surprising that the new strategy seriously aggravated the problem of food insecurity.

Moreover, the assembly industry showed little promise of being able to fulfill the key role assigned to it by international agencies. The industry was unable to create jobs at the rate of rural migration in the 1970s, the period during which Haiti's assembly exports were growing at an average annual rate of 40 percent. During the 1980s, moreover, investment in assembly industries centered on other Caribbean countries, where the labor force was better educated and the internal political situation more conducive to foreign investment.

Predictably, rural-urban migration increased dramatically, and unemployment soared, pushing those with no alternatives toward the leaky boats on the way to the hostile shores of the United States. Clearly the 1981–82 development plan greatly exaggerated the potential for continued growth and employment generation in the urban areas. Furthermore, since what attracts foreign investment in these assembly industries are low wages, employment in these industries has little prospect of providing a way out of poverty for Haitian workers—making the continued migration flow a certainty.

Source: Josh DeWind and David H. Kinley III, *Aiding Migration: The Impact of International Development Assistance on Haiti* (Boulder: Westview Press, 1988).

incentives for capital flight, and remove other distortions that allocate resources inefficiently; (4) revision of tax structures that inhibit growth; (5) promotion of export diversification and expansion; (6) reduction and/or elimination of government subsidies.[49]

Many of the above policy changes are integral components of IMF stabilization programs. According to the AID Latin America Bureau's 1983 strategic plan: "In order to assure that our assistance eases adjustment rather than perpetuates unsustainable policies, our approach has been to make an IMF-supported stabilization program a prerequisite for major AID balance-of-payments assistance."[50] The plan made clear that assistance would be leveraged in ways most likely to promote structural reform and long-run development, adding, "This will sometimes involve coordination with World Bank structural adjustment programs."[51]

World Bank structural adjustment loans (SALS) began in 1980. Their stated aim is to assist in the process of policy and institutional reform in an unfavorable international economic environment. In other words, they are designed to prevent a worsening of economic conditions which are often brought about by IMF structural adjustment programs. Where

SALS and AID balance of payments loans differ from IMF financing is that they both carry long-term maturities.

According to a report by the General Accounting Office (GAO), in actual practice, the degree of conditionality required for AID balance of payments support varies, depending on political criteria. Thus, while the Jamaican government was led by Edward Seaga the required reforms were much less stringent than those imposed on the Dominican Republic. In terms of the effectiveness of these policy reforms, the GAO concluded that AID-IMF-World Bank conditionality did improve the fiscal and current account deficits of the Dominican Republic and Jamaica in the early 1980s. But this did not lead to self-sustaining growth.

What must be kept clearly in mind is that the macroeconomic performance of a country is influenced not only by domestic policies but also by external forces, such as the economic growth rates of the advanced countries as well as of world trade; the level of real interest rates; the availability of external financial capital; and the trade policies of the advanced countries. Thus the GAO report concluded that the AID strategy for increasing exports as the basis of economic growth and to pay debt service obligations was based upon "optimistic assumptions" regarding events in the world economy.

Moreover, under the Caribbean Basin Initiative, development assistance has been increasingly focused on support to the private sector, allegedly to ameliorate constraints to trade and investment expansion in the region.[52] But this focus has come at the direct expense of government programs to improve living conditions for the poor as well as cooperative and community projects based on participation. In other words, the poor are being asked to forego education, health, and improvements in other areas, so that incentives can be showered on the private sector to export more, thus allowing governments to repay the external debt.

In concert with the CBERA, military assistance to Central America and the Caribbean increased sharply (see Table 6.5). Between 1982 and 1984 military assistance to the Caribbean more than quadrupled, then almost doubled again the next year, peaking in 1985 at $46.5 million. The redefinition of U.S. military policy toward the Caribbean began under the Carter administration in mid-1979, in response to the erosion of U.S. power in the region, signaled by the revolutions in Grenada and Nicaragua and the breakdown in Cuba's isolation. But it was the Reagan administration which vigorously pushed the increase in the U.S. military presence and the promotion and coordination of the security forces in the Caribbean, in addition to Central America.[53] The new policy first became evident through the large-scale military maneuvers that took place between 1981 and 1984, which transformed

Table 6.5
U.S. Military Assistance to the Caribbean Basin, 1980–89[1] (in US$ thousands)

	1980	1981	1982	1983	1984	1985	1986	1987	1988	1989
Caribbean										
Antigua-Barbuda	0	0	0	1,067	353	1,483	686	1,142	380	244
Barbados	30	30	56	55	70	192	344	642	89	961
Belize	0	0	20	48	204	919	612	410	325	288
Dominica	0	8	4	1,042	382	1,322	484	525	159	233
Dominican Republic	239	348	3,883	1,096	6,949	4,385	6,997	5,762	3,043	1,959
Grenada	0	0	0	0	2,335	3,450	464	557	625	80
Haiti	128	110	212	339	770	396	1,464	2,221	63	101
Jamaica	0	95	73	3,472	2,936	5,978	9,288	2,712	1,712	12,677
St. Kitts-Nevis	0	0	0	0	32	2,704	451	412	204	168
St. Lucia	0	2	8	1,065	410	225	429	348	136	236
St. Vincent	0	0	1	31	44	85	2,992	318	173	342
Trinidad-Tobago	0	15	0	5	0	39	50	78	70	11
Subtotal	397	608	4,257	8,220	14,116	21,178	24,261	15,027	6,979	17,300
Central America										
Costa Rica	0	31	46	4,084	2,430	14,825	6,787	1,123	1,650	563
El Salvador	2,535	35,412	66,248	69,032	121,598	139,754	130,551	109,779	109,221	87,002
Guatemala	10	4	0	71	2,669	984	3,911	4,239	10,067	15,354
Honduras	2,653	4,711	10,478	24,977	33,631	81,394	98,745	104,916	39,078	26,116
Panama	517	710	807	644	1,258	17,635	3,256	1,965	0	0
Subtotal	5,715	40,868	77,579	98,808	161,586	254,592	243,250	222,022	16,016	129,035
Total CBI	6,112	41,476	81,836	107,028	175,702	275,770	267,511	237,049	166,995	146,335

Source: U.S. Department of Defense, *Foreign Military Sales agreements, Foreign Military Construction Sales and Military Assistance Facts as of September 30, 1989* (Washington, D.C.: DOD, 1989).

1) Includes Foreign Military Sales agreements, Foreign Military Construction Sales agreements, Military Assistance Program, and International Military Education and Training Program.

the Caribbean into a stage set for "war games." The objective of these maneuvers was to pressure Cuba, to plan and prepare for the invasion of Grenada, and to improve the level of training of U.S. forces. By 1984 there were twenty-one U.S. military installations in the Caribbean Basin, 30,000 U.S. troops, plus another 10,000 shipborne troops.[54]

Since 1984 the objective of the maneuvers, as well as of U.S. military assistance, has been to create a regional security system and to train the security forces of the Eastern Caribbean to develop the capacity to act jointly with U.S. regular forces in auxiliary functions. For example, the 1985 exercises named "Exotic Palm" involved the recently created Special Service Units (linked to the police forces) of the Eastern Caribbean, the coast guards of St. Lucia, St. Kitts-Nevis, Dominica, and Grenada, and the defense forces of Antigua, Barbados, and Jamaica. The purpose of the exercises was to practice the invasion of an island.

Along with increased maneuvers the structure of command of the regular U.S. forces in the region has been reorganized to make it more effective and the infrastructure of military bases and installations has been expanded. Honduras has been the focus of this expansion in Central America while in the Caribbean, new installations, along with a new regional training center have been built in Antigua.

U.S. policy has also encouraged Caribbean countries to strengthen their military forces through increased arms purchases. In addition to the subsidized, foreign military sales agreements (included in the data reported in Table 6.5) commercial arms exports licensed under the U.S. Arms Export Control Act increased significantly to the Caribbean, from $1.2 million in 1982 to a high of $5.6 million in 1986.[55] In the Dominican Republic, the proportion of the government budget allocated to military expenditures is reported to have increased from 16.6 percent in 1979 to 22.2 percent in 1985, the same period in which U.S. military assistance to this country expanded rapidly. It is also reported that Jamaica's military expenditures almost doubled in this period, while the military forces of Trinidad-Tobago expanded significantly.[56]

The new U.S. military policy has had a great impact in the English-speaking Caribbean, since these countries either had small military structures or none at all. Elevating the role and status of the military in countries with fragile party systems can be dangerous, generating new contradictions, such as the erosion of civil rights and a reduced space for democratic participation. These countries pose no security threat to the United States, making militarization unnecessary. Moreover, the policy has absorbed substantial economic resources in the region, constituting an obstacle toward its economic recovery and development, both crucial to the common security of the hemisphere.

Export Diversification
and the Problem of Development

The Caribbean Basin Initiative can not be judged either a success or a failure. The scope of its trade provisions and increased developmental assistance was insufficient to have a significant impact on the volume of Caribbean-U.S. trade or Caribbean growth, investment, and employment. However, as we have seen, within the limited terms of the new trade provisions, nontraditional exports from the region have increased since the legislation has been in effect, spurring exports from a number of the Caribbean islands.

While it is still too early to conclude that the CBI has successfully restructured the pattern of Caribbean-U.S. trade around a new set of agroindustrial and labor-intensive manufacturing operations, it is not too early to consider whether this form of restructuring—based on export diversification and centered on export-processing zones—holds the promise for Caribbean development.

To the extent that world market prices for traditional Caribbean exports of primary goods remain depressed (and U.S. trade policy with respect to sugar unchanged), export diversification will alleviate short-run balance of payments problems and provide some new sources of employment. In the long run, however, export diversification will not solve the problem of the vulnerability of the Caribbean economies to fluctuations in international demand. It will continue to be U.S. consumers and corporations rather than Caribbean consumers who determine what is produced and at what price. Export diversification merely redefines Caribbean vulnerability as one export sector replaces another.

The vulnerability of Caribbean economies to the dictates of profit maximization by international capital is well illustrated by the recent experience of Barbados. Prior to the CBERA, Barbados had been the leading Caribbean exporter of manufactured products. Since the inception of the plan, the major corporations operating in the country have closed long-time operations in both the electronics and garment assembly industries in a search for cheaper labor. Note that in 1988 semi-skilled labor in Barbados earned $2.16 an hour, whereas similar labor in the Dominican Republic earned only 55 cents (see Table 5.3). As a result, Barbados' exports to the United States dropped from $202 million in 1983 to $51 million in 1988 (see Table 6.2). This example well illustrates how U.S. policy has stimulated Caribbean economies to compete against each other on the basis of cheap labor, what is being called the "competitive advantage of misery."

The CBERA has also increased the vulnerability of Caribbean economies by making them even more susceptible to the vicissitudes of protectionist sentiments in the United States and specifically, those of the U.S. Congress. Despite the CBERA's twelve-year time span, several provisions have already been revised, limited, or eliminated. For example, ethanol, which had initially been designated eligible under the CBERA, was subject to a new requirement by the Tax Reform Act of 1986 that ethanol producers use at least 60 percent local feedstock to qualify for duty-free status. Firms organized in Jamaica, the Virgin Islands, and Costa Rica are currently idle due to this change in requirements. Costa Rica's cut-flower industry, an early CBERA success story in terms of new investment and export growth, was subjected to countervailing duties as a result of U.S. charges of dumping (pricing below cost). Investment ventures in parakeets and scuba wetsuits have suffered the loss of duty-free treatment due to the pressures of U.S. lobbyists.[57] These examples illustrate the dangers for a developing country of building a development strategy around factors outside its control.

The vulnerability of the Caribbean economies is increased still further by the fact that the new manufacturing industries are largely export-processing industries, located in export-processing or free-trade zones. With raw materials and capital goods imported under duty-free provisions, there is little incentive to develop backward linkages to potential local suppliers. And with wages low, few forward linkages to high-wage industries are generated. In addition, export-processing industries earn less foreign exchange relative to the total value of exports than do primary products, due to the high import content of the projects. An indication of the low value-added of assembly operations and their inefficiency as generators of foreign exchange is provided by examining the dutiable portion of section 807 exports to the United States. In 1986, the total gross value of section 807 exports from the fifteen CGCED countries was $646 million; the dutiable portion—corresponding to Caribbean value added—amounted to only $192 million, or 30 percent of the gross value.[58] For the Dominican Republic, which accounts for over half of the gross value of 807 exports, this ratio was even lower—28 percent.

The total value of exports from the Dominican Republic's free-trade zones has increased impressively in the 1980s, growing by an average annual 43 percent—from $117.1 million in 1980 to $516.8 million in 1988. The foreign exchange captured by the Central Bank from these exports has grown at a much lower rate and, in fact, the proportion of net foreign exchange generated has decreased significantly in this period. In the early period of establishment of the free-trade zones (1975–79) the Central Bank was capturing 45 percent of the value of free-trade zone exports as foreign exchange; by 1988, this proportion had fallen to 25 percent.[59] This data suggest that the new industries attracted to the Dominican free-trade zones are increasingly inefficient generators of foreign exchange due to their low value-added. Thus, even if exports of assembled goods increase significantly, this may not compensate for the loss of foreign exchange from traditional agricultural products.

According to a recent GAO report, traditional exports such as sugar and coffee have an estimated value-added component of 90 percent, while light manufacturing, such as of garments, has a value-added component of approximately 20 percent. Thus, a $1 million decline in sugar exports would have to be offset by a $4.5 million increase in garment exports to maintain the same level of value-added and to generate the same net foreign exchange.[60] According to their calculations, to maintain similar employment levels, a $1 million reduction in sugar exports would have to be compensated by a $6 million increase in textile exports. These comparisons partly explain why the gross export earnings (merchandise trade plus tourism) of the Dominican Republic increased by 6.4 percent per year between 1983 and 1986, but export growth hardly made a dent on growth rates of gross domestic product (see Tables 2.1 and 2.2). Part of the reason is that the net foreign exchange generated amounted to −0.3 percent per year during this period.[61]

Another problem with the free-trade zones is that most provide for unrestricted profit repatriation. This means that foreign corporations are not obliged to keep investing in the country if more profitable opportunities are offered elsewhere. In Chapter 2 it was noted how the repatriation of profits by foreign companies has exacerbated the economic crisis of the region. In addition, most export-processing operations are low-cost investments with minimal capital or job training requirements. This makes them particularly "footloose" and thus not necessarily long-lasting investments that will provide secure employment.[62] Finally, the tax-free provisions of most incentive schemes means that these zones do little to enhance badly needed fiscal revenues while requiring a substantial government investment in infrastructure.

Caribbean governments need look no further than Puerto Rico to see the long-term result of export industrialization strategies, for the same principles governing the CBI were first applied here in the 1950s under Operation Bootstrap. According to Puerto Rican sociologist Emilio Pantojas-García: "In the aftermath of Operation Bootstrap it has become clear that the long-term costs of the Puerto Rican miracle far outweigh its short-term achievements. Twenty percent unemployment, two million Puerto Ricans living in the United States, and 50 percent of the families on the island depending on the food support program—these are just

Table 6.6
Share of Exports to and Imports from Selected Caribbean Countries, 1961–63 and 1983–85

	% of Exports to the U.S.		% of Imports from the U.S.	
	Average 1961–63	Average 1983–85	Average 1961–63	Average 1983–85
Bahamas	91.7	84.0	56.4	52.7
Barbados	6.7	52.7	14.7	45.8
Dominican Republic	74.1	73.3	47.4	34.5
Guyana	18.7	25.0	21.2	21.7
Haiti	54.4	79.9	57.9	69.4
Jamaica	36.0	39.1	27.7	42.8
Suriname	n.a.	24.1	n.a.	32.6
Trinidad-Tobago	25.7	60.5	13.3	40.9

Source: Inter-American Development Bank, Economic and Social Progress in Latin America, Annual Report 1987 (Washington, D.C.: IDB, 1987), p. 126.

a few of the long-term results of Operation Bootstrap. Clearly, the proponents of the CBI do not seem to have learned the lessons of the Puerto Rican experience."[63] It is also important to take into account that while Puerto Rican wages have increased steadily, this has encouraged many companies to move to lower wage areas, requiring the Puerto Rican government to continually devise new schemes to maintain its competitive edge.[64]

The CBI will create some beneficiaries, but these are more likely to be U.S. corporations than Caribbean people. The CBI does provide the basis for the expansion of the operations of U.S. capital in the region, particularly for those industries subject to stiff international competition. It also serves to tie the region even closer to U.S. markets, stimulating certain U.S. export sectors. In the 1980s a number of Caribbean countries became more integrated with the U.S. economy than they were two decades ago (see Table 6.6).

But what is fairly clear is that greater U.S. economic involvement in the Caribbean has done little to solve the economic problems of the region or to enhance the standard of living of the majority of Caribbean people. As the GAO concludes, the CBI has fostered trade and investment opportunities, but these "have not been sufficient to generate broadly based economic growth, alleviate debt-servicing problems, or create lasting employment."[65]

Notes

1. U.S. Department of State, "President Reagan's Address to the OAS on February 24, 1982," Bulletin, March 1982.

2. Richard Feinberg, "The CBI: First Steps Towards Implementation," mimeo 1986 (San German, Puerto Rico: Centro de Investigaciones del Caribe y América Latina, Universidad Interamericana), p. 9.

3. An excellent discussion of the interrelationship between the Reagan administration's policy toward Central America and that toward the insular Caribbean is found in Emilio Pantojas-García, "Restoring Hegemony: The Complementary of the Security, Economic and Political Components of U.S. Policy in the Caribbean Basin during the 1980s," paper prepared for International Relations Working Group of CLACSO meeting, January 26–28, 1988, University of Puerto Rico. This chapter focuses primarily on the Caribbean islands, plus Belize and Guyana (the traditional definition of the Caribbean), although much of the quantitative data refers to the Caribbean Basin (the Caribbean plus Central America and Panama) as a whole.

4. Ibid., p. 3.

5. Richard Newfarmer, "Economic Policy Toward the Caribbean Basin: The Balance Sheet," *Journal of Interamerican Studies and World Affairs* no.1 (February 1985), p. 63.

6. Ibid.; also see Emilio Pantojas-García, "The U.S. Caribbean Basin Initiative and the Puerto Rican Experience: Some Parallels and Lessons," *Latin American Perspectives*, 12, no. 4 (1985).

7. The Reagan administration's initial proposal was for $128 million of the $350 million aid package to go to El Salvador. The islands of the insular Caribbean and Belize would have received only 33 percent of the total, with the remainder divided among the five Central American republics. The final bill approved by Congress reduced El Salvador's share from 37 percent to 21 percent of the total, and increased the share of the insular Caribbean and Belize to 39 percent.

8. U.S. Department of Commerce, *1987 Guidebook: The Caribbean Basin Initiative* (Washington, D.C.: International Trade Administration, 1986).

9. U.S. Department of State, "Report by the U.S. Department of State on the Caribbean Basin Initiative (CBI): Progress to Date," March 1988, p. 2; and U.S. International Trade Commission, *Annual Report on the Impact of the Caribbean Basin Economic Recovery Act on U.S. Industries and Consumers*, 3rd Report, 1987 (Washington, D.C.: US ITC, 1988), p. 1–1, note 3.

10. When the Caribbean Development Bank, for example, refused to exclude Grenada under the Bishop administration from development projects because that "would result in the bank appearing to be operating as an instrument of U.S. foreign policy," funds to the bank were drastically cut.

11. In order for beef and veal products as well as sugar to qualify for duty-free treatment, however, a country must submit an acceptable stable Food Production Plan to the United States designed to show that domestic food production will not be adversely affected by the expected increased export production in response to the CBERA duty-free treatment. U.S. Department of Commerce, *1987 Guidebook*.

12. World Bank, *Caribbean Exports: Preferential Markets and Performance* (Washington, D.C.: IBRD, 1988), p. 65.

13. Emilio Pantojas-García, "The Caribbean Basin Initiative and the Economic Restructuring of the Region," in Projecto Caribeño de Justicia y Paz, *The Other Side of U.S. Policy Towards the Caribbean: Recolonization and Militarization* (San Juan: Projecto Caribeño de Justicia y Paz, 1988), p. 23; and Newfarmer, "Economic Policy Toward the Caribbean," p. 65.

14. Newfarmer, "Economic Policy Toward the Caribbean," p. 66.

15. J. Pelzman and D. Roussland, *Effects on U.S. Trade and Employment of Tariff Eliminations among the Countries of North America and the Caribbean Basin* (Washington, D.C.: U.S. Department of Labor, January 1982), cited in Newfarmer, p. 73.

16. U.S. ITC, *Operation of the Trade Agreements Program*, 39th Report, 1987 (Washington, D.C.: US ITC, 1988).

17. U.S. ITC, *Impact of the CBERA, Fourth Report, 1988*, p. 1–9, note 23.

18. See *Caribbean Action*, no. 1 (1988), pp. 3–5.

19. World Bank, *Caribbean Exports*, p. 10.

20. *Caribbean Action*, no. 1 (1988), pp. 8–9.

21. Other estimates of the loss of foreign exchange earnings to the Dominican Republic are even higher. A GAO report quotes Dominican officials estimating the cumulative foreign exchange loss at $500 million since 1982. See GAO, *Caribbean Basin Initiative: Impact on Selected Countries*, Report to the Chairman, Subcommittee on Western Hemisphere and Peace Corps Affairs, Committee on Foreign Relations, U.S. Senate, July 1988, p. 29.

22. U.S. ITC, *Impact of the CBERA, Fourth Report, 1988*, table 1–1.

23. Ibid., table 1–3. The Department of State ("Report on the CBI," p. 3 and table 1) reports that the decline in Caribbean imports to the United States was reversed in 1987, with imports from beneficiary countries increasing by 0.3 percent. However, the Department of State is going by C.I.F. data rather than customs value data, as reported by the U.S. International Trade Commission. What appears to have increased between 1986 and 1987 is the cost of insurance and freight rather than the value of Caribbean exports.

24. US ITC, *Impact of the CBERA, Third Report, 1987*, table 1–6; and *Fourth Report, 1988*, p. 2–3.

25. Ibid., table 1–9.

26. Pantojas-Garcia, "Restoring Hegemony," p. 27.

27. US ITC, *Operation of Trade Agreements Program*, p. 5–18, and US ITC, *Impact of the CBERA, Fourth Report, 1988*, p. 1–9 and table 1–9.

28. The CGCED includes the CARICOM countries plus the Dominican Republic, Haiti, and Suriname. The data is drawn from World Bank, *Caribbean Exports*, p. 17.

29. Ibid., pp. 16–17.

30. US ITC, *Operation of Trade Agreements Program*, table B-28. The data presented in the text differ from the data in US ITC, *Impact of the CBERA, Fourth Report, 1988*, table 1–6, since the latter refer to all Caribbean Basin countries. Also see Eve Paus, "A Critical Look at Nontraditional Export Demand: The Caribbean Basin Initiative," in E. Paus, ed., *Struggle Against Dependence: Nontraditional Export Growth in Central America and the Caribbean* (Boulder:

Westview, 1988), pp. 197–201, for a detailed analysis of how the various subregions of the Caribbean Basin have responded to the varying provisions of the GSP, 807 and CBI.

31. Department of State, "Report on the CBI," p. 4.

32. World Bank, *Caribbean Exports*, pp. 9–10.

33. Ibid., p. 1–1, and US ITC, *Impact of the CBERA, Fourth Report, 1988*, table 1–1. Preliminary data for 1989 indicate that the U.S. trade surplus with the region increased again. See *CBI Business Bulletin* 6, no. 3 (April 1990).

34. *CBI Business Bulletin* 3, no. 8 (August 1985).

35. U.S. General Accounting Office, "Caribbean Basin Initiative: Need for More Reliable Data on Business Activity Resulting from the Initiative," Briefing Report to the Chairman, Subcommittee on Oversight, Committee on Ways and Means, House of Representatives, August 1986, Washington, D.C., p. 4.

36. U.S. Department of Commerce, "Caribbean Basin Investment Survey," mimeo, November 1988 (Washington, D.C.).

37. US ITC, *Impact of the CBERA, Third Report, 1987*, pp. 3–1 and 3–2.

38. Larry Luxner, "Asian Industries Skip P.R. as They Invest in Caribbean," *Caribbean Business*, 30 June 1988, pp. 1–2.

39. Kevin Power, *The CBI: Caribbean Basin Trade and Investment Guide* (Washington, D.C.: Washington International Press, 1984).

40. Under 936, U.S. subsidiaries operating in Puerto Rico are exempt from U.S. federal income tax as well as Puerto Rican income taxes except for a 10 percent tollgate tax on profits remitted to the U.S. The tollgate tax can be avoided, however, by depositing profits in five-year Certificates of Deposit in Puerto Rico, which can then be remitted tax free upon maturity. The 1986 Tax Reform Act allows the funds being held in CDs to be invested in CBI-designated countries. *CBI Business Bulletin* 5, no. 2 (August 1988), pp. 1–2.

41. US ITC, *Impact of CBERA, Fourth Report, 1988*, pp. 3–10, and *Caribbean Action*, no. 2, 1988, p. 1.

42. US ITC, *Impact of CBERA, Fourth Report, 1988*, pp. 3–11. The TIEA's with St. Lucia and Costa Rica are awaiting the approval of their respective legislatures. According to the *CBI Business Bulletin* 6, no. 10 (November 1989), p. 8, the Dominican Republic officially signed the TIEA in October 1989, and Trinidad-Tobago did so in early 1990 (*CBI Business Bulletin* 7, no. 3, April 1990, p. 9).

43. Ibid. pp. 3–12. See also Ed Konstat, "Low Impact of Caribbean Basin," *Caribbean Business*, 19 October 1989.

44. Ibid., and *Fomento's Caribbean Highlights* 3, no. 4 (March 1988), p. 2.

45. U.S. Department of Commerce, *Caribbean Basin Investment Survey*, tables 7 and 13.

46. Centro de Investigación Económica, Inc. (CIECA, Santo Domingo), CIECA data bank, table 1–3.

47. Gerold Janka, "Estudio de las Zonas Francas Industriales de la Romana, San Pedro de Macorís, Santiago y Puerto Plata," Corporación de Fomento Industrial, May 1986, pp. 5 and 13.

48. This section draws principally upon GAO, *Foreign Assistance, U.S. Use of Conditions to Achieve Economic Reforms*, Report to the Administrator of the Agency for International Development, August 1986.

49. Ibid., pp. 13–14.

50. Ibid., p. 15.

51. Ibid., p. 15.

52. U.S. Department of State, "Fact Sheet on the CBI," 1984.

53. This section is based largely on Jorge Rodríguez Beruff, *Política Militar y Dominación: Puerto Rico en el Contexto Latinoamericano*, (Rio Piedras, P.R.: Ed. Huracán, 1988), chap. 2.

54. Thomas, *The Poor and the Powerless*, p. 343.

55. U.S. Department of Defense, "Foreign Military Construction and Military Assistance Facts as of September 30, 1987" (Washington, D.C.: DOD, 1987). This data, as well as that in Table 6.5 were gathered by Maribel Aponte.

56. Beruff, *Política Militar y Dominación*, pp. 135, 139. The data reported by the U.S. Arms Control and Disarmament Agency indicate an increase in military expenditures for these countries, but the increase is somewhat less (see Table 4.1).

57. US ITC, *Impact of the CBERA, Third Report*, pp. 2–4, 3–2.

58. World Bank, *Caribbean Exports*, table III–12.

59. Centro de Investigación Económica, Inc. (CIECA) data bank drawn from Central Bank data.

60. GAO, *Caribbean Basin Initiative: Impact on Selected Countries*, Report to the Chairman, Subcommittee on Western Hemisphere and Peace Corps Affairs, Committee on Foreign Relations (Washington, D.C.: U.S. Senate, 1988), p. 18.

61. Ibid., p. 20.

62. Ibid., p. 3.

63. Pantojas-García, "The U.S. Caribbean Basin Initiative and the Puerto Rican Experience," p. 122.

64. The U.S. minimum wage became applicable to Puerto Rico in 1981. The labor force employed in the garment industry in Puerto Rico fell from 40,300 workers in 1973 to 33,900 in 1980, partly due to the U.S. recession but also as a result of capital flight or runaway shops. See Helen Safa, "Women and Industrialization in the Caribbean," in Sharon Stichter and Jane Parpart, eds., *Women, Employment and the Family in the International Division of Labor* (New York: Macmillan, forthcoming).

65. Ibid., p. 2.

CHAPTER 7

Beyond Structural Adjustment: Alternative Development Strategies

THE DEVELOPMENT MODELS OF THE PAST, whether designed around import substitution or production for export, have not been able to solve the basic problems of Caribbean development. What is more, these deep-rooted problems have been sharply exacerbated by the present-day economic crisis pervading the region. Past development efforts have bequeathed highly open and vulnerable economies and very unequal distributions of incomes—the legacy of the unequal distribution of access to resources and wealth. The economic crisis and the structural adjustment policies adopted to deal with it have accentuated these inequalities. While the deterioration in standards of living has been more acute among the poor of the region than for the middle and upper sectors, the middle sectors have also suffered from the general cutback in employment in government services, with hundreds of teachers, nurses, and public employees out of work. For the vast majority of people in the region, the possibility of international migration has provided the only hope of individual advancement.

The severity of the current economic crisis has exacerbated other kinds of social problems. The Caribbean is rapidly being transformed into a center for drug trafficking, given its strategic location astride the drug routes from South America. Marijuana is grown in and distributed from Jamaica and Belize, cocaine and heroin make their way to Puerto Rico and the Bahamas for distribution to the U.S. market, and sophisticated money laundering practices have sprung up in many countries—most notably the Cayman Islands. International criminal networks involved in gambling and prostitution have also taken root in countries where they were not involved before. The Dominican Republic now exports prostitutes to Curaçao, St. Martin, Puerto Rico, Europe, and the Middle East.[1] Increasingly, youth are turning to criminal activity to counter unemployment and poverty. Assault, robberies, even assassinations have increased on all of the islands and several, such as Puerto Rico, have entered a stage where fear of delinquency begins to dominate daily life.

Added to a general increase in crime and violence is an increasing incidence of violence against women, as an angry and powerless male population takes out its frustrations on people who are even more powerless. As pressure for economic survival intensifies, domestic violence against women has reached such a point that women's groups in Barbados, the Dominican Republic, and Trinidad-Tobago, as well as other countries, have organized in protest and to demand stronger legislation to counter the trend.

The ramifications of the crisis extend well beyond the Caribbean proper. The increasingly visible and violent activity of Jamaican criminal gangs in the United States, the inroads made by Puerto Rican drug dealers in the U.S. market, and the growing stream of illegal migration to North America, for example, are all a direct consequence of the economic and social crisis in the Caribbean.

Not surprisingly, popular rejection of structural adjustment policies in the region is growing—illustrated by the recent reelection of Michael Manley in Jamaica and by riots, protests, and strikes in Jamaica, Haiti, and the Dominican Republic throughout the 1980s—together with heightened awareness of the need for alternative development strategies if the Caribbean is to overcome the problems of underdevelopment and social decay. Increasingly the contours of these alternatives are being discussed not only in academic circles but also (as we saw in Chapter 4) among mass-based organizations such as women's groups, churches, trade unions, and nongovernmental organizations (NGOs).[2] Women's organizations have been particularly active and in the forefront of an alternative analysis which seeks to illuminate the link between the exploitation of women's time and labor and the reversal of the gains in social development of the decade of the 1970s.[3] To some extent too, the possibility of alternative development strategies is now being discussed within political parties.

On one level, the search for alternative strategies is motivated by immediate short-term considerations which demand a more equitable and balanced approach to current structural adjustment policies. The concern here is how to shape economic policy so that it takes into account the basic needs of the majority of the population and maintains intact the critical social services upon which the region's poor depend.

Viewed in longer term perspective, however, such discussions have increasingly turned to a consideration of the principles which should guide a new development model that would engender a more equitable and participatory process of development in the Caribbean.

In a 1987 symposium on the Caribbean, participants—a broadly representative group of the various social interests in the region— enunciated a set of principles for a new model of development.[4] Intended to guide further discussion, these principles also provide a framework for revamping Caribbean-U.S. relations:

1. *Self-determination:* the shaping of Caribbean development strategies inside, rather than outside, the region.
2. *Participation:* the broad-based involvement of Caribbean people in the definition and implementation of alternative strategies.
3. *Self-reliance:* the building of local structures and capabilities in order to enable the region to reduce its dependence on goods, resources, and assistance from external sources.
4. *Regionalism:* the fostering of cooperation rather than competition among the countries of the region and the strengthening of regional organizations and regional integration.
5. *Equity:* the equitable distribution of assets, resources, and other benefits of development among the various social groups, and among generations as well as both genders.
6. *Sustainability:* the grounding of alternative strategies of development in a sound and secure environment and in local human capacity.

The essential precondition for an alternative development strategy based on these principles in the Caribbean would be U.S. adherence to the principle of noninterference in the internal affairs of other states.

Rather than representing a definite and fixed model, the principles enunciated above instead provide a guide to the character of the changes which would be required in Caribbean societies. The specific contours of the transformation would vary from country to country, depending on particular circumstances. Nevertheless, the aims and objectives— broadly defined—are applicable across the region.

In the sections which follow we will examine more closely the implications of such an alternative development strategy, focusing on the international, regional, and national dimensions of these transformations. In addition, we will analyze the implications of such a course of development at the level of the workplace, the community, and the household.

The Caribbean in the International Economy

Any long-term development strategy premised on the principle of self-determination must include a reevaluation of the role of the external sector in Caribbean development. A structure of production that is organized primarily for and around export production, and which is forever subject to the vagaries of external demand, in effect relinquishes the right to self-determination. Such an economy, particularly if it is also dependent on foreign capital for new investment, will always be subordinated to the whims of foreign consumers and producers, who will thus determine the health of local economies.

In spite of the current trend toward globalization of national economies, local control of economic decision-making is of utmost importance to give substance to the principle of self-determination. Equally important is that the model of accumulation and basic economic activity be internally oriented and geared to the satisfaction of the basic needs of the majority of the population. A model of accumulation premised on self-determination and increased local control of the economy should also provide opportunities for the sustained and progressively widened participation of the local population in economic decision-making.

It should be emphasized that what is being proposed is not an autarchic "de-linking" from the world economy. Even if this were desirable, it is not feasible given the small size and resource constraints that face the various countries of the region. What is being suggested is that national priorities ought to be redirected to the production of those goods and services most needed by the population of the region, in a scheme where exports emerge as an extension of these activities.

Those sectors and commodities which not only substitute for imported products, but also have the potential to be tradeables in regional and international markets, should receive the highest priority. The essential point is that the substitution of imports that is envisaged here is only feasible if the sectors and industries thus targeted can become internationally competitive in the medium to long run—thus avoiding some of the mistakes of import-substitution industrialization in the past.

Comparative Advantage

Another issue has to do with the manner in which international competitiveness is achieved. Rather than basing competitiveness on cheap and unprotected labor—which would be incompatible with the strategy proposed here—international competitiveness should be based on high labor productivity, in turn a function of state support to education, health, and nutrition, as well as worker participation in decision-making.[5]

The proliferation of export-processing zones in the 1980s as the answer to all economic ills has only made the region more vulnerable. In contrast to the majority of import substitution industries, the free-trade zones have been based on the cheapest and most docile labor force, young women, who are in addition denied the right to organize. Moreover, besides the wage bill and utilities, these assembly industries contribute little value-added to national economies, making them inefficient generators of foreign exchange or employment, particularly when compared with the traditional export sectors. The free-trade zones are also not cheap for countries to set up or maintain: they require significant state investments in infrastructure, thus absorbing resources which could have gone into social infrastructure or services. And since attracting U.S. capital rests on incentive tax schemes, these industries contribute little to local public finance. Finally, the minimal capital required of foreign investors in these industries means that they are particularly mobile and thus sensitive to changes in wage rates, state incentives, and political conditions. The export-processing zones can hardly be regarded as a pivotal element of a sustainable development strategy which might enhance the standard of living of Caribbean people.

The Role of Foreign Investment

Since foreign investment has historically played such a large role in determining the structure of production in Caribbean economies, any attempt to reorient the insertion of these economies in the international division of labor will require a careful reevaluation of the role of foreign capital. Despite the controversy surrounding the question, a broad spectrum of both popular and political organizations recognize that foreign capital investments can play a positive role in a nationally focused economic strategy. Foreign investors will remain an important source of finance as well as a potential source of new technology and a potential conduit into new export markets. Properly conceived foreign investments and more creative forms of relations with foreign investors can contribute positively to the economic expansion of the region.

The main concern on the part of most labor organizations is about finding the mechanisms to ensure that the interests of foreign investors correspond to the development priorities laid out by the people of the region and their representative governments. The Oilfields Workers Trade Union of Trinidad-Tobago, for example, insists that overseas interests should be able to demonstrate their potential to generate jobs and to be net earners of foreign exchange. In a 1987 memorandum to the Trinidadian government the union stressed the need to select investments that create the greatest backward and forward linkages with the local and regional economy, and show the potential to transfer technology to the region. They also stressed that foreign investment should not be predicated on extravagant incentive schemes.[6]

The Need to Diversify

Over the long run, it is imperative that Caribbean states engage in a sustained effort to diversify their international economic and political relations. Traditionally, both trade and political relationships have been concentrated on a limited number of countries; today, bilateral relations with the United States predominate. This pattern has reinforced the general subordination of the Caribbean within the world economy, which has historically acted as a constraint on the region's development. Overcoming this limitation should be a major goal; the on-going reorganization of the structure of the global order provides the opportunity. Caribbean countries should move to diversify their trade and investment linkages, taking advantage of the growing economic strength of Japan and Europe in the world economy. A new insertion within the global economy also implies a sustained commitment to building cooperative linkages with other countries of the third world, particularly Latin America.

Given the importance of the external sector and the disproportionate effect which changes in the advanced economies have upon Caribbean growth rates, it is imperative that the advanced industrialized economies adopt coordinated policies to boost world economic growth and thus the demand for the region's exports. A growth-inducing strategy on the part of the advanced countries would probably also depend upon lower real interest rates, which is also crucial in ameliorating the debt crisis.

Canceling the Debt

Economic recovery in the Caribbean depends crucially on the cancellation of the external public debt, including bilateral, multilateral, and commercial debt. Rescheduling is not sufficient: many of the countries of the region have more than repaid the sums initially borrowed from commercial banks through the high interest rates prevailing in the 1980s. Multilateral organizations such as the World Bank, moreover, have refused to even discuss the rescheduling of the debt, imposing severe hardship on already depressed economies. It is imperative that the net resource transfer from the region to creditors be halted.

It is also quite apparent that IMF structural adjustment policies have been designed and are being implemented to allow repayment of the debt at the cost of the well-being of Caribbean populations. It is simply intolerable for economic and social policy to be subordinated to the requirements of debt servicing. At the very minimum, the region's external debt must be restructured so that debt service is reduced to a level compatible with fighting unemployment and poverty.[7]

As the Association of Caribbean Economists points out in their working paper on debt, debt cancellation is crucial, but unless other things change, the debt could be written off tomorrow and by 1999 the region could be in the same situation as it is today.[8] Obviously, other changes must be implemented to generate sustainable economic development, including alternative modes of insertion in the international economy and an alternative model of accumulation.

Regional Integration

The Caribbean countries constitute small economies if considered independently, but together they comprise a population of around 35 million, sufficient in size to overcome the limits of small domestic markets. Moreover, while individual countries have limited resource bases, the region in the aggregate is resource rich.

Since the 1960s, countries in the English-speaking Caribbean have made a number of attempts, which have met with varying degrees of success, to build regional institutions and to integrate economically (see Chapter 5). The most important effort was the creation of the Caribbean Community and Common Market (CARICOM) in 1973. Although intraregional trade subsequently grew, not one country counts CARICOM as its most important source of imports, and progress toward full economic integration has been slow and bumpy.

The regionalist movement has suffered intense pressure in the 1980s. The economic crisis severely affected intraregional trade, restricting both the capacity and willingness of the member states to participate in the integration process.[9] External actors also intervened to limit the scope of this process. The Reagan administration's policy of pursuing bilateral rather than multilateral relations with Caribbean states released a competitive rather than a collaborative dynamic among the region's states. Pressed by the economic crisis, most countries sought to attract foreign capital through competing schemes of incentives and devaluations (to make labor as cheap as possible). Rather than regional unity, the aim became to individually integrate themselves on the best terms with the U.S. market, which had become more accessible through the provisions of the CBI.

CBI-related policies have also promoted projects that spur regional competition and disintegration. The best example was the opening of a banana box factory in Dominica under the Puerto Rican twin plant program. This plant competes with the Windward Island Packaging Co., a paper and cardboard CARICOM industry based in St. Lucia that was the supplier of boxes to Dominica and the other countries of the Organization of Eastern Caribbean States (OECS).

Nonetheless, efforts at more serious integration have slowly been attracting wider support, and as disillusionment with the benefits of the CBI grows, various states have recently strengthened their commitment to regional integration. For the first time in 1975 an organization was formed including states from all of the major linguistic regions of the Caribbean, the Caribbean Development and Cooperation Committee (CDCC) as an adjunct of the United Nations Economic Commission for Latin America and the Caribbean. More recently some of the Spanish, French, and Dutch-speaking countries of the region have expressed interest in becoming members of CARICOM. Currently, Haiti, the Dominican Republic, and Suriname enjoy observer status within the Caribbean Community and have all expressed their interest in full membership. Some members have also proposed extending observer status to Puerto Rico and Cuba in an effort to overcome regional fragmentation.

During 1988–89 the CARICOM heads of state took steps to remove the remaining barriers to free trade and to expedite the establishment of a common external tariff.[10] In addition, a proposal is under discussion to establish a Caribbean stock exchange in order to facilitate transnational investment activity by Caribbean-owned enterprises and, it is hoped, to spur production integration arrangements across the region. Production integration will require careful planning, which in turn implies an active commitment and involvement of the various state and regional authorities. The technical possibilities for successful production integration certainly exist. What is required is the right set of mechanisms and sufficient political will to move the process of regional integration forward.

The future of the regional integration movement also depends on its widening, in two senses. The first, already noted, is the need to broaden the base of participation beyond the original membership of the English-speaking states. Regional economic integration on the widest possible basis is an essential precondition for self-reliance and sustainability, key principles underpinning any alternative development strategy. The second is the need to create structures which allow for greater direct participation of the Caribbean populace in the process.

At a minimum, what is needed is some institutionalized means for nongovernmental organizations—including the churches, trade unions, farmer associations, women's groups, and so on—to have a direct and continuous input in the process of regional decision-making. Probably only in this way can sufficient political will be garnered to overcome the obstacles which have stood in the way of regional cooperation and integration.

It is also important to take note that Caribbean regional integration will assume even greater importance in the next decade given the trend toward regionalization of economic decisions among blocs of "core" countries; namely the recent U.S. Canada free trade agreement and the unification of European economies scheduled for 1992.

A New National Model of Accumulation

We stressed at the outset that any meaningful alternative development strategy in the Caribbean must be aimed at meeting basic human needs and thus eliminating absolute and relative poverty. Moreover, if such a strategy is to succeed, it must be premised upon the broad-based participation of Caribbean people in its definition and implementation. In particular, attention needs to be paid to the participation of women, the key actors in meeting basic needs, and the people whose labor (both paid and unpaid) has been most exploited in the export-oriented growth models of the past. Any alternative strategy must thus be founded on the principle of equity—across genders, generations, social classes, and races—so that the political will is mustered to transform the system of ownership, production, and distribution in such a way that it is geared to the satisfaction of the basic needs of the population.

As Guyanese economist Clive Thomas has pointed out, "accumulation has to be founded on the logic of a dynamic convergence between social needs and the use of domestic resources."[11] In other words, the central element of a model of accumulation geared toward meeting basic human needs is a structure of production oriented toward the structure of desired consumption, subject to domestic resource constraints and sustainability. A second element is a structure of wages and incomes closely linked to productivity increases so that there is a balanced relationship between accumulation (for new investment) and the expansion of the internal market. A third element is a structure of participation in decision-making so that the voices and perspectives of women are sought and incorporated into policies and program design along with those of men.

Diversifying Agriculture

An obvious priority in such a strategy must be the diversification of the agricultural sector. In a context where Caribbean countries currently import millions of dollars of foodstuffs annually, the aim must be to change the region's position as a net importer of food and to enhance farmer incomes. Particular attention must be given to the production of staple foods, to crops linked to the tourist industry, and to those products which constitute vital inputs for agroindustry. Such a set of priorities should result in the saving of scarce foreign exchange while generating employment and expanded trade within the regional market.

The diversification of the agricultural sector requires the modernization of current production arrangements in the region. This must include land reform, so that idle, arable land is put into the hands of those willing to farm. The task of creating landholdings of a viable economic size is a big one, and must be given priority, along with that of improving the character of marketing and storage arrangements. Agricultural cooperatives—including marketing and service as well as production cooperatives—deserve particular state support and should be encouraged, along with other rural organizations, to participate directly in the design and implementation of a new agricultural strategy. The precise mix of measures and structures to be pursued should depend on the choices made by and within rural communities.

Another important consideration for increasing food production is the fact that women in the Caribbean are often the farmers, especially when it comes to food for the family or the local market. Gender bias has traditionally resulted in women farmers being ignored by extension agents or when cooperative associations are formed. Efforts to improve the productivity of the smallholder sector will also have to take into account the interrelated link between women's role in agricultural production and in domestic labor.

None of this implies an abandonment of the traditional export sector, whether in agriculture or in mining, which will continue to be a significant, if unstable, provider of foreign exchange. However, the traditional export sector must become more competitive, through technological change, and become more directly linked to the other sectors of production within the local economy. Moreover, careful attention will have to be given to the future world market prospects of some of the region's primary commodity exports, such as sugar and bananas. The trend toward the substitution of nonsugar sweeteners for sugarcane, and the severe reduction in the region's access to the protected U.S. market, suggest that it is imperative for Caribbean sugar producers to begin planning how to convert excess sugarcane producing land to foodstuffs or new agroexports compatible with the domestic market. Likewise, the possible loss of the privileged access of Caribbean banana exports to European markets calls for careful planning of both agricultural and export diversification.

Redefining Import Substitution

The second main prong of a new model of national accumulation relates to the reorientation of the process of industrialization. Priority should be given to new industries which use local and regional raw material inputs and which are employment-intensive. The targeted industries should be either intermediate industries with a regional market or wage goods industries whose products form part of the basic consumption of the domestic and regional population. Whereas in the past import substitution focused on the production of luxury goods produced largely with imported inputs in assembly-type industries, the approach being proposed here emphasizes the priority of basic goods, redefining the concept of import substitution industrialization. Specifically, we propose that emphasis should be placed on those commodities which are used directly or indirectly in the production of most other commodities.[12] In this way it should be possible to overcome the limitations of previous import-substitution strategies which involved massive imports of raw materials, developed few linkages between sectors in the local economy, and generated minimal employment. It should be emphasized again that a basic underlying principle for the establishment of import substitution industries should be their international competitiveness, at least in the medium term.

Rethinking the Role of Tourism

Finally, the tourist sector will continue to play a vital role in the economy of the region as a generator of foreign exchange. However, this sector is currently characterized by low value-added (approximately 60 percent of the inputs of this industry are imported).[13] A high priority should be given to developing the backward and forward linkages, particularly in agriculture and the textile and furniture industries, to make the tourist sector a more efficient generator of foreign exchange.

Moreover, since the tourist industry tends to put the Caribbean islands in competition for tourist dollars, it will be important to develop a regional strategy for tourist development that can benefit the region as a whole. For example, currently the Caribbean loses access to foreign exchange through the common practice in which visitors prepay for their hotel accommodations through U.S. airlines. If these hotels are foreign owned, prepayment will not necessarily engender foreign exchange which passes through local central banks. A regional marketing center based in the United States might be one way to promote locally owned tourist facilities; such an organization could also develop the different segments of the tourist market (business, education, health tourism, etc.) to the benefit of all.[14]

Reconsidering the Role of the State

The alternative model of national development sketched out here necessarily depends upon the state playing a crucial role in the orientation of economic life. While private enterprise will certainly remain central, and even dominant, in the process, the state will need to act as both catalyst and manager of the process of economic transformation. Not only will macroeconomic policy have to be geared to the requirements of a new mode of accumulation, but in critical sectors and industries, particularly where the investments requirements are large or where the time horizon is longer than that typical of private enterprise, there will be a need for direct state involvement in the process of production.

Implied in this model is not the traditional mixed economy which centers on state and capitalist enterprises. Rather, what is being proposed is a more heterogenous productive structure encompassing, besides the above, small-scale enterprises and cooperatives. NGOs have a critical role to play in this new structure, for they have been effectively channeling what have been up to now activities of the informal sector and providing poor men and women with an institutional framework to make such activities stable and profitable. NGOs have also been more successful than the state in promoting cooperative development.

The state also has a vital role to play in the protection of the environment and in the provision of social services and physical infrastructure, all vital elements in the construction of a more equitable society and sustainable economy. Quite apart from the well-being of their own populations, the importance of natural resources and tourism in any alternative development strategy makes it essential that Caribbean governments not allow the region to turn into a toxic waste dump. Moreover, the development of the tourism sector needs to be monitored to protect the very resources that attract people to the region—clear air, water, beautiful beaches, and so on.

Social services across the region have been decimated by the current structural adjustment policies. An urgent priority is to restore these services to at least the levels of the 1970s and targeting these services to the most vulnerable groups, particularly poor women and children.

Their improvement over time will be necessary for any project hinged on expanded production and the principle of equity.

For this alternative model of development to succeed, the entire functioning of the state and of society at large must be subject to the "logic of the majority": that is, substantive economic and political transformation is predicated upon it being a project implemented and designed by the majority.[15] This in turn requires that the entire political process be geared toward the democratization of power in society and to the protection of the fundamental human and civil rights of the population, including the rights to free expression, organization, and assembly, and guarantees against repression and torture.

The process of democratization should not be conceived of as being restricted merely to the institutions of the state. In order to succeed, the whole gamut of social institutions, from the workplace to the community, and including the home and family, must be transformed. This requires organization and education—especially programs of non-formal and popular education—to secure the sustained transformation of attitudes and behavior that such a process of democratization involves.

Democratization at the Workplace

A sustainable strategy of development organized around the satisfaction of basic needs must place in the forefront the interests of the workforce— necessarily the main agent of the transformation. A central element of this strategy must include the planned and effective implementation of the right to employment.[16] The right to employment must include the right to work without coercion; the right to free collective bargaining and effective representation; and the right to participate in the organization of the work process. It must also include the right to training, to health protection, and most importantly, an end to discrimination based on gender, race, or ethnicity.

The Caribbean has a rich history of trade union struggle and representation, stretching back over a century. The gains have not always been easy and have been achieved only through sustained organization and militancy. More recently, in the wake of the export-oriented structural adjustment strategies—aimed at attracting foreign capital with the lure of cheap labor—there has been a disquieting mood of hostility on the part of certain states and social sectors to trade union activity, particularly in the export-processing zones.

Again, the negative impact of the structural adjustment process is being borne disproportionately by poor women. A similar pattern is manifest in much of the recent anti-union agitation, which has proscribed, for example, the organization of workers in the free-trade zones in Jamaica and the Dominican Republic where the overwhelming majority of workers are women. Special measures must be taken to guarantee the right of trade union representation to them. Moreover, states must be called upon to protect workers in these zones from such abuses as the lack of payment of adequate wages, undue overtime, excessive production quotas, and sexual harassment.

In general, states must make a deliberate effort to ensure gender equity at the workplace, including equal pay for equal work and for jobs of comparable worth, and the training of women workers and youth, who have been disproportionately hit by unemployment in the current crisis.[17] In addition, it should be taken into account that women workers need special support services to enable them to continue to take care of their families, and these should be provided by management, the unions, or the state, or some combination of these. Among these are child care, adequate health care and maternity leave, and improved transportation. But the importance of these support services will never be recognized let alone acted upon without greater female participation in the leadership of the trade unions and greater gender awareness at all levels within the unions. Such participation is a precondition of workplace equality, as is a vibrant and effective women's movement with the space and power to implement needed changes.

The informal sector has provided an important cushion for the underemployed of the region. It should not be seen, however, as a panacea for solving employment problems in the region. Care should be taken that the informal sector is not abused as a source of cheap labor by national or multinational firms wishing to skirt minimum wages, regulation, labor organizing, and the like, through subcontracting. The role of NGOs, through their organizing of people in this sector and placing their needs before the government, will be critically important in providing the institutional framework to make informal sector activities stable and profitable.

Finally, the call is increasingly heard across the region for the rights of workers to be extended beyond those of trade union-led collective bargaining at the workplace, to incorporate a more wide-ranging system of worker participation in the organization of production activities in the enterprises and within the economy in general. The Oilfields Workers Trade Union in Trinidad-Tobago, for example, has called for a system of workers councils in all key sectors of the economy to engage in participatory sectoral planning.[18] Suffice it to say that expanded, sustainable production and equity in the Caribbean will require a fundamental reorganization in the way production and decision-making are organized at the level of the workplace.

Community Participation

Significant segments of the population currently remain outside the formal economy and thus would not be directly affected by any program of worker participation. This makes the community another vital arena for increasing the participation of people in development. Moreover, the salience of community-level action is underscored by the surge in the number of grassroots groups and community-based local development organizations across the region over the past decade, as we saw in Chapter 4, largely in response to the failure of official authorities to adequately provide the resources to address the needs of local communities.

Given the increasingly vibrant state of community organization, and the need to extend the structures of democratic participation which form an essential component of an alternative strategy of development, national governments must encourage these organizations in order to harness the human and material resources of the communities. In addition, communities are a vital element to take into account in the formulation of general development plans. Not only do community-based enterprises, especially in rural communities, have the potential to contribute significantly to employment generation and the maintenance and extension of social services, but community organizations should provide the initial and essential definition of what constitute "basic needs." In this sense they are, indeed, indispensable to the whole strategy of development envisaged here.

The strengthening of community organizations requires that special attention be paid to the active participation of women in their leadership and to the use of an analysis which considers how gender roles are constructed and reproduced to determine needs and priorities for action; that is, specific attention has to be given to the differential impact of policies on men and women. It must also recognize that these organizations need training—in nonformal and popular education techniques—for increasing popular participation.

Given that community ties in the Caribbean often extend across national borders and include permanent migrants to the United States and Great Britain, and that migrants' remittances are both an important source of foreign exchange as well as household income, creative ways are needed to harness such remittances for community development. For example, governments might consider offering matching funds or tax breaks or access to foreign exchange for remittances sent explicitly to community organizations for community development projects.[19]

Equity in the Household

Equity, as defined in the development strategy outlined here, requires recognition of three elements at the household level: (1) the value of women's unpaid labor; (2) the link between production and reproduction; and (3) the existence of gender hierarchies within the household.

Women's unpaid work in domestic tasks contributes to a higher household standard of living than would otherwise be the case. Nonetheless, domestic labor is rarely considered to be "work," often not even by the women themselves, and its importance in social reproduction (reproducing the capacity to work as well as the socialization of the next generation of workers) is rarely acknowledged. Recognition of the link between production and reproduction requires that existing inequities within the household be addressed. Quite apart from their personal cost, existing inequities also involve important social costs. Long hours of domestic work, due to the rudimentary conditions in which it is often carried out, impose a heavy physical toll on women that limits their effective participation in directly productive activities in the wider economy. Moreover, it restricts their participation in community life, in political parties and unions, and in social activity in general.

Special attention should be given to female-headed households, in which women carry not only the full burden of domestic labor, but also that of maintaining their families. Of all households, these are clearly the most disadvantaged in terms of income levels, given women's generally lesser earning power as compared with men.

It is essential that an alternative development strategy prioritize the need to improve conditions of human reproduction and enhance the conditions under which domestic labor is performed. This involves attention to the provision of social services and basic infrastructure (for example, potable tap water), the search for more appropriate domestic technologies to make domestic tasks less time-intensive as well as environmentally sustainable (e.g., appropriate stoves), and redressing the inequalities in the household gender division of labor.

The existence of a gender hierarchy within the household, which limits women's access to resources—whether training, land, credit, or family planning—and to leisure, must also be recognized. Unequal power relations between men and women deny women the resources and time to participate in society on an equal footing with men. An alternative model of development based on the principle of equity thus requires a long and sustained effort to redefine traditional gender roles within the household, the community, the workplace, and the state.

Conclusion

We have not sought to present a definitive "blueprint" of an alternative development model applicable to all Caribbean states. Rather, we have sought to outline general principles to guide the search for such alternative strategies, based upon an analysis of the historical experience of the Caribbean and upon a basic commitment to the values of freedom, equity, and popular participation in the organization of society.

More specifically, we have sought to distill the basic perspectives emerging within the increasingly active network of progressive social and political movements within the Caribbean. Our focus has by no means been exhaustive, but we have attempted to address the main and most vocal demands that are emerging from the region. Ultimately, however, the shape of the future development of the Caribbean will depend on the capacities of the people of the region, collectively and in their separate territories, to define, struggle for, and implement a new vision of Caribbean development.

As we approach the closing decade of the twentieth century it is all too evident that an alternative model of Caribbean development, designed to benefit the majority of Caribbean people, requires a much greater awareness among the American public of the need for fundamental changes in U.S. policy toward the region. A new U.S. economic, political, and military policy is required that is based on respect for the right to self-determination and regionalism. Moreover, U.S. policy must recognize that enhancing the standard of living of the majority of Caribbeans—in a form and manner that they themselves determine— is the precondition to the common security of the hemisphere.

Notes

1. Cristina Calvalcanti, Carmen Imbert, and Margarita Cordero, *Prostitución: Esclavitud Sexual Femenina* (Santo Domingo: CIPAF, 1985).

2. See Coordinadora Regional de Investigaciones Económicas y Sociales (CRIES), "The Contemporary Caribbean: Economic Crisis, Social Movements, and Alternative Development Strategies," report prepared for OXFAM-America, July 1988.

3. The active role of women in denouncing structural adjustment policies was particularly evident at the November 1988 10th Anniversary Consultation and Symposium of WAND (the Women and Development Unit of the University of the West Indies based in Barbados) which brought together women's grassroots organizations and leaders from throughout the region.

4. The principles are drawn from The Development Group for Alternative Policies, *The Caribbean Basin Initiative: Caribbean Views*, Report of a Congressional Study Mission and Symposium on the Caribbean Basin Initiative, Sep-

tember 18–19, 1987, to the Committee on Foreign Affairs, U.S. House of Representatives (Washington, D.C.: U.S. Government Printing Office, 1987), p. 6.

5. Presentation by Norman Girvan at the Seminar on "Puerto Rico in the Caribbean," Institute of Caribbean Studies, University of Puerto Rico, May 1989.

6. Oilfields Workers Trade Union (OWTU), *Memorandum to the Government of Trinidad-Tobago* (Trinidad: OWTU, 1987), p. 16.

7. Ibid., p. 26.

8. Association of Caribbean Economists, Working Group on External Debt, "Debt and Development Strategies in the Caribbean," paper presented at the Second Conference of Caribbean Economists, Barbados, May 1989, p. 4.

9. For example, between 1981 and 1984 intra-CARICOM trade declined from US$590 to US$445 million. The Economist Intelligence Unit, *Quarterly Economic Review* no. 1 (1988), p. 6.

10. *Washington Report on Latin America & the Caribbean* 4, no. 19 (1989), p. 1.

11. Clive Thomas, *The Poor and the Powerless* (New York: Monthly Review Press, 1988), p. 364.

12. Ibid., pp. 364–66.

13. GAO, *Caribbean Basin Initiative: Impact on Selected Countries,* Report to the Chairman, Subcommittee on Western Hemisphere and Peace Corps Affairs, Committee on Foreign Relations, U.S. Senate, July 1988, p. 17.

14. See Alister McIntyre, "Developing Tourism," *Caribbean Affairs* 1, no. 1 (1988), pp. 174–75; and B. Zargaris and L. Emery, "Tourism: the Orphan of Caribbean Programs," *Journal of Tourism Research* 26 (1988), pp. 24–28.

15. Thomas, *The Poor and the Powerless,* p. 361.

16. Ibid., p. 357.

17. Caribbean Congress of Labour, *A Trade Union Programme for the Structural Transformation of the Caribbean* (Barbados: ICFTU/CCL, 1986), pp. 28–29.

18. Oilfields Workers Trade Union, *Memorandum,* pp. 5–6.

19. For other proposals on how migrant remittances might be harnessed for development purposes see Robert Pastor, "Migration and Development in the Caribbean Basin: Implications and Recommendations for Policy," Commission for the Study of International Migration and Cooperative Economic Development Working Paper #7, Washington, D.C., 1989.

CHAPTER 8

Out of the Shadow: Alternative U.S. Policies Toward the Caribbean

GIVEN THE COMPLEX and multifaceted links between the United States and the Caribbean, a new U.S. policy toward the region must be based on the recognition of our interdependence and of the importance of our mutual economic well-being. The policies of the Reagan administration—designed to aggressively promote the interests of capital regardless of the costs to labor, and to exploit the inherently unequal regional power relationship wherever possible—have worsened the economic crisis of the Caribbean and heightened social tensions. In so doing, these policies have in fact hurt the long-run interests of the United States. An alternative U.S. policy toward the region, aimed at fostering sustainable, participatory, and equitable development, is better suited to serving our mutual interests.

The previous chapter highlighted some of the ways in which Caribbean peoples themselves are attempting to define the contours of new strategies of development, strategies that are based on popular participation in decision-making. Key in this search is how to reconcile concerns for both growth and equity—across social groups, genders, and generations. A more viable U.S. strategy toward the region should start from the ideas, aspirations, and energies of Caribbean people as well as from their local, national, and regional organizations.

The first element of an alternative U.S. policy is acceptance of the goal of self-determination. It is time that we recognized that self-determination is consistent with U.S. national interests when it is inspired by the people of the region and geared to benefit them. Caribbean history provides substantial evidence to show that externally imposed models have not worked. We must allow Caribbean people to assume the leadership in defining solutions to their own problems. Moreover, a pragmatic policy proposal must recognize that the magnitude of resources required to engender sustainable Caribbean development is unlikely to be forthcoming from the U.S. Congress in a time of mounting budget deficits. Without the participation of Caribbean people in constructing their own modes of development, the goal of increasing the standard of living of the region will be unattainable.

A second element of an alternative U.S. policy, derived from the first, requires not only acceptance but promotion of the goal of regional integration. The recent U.S. administrations, rather than fostering regional integration and regional institutions, have been promoting competition rather than cooperation among the countries of the region. This, we feel, is to the detriment of Caribbean peoples, making it more difficult for the nations of the region to speak with a common voice about solutions to regional problems.

In the following, we outline some of the more specific aspects of an alternative U.S. policy toward the Caribbean which respond to the alternative visions of development emerging from the region. We first discuss the short-run measures necessary to alleviate the current economic crisis—debt relief and the temporary restoration of sugar quotas. We then turn to longer term U.S. policies that influence Caribbean growth and development options: trade, migration, development aid, and military assistance. The chapter concludes with a discussion of U.S.-Cuba relations and those between Puerto Rico and the Caribbean, countries whose participation is crucial if the region is to achieve prosperity as well as stability in the long run.

Out of the Debt Shadow

For many Caribbean countries any possibility of embarking on a new path of growth and development depends upon lifting the intolerable burden of debt. The experience of the 1980s has demonstrated the dangerous social consequences of repaying foreign debt by squeezing a domestic surplus through the implementation of structural adjustment policies. The price of unbridled profit maximization by international finance capital and of unwise development projects for which governments incurred debt has fallen disproportionately upon the most disadvantaged groups in the Caribbean, particularly poor women. The consequences are seen not only in human suffering but also in social dislocation and disintegration.

It is increasingly evident that no one benefits from the debt crisis. Only by resolving it on a long-term basis will third world countries again play a positive role in stimulating global economic growth. As recognition of this reality has grown so too has an international consensus that bold steps must be taken to solve the debt crisis, steps that include outright debt reduction and forgiveness.[1]

The Reagan administration was a staunch opponent of debt reduction. Instead, the 1985 plan developed by then Treasury Secretary James Baker focused on proposals for new lending by commercial banks and international financial organizations combined with some debt rescheduling to those countries that implemented adjustment programs based on "free market" economic policies. By 1988 it was evident that new international lending had been at most modest and that the capital flows projected under the "Baker Plan" were insufficient to repay the debt, not to mention to spur growth. Even officials of the International Monetary Fund (IMF) and the World Bank were beginning to discuss how to reduce third world debt and not only how to restructure it.[2]

This is the context in which the Bush administration launched the "Brady Plan" in March of 1989, officially recognizing for the first time that some debt reduction would be necessary to revitalize third world economies.[3] At the crux of the plan is the expectation that commercial banks will act voluntarily to reduce the size of third world debt if given appropriate incentives. The "carrot" is the use of World Bank and/or IMF resources to reduce the debt principal or to guarantee payment of a portion of the interest owed to the commercial banks once the commercial banks agree to reduce the total amount of debt owed. The "stick" is the threat of congressional action, such as requiring the Federal Reserve Board to set stiffer reserve requirements for banks that are heavily exposed in the third world.[4]

The specifics of the Brady Plan were to be worked out in country-by-country negotiations among concerned parties; the aim, however, was to achieve what appeared to be a rather minimal reduction in the outstanding third world debt, on the order of 20 percent of the debt of the thirty-nine most heavily indebted countries.[5] Critics immediately asked how such a small reduction in the total debt could renew growth and spur development. Moreover, the plan did not address a disturbing dynamic of the current debt crisis: that banks make new loans to debtor nations that simply go to pay off interest on old loans. Even though it creates more principal (which will never be repaid), this maneuver keeps interest payments flowing and lets banks avoid having to declare old loans "nonperforming," which would mean taking a loss against current profits. Finally, there is the question of why multilateral institutions—which are ultimately financed by taxpayers—should have to pick up the tab to maintain the profitability of commercial banks.

The Brady Plan, like the Baker Plan before it, sides with the lenders over the debtors and is clearly calibrated to protect the interests of the banks, prevent default, and strengthen policies of structural adjustment in the third world. It springs not from concern over the damaging consequences of debt payments and structural adjustment on the third world's poor, but from the worry that the cost will become so high that social explosions—like the February 1989 riots in Venezuela—will favor the rise of debtor-nation governments that refuse to continue payments.

From the third world, however, comes a very different argument—that the debt is illegitimate. This argument, advanced by more and more grassroots organizations, political parties, and community, church, and political leaders, applies especially to commercial debt, much of it extended by banks flush with petrodollars in the early 1980s, and most spent not on productive investment but rather on consumption that usually benefited only the wealthy in debtor nations. Also gaining currency in Latin America is a related argument—that the debt has already been paid off. If one takes into account the high interest rates of the early 1980s, the reduced primary export prices of this period, and illegal capital flight, the net transfer to the advanced countries has surpassed the value of the initial debt incurred by most third world countries.[6]

Whatever one's conclusions about the legitimacy of the debt, even the most optimistic economic projections cannot foresee conditions under which the debt will be repaid. Default is inevitable, and rather than advocating short-term measures to continue payments for the next year or two, U.S. policy should accept reality and look for the most orderly way possible of writing off the debt, even if it means that some commercial banks fail. And if we accept that structural adjustment policies have had devastating results for the poor majorities of these countries, and that U.S. policy should instead support equitable, participatory development, then it is illogical to continue using IMF and World Bank assistance, let alone U.S. aid, to press for full payment. U.S. citizens have a far greater interest in the long-term sustainable development of the Caribbean, an interest we share with the citizens of the region.

Since the debt of many Caribbean countries is either bilateral or multilateral rather than commercial (see Table 2.10), any solution to the Caribbean debt crisis must include not only commercial debt forgiveness, but a significant change in U.S. bilateral debt policies and in those of the multilateral donors.

The need for genuine concessionality in terms of official, bilateral debt was agreed upon in June 1988 by the Group of Seven industrial countries (known as the Paris Club) at their fourteenth Economic Summit in Toronto. The group, which besides the United States includes Canada, France, Italy, Japan, the United Kingdom, and West Germany, agreed to reduce the bilateral debt of the poorest debt-distressed countries through some combination of reduced interest rates, longer repayment periods, and partial write-offs of debt service obligations.[7] Apparently at the insistence of the United States, however, the beneficiaries must be undertaking internationally approved structural adjustment programs.

The extent to which Caribbean countries will potentially benefit from these new initiatives depends largely on which countries are to be included among the poorest or most debt-distressed. The Paris Club of donors has generally relied on the World Bank's eligibility criteria for loans with the most concessionary terms, currently encompassing those countries with per capita incomes of less than $420.[8] By this definition, Haiti would be the only Caribbean country eligible for debt relief. For the most debt-ridden Caribbean countries to benefit from this legislation, the standard would have to include what are currently defined as lower middle-income countries, those with per capita income levels of less than $1,570. Redefining the poorest countries by this standard would allow the two countries with the largest bilateral debt with the United States, Jamaica and the Dominican Republic, to be included along with the other countries in the region in most need of debt relief.

A genuine commitment to Caribbean economic development requires the U.S. government to take the following actions:

1. Cancel all bilateral debt incurred by the poorest Caribbean nations, without conditionality. A move to convert debt incurred for development assistance loans to grants in the case of the poorest Caribbean countries would be the strongest demonstration of a new U.S. commitment to solving Caribbean development problems and signal our resolve to end the global debt crisis. Moreover, debt relief should not be conditioned on the implementation of structural adjustment programs, which, as we have shown, are counterproductive to a growth-with-equity development strategy.

The total bilateral debt of the region is rather small in terms of forgone U.S. Treasury receipts; since 1980 development assistance to the Caribbean has totaled only around $2.0 billion (see Table 6.4), equal to about half of the total outstanding bilateral debt of the Caribbean, excluding Cuba (see Table 2.10). The political pay-off of bilateral debt forgiveness, nonetheless, is large, as it demonstrates a new U.S. commitment to the well-being of the Caribbean, and for

certain countries, such as the Dominican Republic, would bring substantial debt relief.[9]

2. Urge the multilateral banks (the World Bank, the Inter-American
Development Bank) to reschedule their debt, and to take steps toward
debt forgiveness for the poorest Caribbean nations. The multilateral
banks have been the least willing to consider rescheduling debts out
of fear that such a move would jeopardize their ability to borrow in
international capital markets. Moreover, the multilateral banks are now
collecting more in principal and interest on past loans from Latin
America than they are providing in new loans, clearly an untenable
situation from the perspective of the region's recovery and future
growth.[10]

The United States should maintain its commitment to the viability
of the multilateral lending institutions by timely infusions of capital—
the need for which is particularly pressing in the case of the Inter-
American Development Bank—in exchange for greater flexibility on
the part of these organizations in debt rescheduling. Debt rescheduling
should include reducing and in some cases canceling interest payments
on loans and/or lengthening the grace period for repayment of principal
on both new and existing loans. The United States should also take
the lead in reevaluating the policies of structural adjustment pursued
by the multilateral institutions and in proposing a new set of criteria
for them to follow, described below.

3. Press for changes in structural adjustment policies so that these
facilitate renewed economic growth and sustainable development in a
manner consistent with eliminating poverty. The United States should
give serious attention to the various proposals that have come out of
the ongoing North-South dialogue for reforming the IMF and changing
the priorities and content of structural adjustment policies imposed on
third world governments by this as well as the other multilateral
institutions.[11] Rather than prioritizing draconian stabilization policies
aimed to enforce third world debt service, adjustment programs should
be designed to spur growth in a manner complementary with improving
the distribution of income. As the Working Group on Debt of the
Association of Caribbean Economists argues, economic and social policy
should never be subordinated to the requirements of debt servicing,
but rather, debt servicing should be a residual of development planning.[12]

A crucial component of an "adjustment with growth" program must
be the guarantee that the program not adversely affect the standard of
living of the majority of the population—the rural and urban poor.
This requires that minimum consumption standards be taken into
account in the design of programs aimed at the contraction of aggregate
demand. Recommendations to eliminate government fiscal deficits must
be designed so that cuts in social services, subsidies, and other

government programs not fall disproportionately upon the poorest sectors of the population, specifically poor women and children. Debt-servicing obligations must then be designed and rescheduled in such a way as to maintain these minimum consumption standards as well as an adequate rate of economic growth.

4. Urge the nation's commercial banks to broaden and extend recent efforts toward debt reduction. An increasing number of commercial banks have now undertaken bad-loan provisioning— holding a certain portion of their profits as reserves in case of defaults or losses due to discounting of debt. In the secondary loan market in third world debt issues, debt obligations are traded at a discount from face value, reflecting market expectation regarding these countries' ability to repay their external debt.[13]

The growth in the secondary market in debt issues has been accompanied by debt buy-backs, "debt-for-nature swaps," and debt-equity swaps. Debt buy-backs allow countries to purchase their own discounted debt securities.[14] Debt-for-nature swaps involve the purchase of discounted debt by international environmental groups which are then redeemed in local currency bonds and donated to local environmental groups for conservation and other environmental purposes.[15] Debt-equity swaps, which seem potentially harmful to the long-run goal of third world development, involve a trade of external debt commitments for local assets, requiring the country to incur future commitments with respect to profit remittances in return for short-term debt relief. Such schemes may also substitute for direct foreign investment, thus reducing the actual capital inflow, while "denationalizing" the most viable economic sectors. They also do not ensure that the secondary market discount is actually captured by the debtor country.[16]

The potential of the secondary market in debt issue to ameliorate the debt crisis will depend largely on the willingness of the commercial banks to allow buy-back programs and on whether official development assistance is forthcoming to fund the direct purchase of discounted debt in local currencies by the debtor nations themselves.[17] But such a strategy, while providing some debt relief to third world countries, basically requires taxpayers to subsidize commercial banks. More preferable would be a U.S. policy that actively encouraged the commercial banks to engage in voluntary debt reduction by writing off their loans to the poorest Caribbean and other third world countries.[18]

U.S. Sugar Quotas: Easing the Crunch

The Caribbean economies have suffered a severe jolt from the changes in U.S. sugar policy that were instituted by the Reagan administration. The maintenance of high domestic sugar prices at no cost to the U.S.

Treasury has been attained by restricting imports to the U.S. market with the result that Caribbean sugar export revenues have been drastically reduced. The reduction of U.S. sugar imports has created a most contradictory situation, leading to a significant expansion of domestic sugar production in response to artificially high prices, while domestic producers remain high-cost-producers in comparison to their Caribbean counterparts.[19] While U.S. sugar and beet producers make super profits, Caribbean sugar mills have been shut down, thousands have been thrown out of work, and export earnings have floundered.

In the short run, it is imperative that Caribbean economies be given some immediate relief, since the sudden changes in U.S. sugar policy have been most disruptive for these economies and have compounded the economic crisis which the Caribbean Basin Initiative is supposedly to resolve. The Dominican Republic, for example, the largest producer in the region, has lost approximately $500 million in sugar export revenues, export earnings which have not been compensated for by the growth of the nontraditional exports promoted by the Caribbean Basin Initiative (CBI).

In the long term, however, the prospects for the Caribbean sugar sector appear bleak, given the trend favoring the consumption of nonsugar sweeteners. Nonsugar sweeteners currently make up 55 percent of the U.S. sweetener market.[20] Another problem which Caribbean sugar producers must recognize is that their comparative advantage has long rested on cheap manual labor. In the Dominican Republic, for example, domestic labor shortages have led to increased reliance on the import of cheaper migrant labor from Haiti. These migrants, who work in the most deplorable conditions, now constitute approximately 80 percent of the workers in this industry.[21] Cuba is the only island to have successfully mechanized cane harvesting, altering its comparative advantage in this crop from cheap labor to technological advance.

The current crisis in the Caribbean sugar industry provides an opportune moment for sugar producing countries to reevaluate the role of this sector and to explore how sugarcane acreage could be converted to domestic food production. As noted previously, food imports have been a growing component of Caribbean imports, absorbing scarce foreign exchange.

In order to restore the ability of Caribbean countries to realize short-term export earnings as well as to encourage the long-term goal of achieving food self-sufficiency, we propose the following transition program:

1. Caribbean sugar quotas should be restored to at least their pre-CBI level (1983–84) for a specific period of time, to be negotiated with Caribbean governments. The Caribbean Basin Economic Recovery

Expansion Act of 1989—also known as CBI-II or the "Gibbons Bill," after the chair of the House Ways and Means Trade Subcommittee who sponsored the legislation—recommended that a floor be legislated on Caribbean sugar quotas. The minimum Caribbean quota, however, was to be the 1989 aggregate level of 371,449 metric tons. The provision in the current bill (H.R. 1233) is much less favorable to Caribbean producers than an earlier (1987) version of the bill, which provided for Caribbean sugar quotas to be restored to their pre-CBI level (1983–84). The difference between the two proposals amounts to approximately $200 million in annual export earnings for Caribbean sugar producers.

We propose that quota levels be restored to their pre-CBI level for a specified period of time, such as five years, to allow a transition agricultural diversification program to be put into place. The increased Caribbean quotas to the U.S. market could be accommodated by lowering the guaranteed U.S. price of sugar, thus creating a gap between domestic supply and demand. This would encourage inefficient U.S. producers to get out of sugar production while also benefiting the U.S. consumer.

2. Caribbean countries benefiting from the restoration of sugar quotas should be asked to prepare a plan for the conversion of what would otherwise be excess sugarcane land to food production. U.S. development assistance (discussed below) should then be channeled to this agricultural diversification program, prioritizing food production by small farmers and cooperatives.

U.S. Trade Policy: Making Changes

One of the contradictory aspects of U.S. trade and aid policy toward the Caribbean Basin has been its stress upon creating more open, export-oriented economies in the region, while keeping U.S. doors closed to many Caribbean exports. The Reagan administration, while espousing the rhetoric of the benefits of free trade, did little to significantly reduce tariffs and quotas on key Caribbean exports or the nontariff barriers which restrict Caribbean access to the U.S. market for many products.[22] The success of either the U.S.-promoted export-oriented strategy for the region or the more sound objective of export diversification depends on the willingness of the United States and other advanced economies to accept Caribbean exports.

Legislation to extend and broaden the CBI, known as CBI-II or the Gibbons Bill, was first introduced in Congress in August 1987, and then reintroduced in revised form as the Caribbean Basin Economic Recovery and Expansion Act of 1989. This bill extends the provisions of the initial CBERA legislation to the year 2007, and further liberalizes one-way trade.[23] One of the new provisions would allow textile products eligible under the guaranteed access levels (GALS) program—which applies to apparel produced exclusively from U.S.-made, formed, and cut fabric—to enter the U.S. totally duty free. In other words, duties currently paid on the value-added portion of apparel articles produced in the Caribbean would be eliminated; recall that the value of U.S.-made components already enters duty free under section 807 of the U.S. Tariff Code. The level of apparel imports under the GALS program would continue to be determined through bilateral agreements.

In the 1987 version of the bill, *all* products made entirely of U.S.-made parts or components would have been entitled to duty-free treatment. More important for Caribbean development prospects, other products, previously excluded under the original CBERA legislation, would have been allowed to enter duty free up to specified quantities, to be determined according to the level of past exports to the United States, with duty-free quotas increased by 3 percent annually. This provision could have encouraged Caribbean exports of textiles and apparel not consisting wholly of U.S.-made, formed, and cut fabric, as well as footwear, leather goods, watches, tuna, and petroleum products.

The 1989 legislative proposal replaced duty-free treatment with a more moderate 50 percent reduction in the level of existing tariffs applicable to these products. Even this more limited proposal met stiff opposition from protectionist congresspeople and during deliberations in the House Ways and Means Committee, products such as leather footwear, petroleum and its derivatives, and tuna were exempted from any duty reduction.[24] The revised bill finally approved by the U.S. House of Representatives in October 1989 further reduced provisions to cut duties on many apparel and leather items. The modified CBI-II legislation was still under consideration by the U.S. Senate in early 1990.[25]

There is little question that favorable access to the U.S. market is crucial for Caribbean economic growth. But not all of the proposed CBI-II provisions are equally beneficial for Caribbean countries. U.S. trade policies that encourage turning the region into export-processing platforms, based on cheap and submissive labor, go against the effort to construct more equitable and viable Caribbean economies. And trade preferences which are tied to the use of U.S. inputs and components undermine efforts to construct more vibrant and self-reliant economies.

The proposal for duty-free treatment of all products made exclusively from U.S. parts and components will not necessarily benefit the Caribbean since this provision could further discourage Caribbean input production by rewarding the substitution of U.S.-made inputs for those produced in the region, and further discourage investment in those industries with potentially the greatest links to the local economy. Similarly, duty-free treatment for apparel made totally from U.S.-made, formed, and cut cloth might not have particularly beneficial effects on Caribbean economies, since such treatment encourages the further expansion of apparel production with the lowest local content. Recall that Caribbean apparel production already is characterized by its low value-added, generally 30 percent or less. Duty-free treatment under the GALS program, however, would make garment operations in the region more profitable for U.S. companies.

What trade measures would favor Caribbean development? U.S. trade policy favoring duty-free treatment of Caribbean products with a high rather than a low value-added requirement would generate the greatest domestic linkages, and thus overall Caribbean employment and income. The objection is often raised that such a policy would hurt U.S. labor. Indeed, this is often the rationale used by U.S. industries to get labor and Congressional support for protectionist tariff legislation. We strongly disagree, since we believe the best interests of U.S. labor would be served by development strategies which increase Caribbean wages and incomes, reduce unemployment levels, and foster the expansion of the trade union movement. Without such developments, U.S. plant closings will continue unabetted until U.S. and Caribbean wages are equalized downward.

Some U.S. labor groups have already come to a similar conclusion. As the International Ladies' Garment Workers' Union has argued: "If we sincerely want to help our neighbors, we should develop programs that concentrate on building infrastructure and encourage growth in the internal market and in the building of local economies. We should seek to encourage the development of free labor movements in order to help to improve conditions in these countries."[26]

Another issue is the manner in which trade concessions for the Caribbean are formulated and negotiated. The Reagan administration, by unilaterally designing trade preferences and then implementing them bilaterally rather than regionally, turned U.S. trade policy into a political lever to favor those countries subservient to U.S. policy goals. By ignoring regional institutions and regional development and trade programs, this policy discouraged regional cooperation and spurred competition among the governments of the region.

The central elements of a new U.S. trade strategy aimed at promoting Caribbean development would include the following:

1. Multilateral, rather than bilateral, trade agreements designed to strengthen regional institutions and the process of regional integration should be negotiated through regional organizations such as the Caribbean Common Market (CARICOM).

Special trade concessions should be evaluated for their potential developmental impact and be designed to favor products with the greatest, not the fewest, local linkages. Moreover, planning for export diversification should be carried out in the context of CARICOM planning for production integration to ensure compatibility between production for export and that for the regional market.

2. Preferential access to the U.S. market by Caribbean-based producers should be conditioned on the extension, protection, and enforcement of internationally recognized workers' rights.[27] Current CBERA legislation gives only cursory treatment to workers' rights, including these as only one of a number of discretionary criteria the president may invoke in determining whether to designate a country a beneficiary.[28] It is quite clear that the CBERA has encouraged the proliferation of export-processing zones where workers rights are consistently violated. Governments and enterprises in export-processing zones which do not meet minimum standards of labor legislation—such as the right to organize and the protection of labor from abuses (e.g., the lack of payment of minimum wages, undue overtime, and excessive production quotas) should be disqualified from U.S. tariff exemptions (whether CBI-II or section 807 regulations).

U.S. trade legislation should also take into account that Caribbean export-processing zones employ predominantly women. Working women need special support services, which should be provided by management, unions, the state, or a combination of these. These support services include child care, transportation, and adequate health care (particularly in relation to occupational health and safety hazards).

3. U.S. trade concessions and tax and investment incentives which favor the assembly of U.S.-made components in the Caribbean should be tied to strong U.S. plant-closing legislation, governing both notification and indemnization of workers and their communities.

U.S. Migration Policy: Making Room

The U.S. Immigration Reform and Control Act of 1986 (IRCA) provided the opportunity for more than 1.7 million undocumented workers and 1.3 million agricultural guest-workers to apply for legal residence status.[29] Moreover, the act sought to control the growing flow of undocumented migrants to the United States by instituting employer sanctions against hiring these workers and by strengthening border controls. The legislation, however, ignored the underlying reasons that spur both legal and illegal migration to the United States: economic conditions in the Caribbean Basin.

Rather than an enhanced infrastructure for apprehension of undocumented migrants, a sound migration policy must be linked to strategies to improve living and working conditions in the Caribbean. As we will suggest below, attaining this objective requires a comprehensive change in U.S. development assistance policy toward the Caribbean.

A recent study suggests that employment prospects in the Caribbean islands are deteriorating rapidly and are certain to worsen, stimulating even higher levels of undocumented migration, unless bold steps are taken soon to promote Caribbean development.[30] Maintaining unemployment rates in the year 2010 at their regional level in 1980 requires that 3.2 million jobs be created in the Caribbean islands in a thirty-year period. A more modest objective (certain to spur even higher rates of international migration than in the 1980s) would be to prevent unemployment rates from rising more than 50 percent above 1980 levels; this minimal aim would require the generation of 1.9 million new jobs. To generate this number of new jobs would require new investment in the range of $61 billion (or $2 billion annually) for the minimalist scenario, to $112 billion (or $3.7 billion annually) to maintain the existing unemployment rates (and presumably migration) at the current rate. Reducing current rates of unemployment and migration would require new investment on the order of $158 billion or an annual rate of $5.3 billion. It is clear that efforts stronger than the CBI will be needed to generate sufficient jobs in the Caribbean, and at wage levels high enough to overcome poverty, to stem current levels of migration from the region.

If a goal of U.S. policy is to discourage undocumented migration, it may be necessary not only to take more responsibility for increasing the standard of living in the Caribbean, but also to expand the quota for legal migrants from the region, and to extend the amnesty period for undocumented workers under IRCA.

It is estimated that perhaps from 1 to 3 million undocumented workers did not apply for amnesty under the IRCA because of fear of not being able to comply with all the legal requirements. These, plus those who subsequently entered the country illegally, constitute a mass of exploitable workers that the law is not protecting. Clearly, IRCA has reinforced the segmentation of immigrants into documented and undocumented classes. Moreover, the stiff employer sanctions for employing undocumented workers plus other enforcement mechanisms may have induced increased discrimination against Hispanic and black citizens from the Caribbean. Concretely, we recommend the following measures:

1. The amnesty period under the IRCA should be extended for one year to cover those who did not apply. More resources need to be made available to fund the English and civics courses necessary to satisfy Immigration and Naturalization Service requirements for residency under the IRCA. Advocacy groups estimate that there is a large shortage of adequate courses for all those who need to take these exams during

the next two years. Those applicants who cannot comply with the literacy and U.S. history and government proficiency requirements should be granted a time extension.

2. Existing civil rights legislation should be rigorously enforced to protect Hispanic and black citizens from the Caribbean from discrimination by employers.

3. The 1980 Refugee Act should be extended to immigrants from Haiti. This act has been applied primarily to refugees from countries with socialist governments. The current political situation in Haiti merits a case-by-case judgment on residency applications from citizens of that country.

4. Legislation should be enacted to facilitate voluntary remittances by immigrants to their home countries to foster economic development. As was discussed in Chapter 3, remittances already constitute an important source of foreign exchange for many Caribbean governments and a vital source of income for many Caribbean households. The U.S. tax code should be reviewed and amended to encourage these remittances by Caribbean immigrants to their home countries. Similarly, Caribbean governments should be encouraged to provide incentives to stimulate savings by agricultural guest-workers and other migrants, and to channel these funds into productive investment in the local economy.

U.S. Development Assistance: Changing Priorities

U.S. development assistance will continue to be a crucial complement to regional attempts to build more viable economies, geared to raising the standard of living of the region's poor. Such assistance must be maintained, even as growing U.S. fiscal deficits exert pressure on Congress to reduce it. But perhaps even more important, if U.S. assistance is to contribute to sustainable Caribbean development, the focus of U.S. programs in the region must be substantially changed from those of the Reagan era.

Under the Reagan administration, development assistance prioritized U.S. bilateral assistance to the detriment of regional institutions and programs. Moreover, the focus on structural adjustment and export promotion favored the private sector, particularly business groups, to the detriment of public programs favoring the region's poor. The Bush administration is continuing the Reagan administration's approach of emphasizing "private-sector, market-led" policies, while reducing assistance to government-sponsored development projects.[31] This strategy has been extremely harmful, serving to promote neither growth nor sustainable development. At best, it has only served to integrate the region more closely to the United States, by strengthening the ties between local elites and U.S. capital, while reproducing poverty and the Caribbean as a low-wage area.

During 1988 Representative William Crockett introduced legislation which attempts to redirect U.S. development assistance in a manner consistent with regional aspirations. The "Crockett Bill" was the product of a consultative process which included Caribbean nongovernmental organizations as well as regional and U.S. policy-makers.[32] The bill (on which no action was taken during 1988) was reintroduced in Congress as the Caribbean Regional Development Act of 1989. We strongly support its proposed new objectives for U.S. development assistance. These include the following:

1. To help the poor (including women, the landless, subsistence food producers, urban workers, the unemployed and indigenous populations) to participate in the development of their societies through a process of equitable economic growth that enables them to increase their incomes and their access to productive resources and services, to protect and advance their rights, and to influence decisions that affect their lives.
2. To support development that is environmentally sustainable.
3. To promote Caribbean self-reliance by providing assistance to indigenous national and regional governmental and nongovernmental institutions that have the capacity or potential to carry out development programs effectively.
4. To support food production for national and regional consumption.
5. To promote the diversification of industrial and agricultural production, the development of new products, and the integration of agricultural production with the development of industry and tourism.
6. To help advance the process of regional economic integration by channeling assistance through regional organizations to the maximum extent possible.
7. To support those national programs of economic adjustment that promote the policies enumerated in this section in order to help ensure that the burdens created by adjustment are not borne by the poor.
8. To support employment generation while avoiding the displacement of traditional lines of small-scale production.
9. To preserve and reinforce traditional Caribbean culture and social values.[33]

The proposed bill redirects current development assistance efforts to give priority in the use of development funds to Caribbean institutions that represent, work with, and benefit the poor and include their participation in decision-making. The use of Economic Support Funds is changed from supporting imports for the private sector, to supporting those required by small and medium-sized industries, farms, and cooperatives and for key consumer items in short supply. To the extent that economic support assistance is made available to promote national economic policy reforms, these reforms are required to be consistent with the aims noted above as well as with the following programmatic priorities: food self-sufficiency, integrated rural development, community-based agroindustries, financial resources for small and medium-sized farm and manufacturing enterprises, the expansion of a domestically linked tourist sector, regional integration, upgrading technical and managerial skills, and programs designed to sustain the renewable natural resource base of the region.[34] In addition, the bill makes clear that support for the private sector linked to export promotion and diversification must be consistent with the stated objectives. The proposed bill is also commendable in its explicit support for women's role in development and for the effective protection of workers' rights.

Given the need to reorient U.S. development aid priorities in the Caribbean, we recommend the following specific measures:

1. The Crockett Bill and the reorientation of development assistance programs in the region to meet its objectives should be placed on the congressional agenda for 1990. In order to undo the harm caused by structural adjustment policies during the decade of the 1980s, it will be especially important to rebuild the role of the state in the social reproduction of the poor. In particular, it is crucial that education and health services as well as programs that support poor rural and urban women and their children be restored to pre-crisis levels.

2. The level of U.S. development assistance for the Caribbean should be maintained at at least the average level of 1982–87, $258 million (see Table 6.4). While the House Foreign Affairs Subcommittee on the Western Hemisphere recommended an increased sum for the Caribbean in fiscal year 1990–91 over the previous year, the total, $153.6 million, is still below the average level of the 1980s.[35] It must be recognized that the average level of U.S. development assistance to the Caribbean in the 1980s was woefully inadequate to meet the investment needs of the region, as noted in the discussion of employment generation in the previous section.

In this period of growing U.S. budget deficits, every attempt should be made to maintain development assistance by converting U.S. military assistance funds (including Economic Support Funds) to development purposes. In the 1982–87 period, the United States provided Caribbean governments with an annual average $27 million a year and its allies in Central America with an annual average $328 million in military assistance, not including special training costs (see Table 6.5). Achieving peace in Central America through diplomatic means is essential to establish the preconditions for development in Central America and to free revenues for a serious development effort in the Caribbean Basin.[36]

3. All development assistance should be based on strong support for human rights, democratic reform, and the rule of law, without which it is counterproductive. Any aid to the government of Haiti should be absolutely conditioned upon free and fair elections and the guarantees of the new Haitian constitution, which include the right to organize. Without some movement toward a genuine governmental interest in development, official development assistance efforts will be totally wasted.

U.S. Military Policy: Letting Go

By now it is clear that the militarization of the region under the Reagan administration was counterproductive to U.S. long-run interests in the Caribbean. Not only was increased military assistance unnecessary—since the area is not a security threat to the U.S.—but the military build-up has had negative consequences. The use of the Caribbean as a training ground for U.S. forces in Central America heightened tensions in the region and generated renewed anti-Americanism. The training of local police forces as "security forces" in the Eastern Caribbean, as well as the build-up of military assistance to Jamaica and the Dominican Republic, rather than strengthening democracy, has strengthened those sectors of Caribbean society most disposed to undermining it. Besides the social and political costs of militarizing the region, these policies have had economic costs, diverting local resources from much-needed social programs.

It is clear that limited resources would be better employed by substituting a dangerous military build-up with an energetic effort to institutionalize peace in the region. Specifically we recommend:

1. The U.S. military presence and the scale of military exercises throughout the region should be drastically reduced and U.S. military assistance rechanneled to development purposes. It will be particularly important for the U.S. to abstain from providing any military assistance to Haiti as long as that country remains under military rule.

2. Avenues should be explored to create a "peace zone" in the Caribbean in the interests of our common security. Since 1979 the governments in the region as well as nongovernmental organizations (NGOs) have been discussing the possibility of creating a peace zone

in the Caribbean, built around the principles of nonalignment, ideological pluralism, and nonintervention. Specifically, the concept of a peace zone includes the "peaceful solution of conflicts; the need to strengthen bonds as well as the cooperation currently existing among the States of the Caribbean Basin; the elimination of colonial territories or those externally dominated in the region; prohibition of the establishment of new military bases in the region, and the dismantling of those already existing; the interdiction of all support or financing to mercenary groups; and the prohibition of installation or the maintenance of nuclear arms."[37]

Reconciliation with Cuba

After thirty years of confrontation, the time has come for a new U.S. policy toward Cuba, based on negotiated solutions to bilateral issues and respect for self-determination and international law. The involvement of both Cuba and the United States in negotiations with Angola and South Africa shows that diplomacy can yield fruitful results and the benefits of cooperation rather than confrontation.

Probably no factor would do more to reduce tensions in the region and create a climate conducive toward the generation of creative development solutions than the normalization of U.S.-Cuban relations. The U.S. policy of isolating Cuba from the community of the Western Hemisphere has had severe costs both for Cuba and for the nations of the region. There is much to be learned from the Cuban experience, particularly in the areas of health, education, and tropical agriculture. Normalization of U.S.-Cuban relations would more than likely open a full debate in the region over the positive and negative lessons of this experience, enriching the search for development options.

Normalization of U.S.-Cuban relations would require the following steps:

1. The restoration of full diplomatic relations and a resumption of trade and economic relations between the two countries. Over the last decade the United States has become increasingly isolated in the hemisphere in its refusal to establish full diplomatic relations with Cuba. Moreover, as Cuba becomes an increasingly important and respected member of the Latin American community, the costs for the United States of maintaining this adversarial policy rise.

2. The resolution of regional and global security issues. As noted above, the U.S.-Cuba dialogue on southern Africa provides an important precedent with respect to the potential role of diplomacy in solving issues of mutual interest. Normalization of diplomatic and economic relations would set the stage for further cooperation on such issues of

increasing U.S. public concern as securing peace in Central America and maintaining the Caribbean as a nuclear free zone.

3. Long-term reconciliation between the United States and Cuba. The process of reconciliation has been set back recently by the cultural warfare directed at Cuba by U.S. funding of Radio and TV Martí. These instruments of propaganda not only irritate the Cuban government but waste U.S. taxpayers' dollars, revenues which could be redirected to Caribbean development purposes.[38]

The process of reconciliation should be fostered through greater cultural and intellectual interchange between U.S. and Cuban citizens. This, in turn, requires the U.S. government to respect the right to travel—of U.S. citizens to Cuba and of Cuban citizens to the United States. We call on the U.S. government to lift the current Treasury Department regulations which effectively deny ordinary U.S. citizens this basic right and urge the State Department to revise its current procedures with respect to granting visas to Cuban citizens to visit the United States.

Puerto Rico in the Caribbean

The government of Puerto Rico is attempting to expand its role in the Caribbean through various mechanisms, including the twin plant program and 936 investment program discussed in Chapter 6, and the greater use of the skills of Puerto Ricans in the development process of other Caribbean countries. Perhaps the most controversial issue is the fate of section 936 of the U.S. tax code, both in terms of what it means for the Puerto Rican economy, and in terms of its potential as a source of development financing for Caribbean countries.

Section 936 is a loophole in the tax code that permits the entrance of massive corporate profits to the United States tax free, so long as they have remained in Puerto Rico for five years. While this loophole has reduced U.S. tax revenue, it has stimulated the development of the financial sector in Puerto Rico. In 1988, Section 936 funds accounted for more than $6 billion in deposits in local commercial banks. Nonetheless, the existence of these deposits has done little to stimulate productive investment in the Puerto Rican economy, or as yet, in the Caribbean.[39] What the abundance of 936 funds in the Puerto Rican banking sector has stimulated is increased indebtedness, particularly for personal consumption. The social consequences of growing personal indebtedness include a steady increase in the filing of personal bank-ruptcies and acute economic pressures on households among all sectors.

Another issue is the extent to which 936 funds will be employed to promote productive investment and growth in the other Caribbean economies, as intended by Congress, and who precisely is to benefit from these investments. The few loans which have been approved thus far suggest an alarming trend: the most likely loans to be approved involve U.S. multinationals or other large-scale public or semi-public corporations. Rarely is consideration given to small producers or cooperatives, or to the organizations or NGOs that might represent them.

Finally, Puerto Rican people themselves must have input into the decisions regarding both the status of Puerto Rico and Puerto Rico's role in the region. Will Puerto Rico remain the "handmaiden" of U.S. capital, primarily fostering the interests of U.S. multinationals and the greater integration of the region to the U.S.? Or will Puerto Rico achieve the autonomy to join the Caribbean community of nations and the collective search for more viable and equitable models of development?

Our specific recommendations focus on the following modifications of section 936 of the U.S. tax code:

1. Restrictions on the use of 936 funds deposited in Puerto Rican banks should include the earmarking of an increasing percentage for loans to finance investment in development-related projects in Puerto Rico, while gradually eliminating the use of 936 funds for consumption loans. To achieve this shift in the use of 936 funds, new regulations should induce longer maturity of deposits and increase the proportion of these deposits in local institutions, particularly in small banks and savings and loan associations.

2. A proportion of 936 funds should be earmarked as an investment fund for Caribbean development to be administered by the Caribbean Development Bank and possibly the Inter-American Development Bank, to ensure full coverage of the region. Priority access to this fund should be given to small businesses, cooperatives, and NGOs working with communities or other local organizations to further development projects in the region.[40] A further proportion of these funds should be earmarked for infrastructure projects presented by Caribbean governments, since infrastructure is considered to be a major bottleneck for Caribbean development.

3. Ultimately, this loophole for U.S. corporations should be closed. U.S. corporations operating in Puerto Rico should contribute their fair share to both the U.S. and Puerto Rico's treasury. A time limit should be imposed on continuation of section 936 giving the government of Puerto Rico sufficient time to prepare revisions in its tax codes.

Conclusion

We have attempted in this chapter to sketch an outline of alternative U.S. policies which would foster the broader welfare of both U.S. and

Caribbean peoples. Our proposals are based on the premise that the standard of living of U.S. citizens is inextricably linked to those of citizens in the Caribbean, and that promoting sustainable and participatory Caribbean development is very much in our shared interest.

We have also challenged the content and assumptions behind the policies of Reagan and Bush administrations, arguing that these policies were designed to benefit U.S. capital rather than the people of the region or the average U.S. citizen. Structural adjustment policies have lowered real wages in the region, while the Caribbean Basin Initiative has provided the structure for U.S. capital to become more competitive, drawing upon the Caribbean as a cheap labor reserve. The overall effect has been to integrate the Caribbean more closely to U.S. markets, improve the U.S. trade balance, and enhance the profitability of U.S. multinationals and finance capital.

The primary losers have been the poor of the region. Structural adjustment policies, combined with the rechanneling of development assistance in service of "the private sector," squeezed a domestic surplus for debt repayment, but at the cost of increased misery and social instability. U.S. citizens also lost, in terms of jobs lost to runaway shops and new flows of potentially cheaper migrant labor to this country. They also lost in terms of long-term security, since a genuine regional security policy must ensure the economic well-being and a sustainable quality of life for the people of the Caribbean.

Overcoming the harmful effects of the economic and social crisis of the 1980s and of misguided U.S. policies toward the region will not be an easy task. It will take all of the creative energies of Caribbean and North American people together to ensure that the 1990s not become the second lost decade for development.

Notes

1. For example, see the following reports which represent a broad range of political perspectives: Inter-American Dialogue, *1986 Report* (Washington, D.C.: Inter-American Dialogue, 1986); Georges Fauriol, *The Third Century: U.S.-Latin American Policy Choices for the Third Century* (Washington, D.C.: Center for Strategic and International Studies, 1988), p. 26; United Nations Center for Trade and Development (UNCTAD), *Trade and Development Report, 1988* (New York: United Nations, 1988), Ch. 4.

2. "New Goal: Third World Debt Reduction," *New York Times*, 4 October 1988.

3. *Congressional Quarterly*, 11 March 1989.

4. During 1989 two bills were introduced in Congress which would require banks to maintain good-sized reserves against potential loan losses unless they cooperated in easing the debt burden. See *Congressional Quarterly*, 27 May 1989 and 1 July 1989.

5. *Congressional Quarterly,* 18 April 1989.

6. The most detailed analysis of the net transfer of resources to creditor nations is provided by the *GATT-Fly Report* (Toronto) 10, no. 1 (February 1989).

7. "Summit Adopts Debt Relief Plan to Help Poorest Countries," *IMF Survey,* 27 June 1988.

8. World Bank, *World Development Report, 1988* (Washington, D.C.: World Bank, 1988), table 1.

9. U.S. AID is the largest creditor of the Dominican Republic, holding 21.7 percent of that country's external public debt. See Association of Caribbean Economists (ACE), Working Group on External Debt, "Debt and Development Strategies in the Caribbean," paper presented at the Second Conference of Caribbean Economists, May 1989, Barbados, p. 26.

10. Inter-American Dialogue, "Discussion Paper on Economic Issues," November 1988 (Washington, D.C.), p. 4.

11. The rationale and programmatic content for such a change in IMF priorities is well laid out in "The Group of 24 Deputies Report," *IMF Survey,* 10 August 1987, pp. 2–3.

12. ACE, "Debt and Development Strategies," p. 67.

13. This section draws on Frank Sader, "Debt Swaps—'The Hottest Game in Town'," mimeo, September 1988 (University of Massachusetts, Amherst).

14. Bolivia was allowed to cut its debt almost in half through this mechanism; Chile purchased approximately one-third of its debt at a discount of 89 percent. See General Agreement on Tariffs and Trade (GATT), "Developments in the Trading System, October 1987-April 1988," Report by the Secretariat, June 1988, p. 154; Ricardo Ffrench-Davis, "Conversión de Pagares de la Deuda Externa en Chile," *Colección Estudios CIENPLAN* (Santiago), no. 22 (December 1987), p. 42.

15. Debt-for-nature swaps have been concluded by the World Wildlife Fund (WWF) with Ecuador and Costa Rica, and by Conservation International with Bolivia. See GATT, "Report by the Secretariat," p. 156.

16. See Ffrench Davis, "Conversion de Pagares," p. 55, and John Williamson, *Voluntary Approaches to Debt Relief,* Policy Analyses in International Economics #25 (Washington, D.C.: Institute for International Economics, 1988), pp. 28–29.

17. A number of proposals have been made with respect to the need to organize a new international debt facility (either under the auspices of the IMF, or the World Bank, or as a new entity) to purchase third world debt. The value of the various proposals from the point of view of debtor countries depends largely on the extent to which the discount on debt issues in the secondary market is passed on to the debtor country and whether interest rates on outstanding debt would be reduced. A good summary of the many proposals is found in UNCTAD, *Trade and Development Report, 1988,* ch. 4. Also see the discussion in Williamson, *Voluntary Approaches to Debt Relief.*

18. At the fifteenth annual economic summit meeting in Paris in July 1989, the heads of state of the Group of Seven for the first time spoke out in favor

of commercial banks reducing their outstanding loans by taking a hit on profits, sending a message to the banks that they should actively pursue debt reduction negotiations. The implication was that the governments of the advanced, industrialized nations were not willing to bail them out. See *Congressional Quarterly*, 24 July 1989.

19. The sugar price support program has resulted in a 21 percent increase in sugar beet acreage and an 11 percent increase in cane acreage in the United States since 1982. In 1987 the U.S. (wholesale) sugar price was 21.76 cents per pound whereas the world market price was around 10 cents. Whereas cane sugar produced in the Caribbean costs an average 15 cents per pound to produce and refine, U.S. cane sugar costs 26.5 cents and beet sugar 21.03 cents per pound. *Caribbean Action*, no. 1 (1988), pp. 8–9.

20. Ibid., p. 7.

21. Paul Latortue, "Haitian Migration to Santo Domingo," paper presented to the Meeting of the Association of Caribbean Economists, 23 October 1988, Santo Domingo.

22. See U.S. General Accounting Office, *The Caribbean Basin Initiative* (Washington, D.C.: Government Printing Office, 1988), pp. 27–28, and Dominick Salvatore, ed., *The New Protectionist Threat to World Welfare* (New York: North-Holland, 1987).

23. The following discussion is drawn from U.S. International Trade Commission, *Annual Report on the Impact of the Caribbean Basin Economic Recovery Act on U.S. Industries and Consumers, Third Report* (Washington, D.C.: USITC, 1988), pp. 3–7 to 3–9; the draft of H.R. 1233 introduced in Congress on March 2, 1989; and the *CBI Business Bulletin*, various issues.

24. *CBI Business Bulletin* 4, no. 7 (August 1989), p. 3.

25. *Washington Report on Latin America and the Caribbean* 4, no. 20 (10 October 1989), p. 1, and *CBI Business Bulletin* 7, no. 3 (April 1990), p. 8.

26. "Statement of Jay Mazur, President, International Ladies Garment Workers' Union, AFL-CIO, on H.R. 3101, The Caribbean Basin Economic Recovery Expansion Act of 1987," 28 March 1988.

27. The internationally recognized worker rights are defined in section 502(a)(4) of the U.S. Trade Act of 1974. The proposal here, governing trade concessions, parallels that governing development assistance proposed in the Crockett Bill (Caribbean Regional Development Act of 1988, sec. 4 [b]).

28. The House Sub-Committee on Trade added a provision to the 1989 legislation requiring CBI-II beneficiary countries to comply with internationally recognized worker-rights, and requiring the president to review CBI country eligibility biannually.

29. Immigration and Naturalization Service (INS), "Provisional Legalization and Application Statistics, July 20, 1989," INS Statistical Division (Washington, D.C.).

30. Thomas J. Espenshade, "Projected Imbalances between Labor Supply and Labor Demand in the Caribbean Basin: Implications for Future Migration to the United States," The Urban Institute, January 1988 (Washington, D.C.), p. 16 and tables 14–18. The data in the text are drawn from Espenshade's middle scenario regarding assumptions with respect to the growth in the demand and supply of labor.

31. *Congressional Quarterly*, 25 February 1989, p. 407.

32. The 1988 bill (H.R. 4943) was the result of two congressional study missions and consultations in the Caribbean organized by the Washington-based NGO, The Development GAP, in September 1987 and February 1988, on behalf of the Subcommittee on Western Hemisphere Affairs and the Subcommittee on International Economic Policy and Trade of the Committee on Foreign Affairs. See "United States-Caribbean Economic Relations," Report of a Congressional Study Mission and Consultation on Proposals to Strengthen United States-Caribbean Economic Relations, February 6–7, 1988 (Washington, D.C.: U.S. Government Printing Office, 1988).

33. Drawn from draft amendment to the Foreign Assistance Act of 1961, ch. 2, mimeo (n.d.), pp. 15–16. The Crockett Bill is also cited as Title 6 of HR 2655. According to the *Congressional Quarterly* (22 April 1989), the House Foreign Affairs Subcommittee on the Western Hemisphere approved its portion of a fiscal 1990–91 foreign aid bill, incorporating this amendment, on 13 April 1989.

34. Ibid., section 6103, pp. 17–21.

35. *Congressional Quarterly*, 22 April 1989, p. 906.

36. On the crisis in Central America, see Richard Fagen, *Forging Peace: the Challenge of Central America* (New York: Basil Blackwell, 1987).

37. Andres Serbin, "Peace in the Caribbean: Is it an Achievable Utopia in a World Full of Threats?," *Caribbean Affairs* 1, no. 4 (1988), p. 160.

38. The start-up costs of Television Martí have been estimated as $40 million, with annual operating expenses of $15.5 million; J. Treaster, "Cubans are Curious to see U.S. TV," *The New York Times*, 21 February 1989.

39. In 1988 Puerto Rico had an investment to GDP ratio of less than 15 percent, much lower than for developing economies as a whole, where it is on the order of 23 percent. See Estudios Técnicos, Inc. (San Juan), "Prospects for the Puerto Rican Economy," Report presented to the Young Presidents' Organization, September 1988.

40. A bill is currently pending before the House Committee on Trade, as an amendment to the Gibbons Bill, which would earmark $100 million annually of 936 funds for such a development program. For a more detailed critique of section 936 and an alternative proposal, see Emilio Pantojas-García, "The Government of Puerto Rico's Caribbean Development Program: Comments on the Report to the Committee on Ways and Means of the U.S. House of Representatives," prepared for the Caribbean Project for Justice and Peace, San Juan, n.d.

About the Book

Most people in the Caribbean are poor, and the economies of their countries, shaped by colonizing powers, remain highly dependent on international markets. Caribbean nations that have tried to follow a more autonomous course have found themselves at odds with the United States, which sees the region as part of its own sphere of influence. Washington has tried to bind the region more closely to the U.S. economy as a source of cheap labor and as a market for U.S. goods, while pushing Caribbean governments to repay onerous foreign debts at the expense of the living standards of their people.

In the Shadows of the Sun examines the region's disastrous experience in the 1980s, when sharp economic declines resulted from the debt crisis and the poor performance of regional exports. It focuses on alternative development strategies that have emerged in recent years, based on the goals of meeting basic needs and ending poverty; of eliminating discrimination based on gender, race, and ethnicity; and of promoting democratic participation. Proposing a U.S. policy toward the region that might provide conditions more favorable to alternative development strategies and mutual cooperation, the authors place special emphasis on alleviating the burdens that the economic crisis places on women in their roles as both breadwinners and caregivers.

The product of a collaborative research effort among Caribbean scholars and U.S. experts on the region, this book is the most recent in a distinguished series of books from Policy Alternatives for the Caribbean and Central America (PACCA).

About the Authors

Peggy Antrobus is director of the Women and Development Unit (WAND), which she established in 1978 within the extension division of the University of the West Indies in Barbados. She was born in Grenada and received her training in economics, social work, and nonformal education at universities in Great Britain and the United States. She has worked in various Caribbean countries with both governments and nongovernmental organizations. Since 1974, when she was appointed by the government of Jamaica to set up their Women's Bureau, her work has focused on programs aimed at enhancing women's roles in development. She is a founding member of the network of third world feminists known as Development Alternatives with Women for a New Era (DAWN).

Lynn Bolles is associate professor of women's studies at the University of Maryland, College Park. A social anthropologist, she received her Ph.D. from Rutgers University and previously was director of Afro-American studies at Bowdoin College. Her research has focused on women in the urban working class in Jamaica and women in trade unions throughout the English-speaking Caribbean. Among her published works is the monograph *My Mother Who Fathered Me and Others: Gender and Kinship in the English-Speaking Caribbean*. She is consultant to the Women's Studies and Development Program at the University of the West Indies and an editor of the journal *Feminist Studies*.

Carmen Diana Deere, the project coordinator, is professor of economics at the University of Massachusetts, Amherst. She received her Ph.D. in agricultural economics from the University of California, Berkeley, and has carried out research on rural women, agrarian reform, and agricultural policy throughout Latin America and the Caribbean.

She is the author of *Household and Class Relations: Peasants and Landlords in Northern Peru* and coeditor of *Rural Women and State Policy: Feminist Perspectives on Agricultural Development in Latin America* and *Transition and Development: Problems of Third World Socialism*. During 1984–85 she served as advisor to the national-level study on rural women carried out by the Center for the Study for Feminine Action (CIPAF) in the Dominican Republic and is currently engaged in research on agrarian issues in Cuba. She was co-chairperson of Policy Alternatives for the Caribbean and Central America (PACCA) from 1984 to 1989.

Edwin Melendez is assistant professor in the Department of Urban Studies and Planning, Massachusetts Institute of Technology. He holds a Ph.D. in Economics from the University of Massachusetts, Amherst, and previously taught Puerto Rican Studies at Fordham University. His recent research focuses on the economic crisis, development strategies, and political change in Puerto Rico and on wage inequality and employment and training of Latinos in the United States.

Peter Phillips is currently minister of state in the office of the prime minister of Jamaica. Until February 1989, Dr. Phillips was on the faculty of the Consortium Graduate School for the Social Sciences of the University of the West Indies/University of Guyana, located at the University of the West Indies campus at Mona, Jamaica. He has published a number of articles and chapters in various books on aspects of Caribbean development and more specifically on the historical development of the U.S.-Caribbean relationship.

Marcia Rivera is director of the Center for the Study of Puerto Rican Reality (CEREP) in San Juan. She received her graduate training in Urban Sociology and Economics at the University of London. Her recent research has focused on women in the informal economy, on the economic crisis in the Caribbean, and on political change in Puerto Rico. She is on the executive boards of PACCA and the Latin American Council of Social Sciences (CLACSO), a founding member of the Regional Coordinator of Socio-Economic Studies (CRIES), and a member of the board of directors of the Conservation Trust of Puerto Rico.

Helen I. Safa is professor of anthropology and Latin American Studies at the University of Florida, Gainesville. After receiving her doctorate at Columbia University, she taught at Syracuse University and Rutgers University and was director of the Center for Latin American Studies at the University of Florida. She is the author of *The Urban Poor of*

Puerto Rico and the editor of *Migration and Development, Women and Change in Latin America, Toward a Political Economy of Urbanization in Third World Countries* and other books. Her articles and reviews on migration, housing, race, ethnicity, education, and women and national development have appeared in a variety of scholarly journals. Her current research centers on women in the industrialization process in Cuba, the Dominican Republic, and Puerto Rico. She is past president of the Latin American Studies Association and former chair of the Advisory Committee for the American Republics, Council for International Exchange of Scholars (Fulbright).

Index